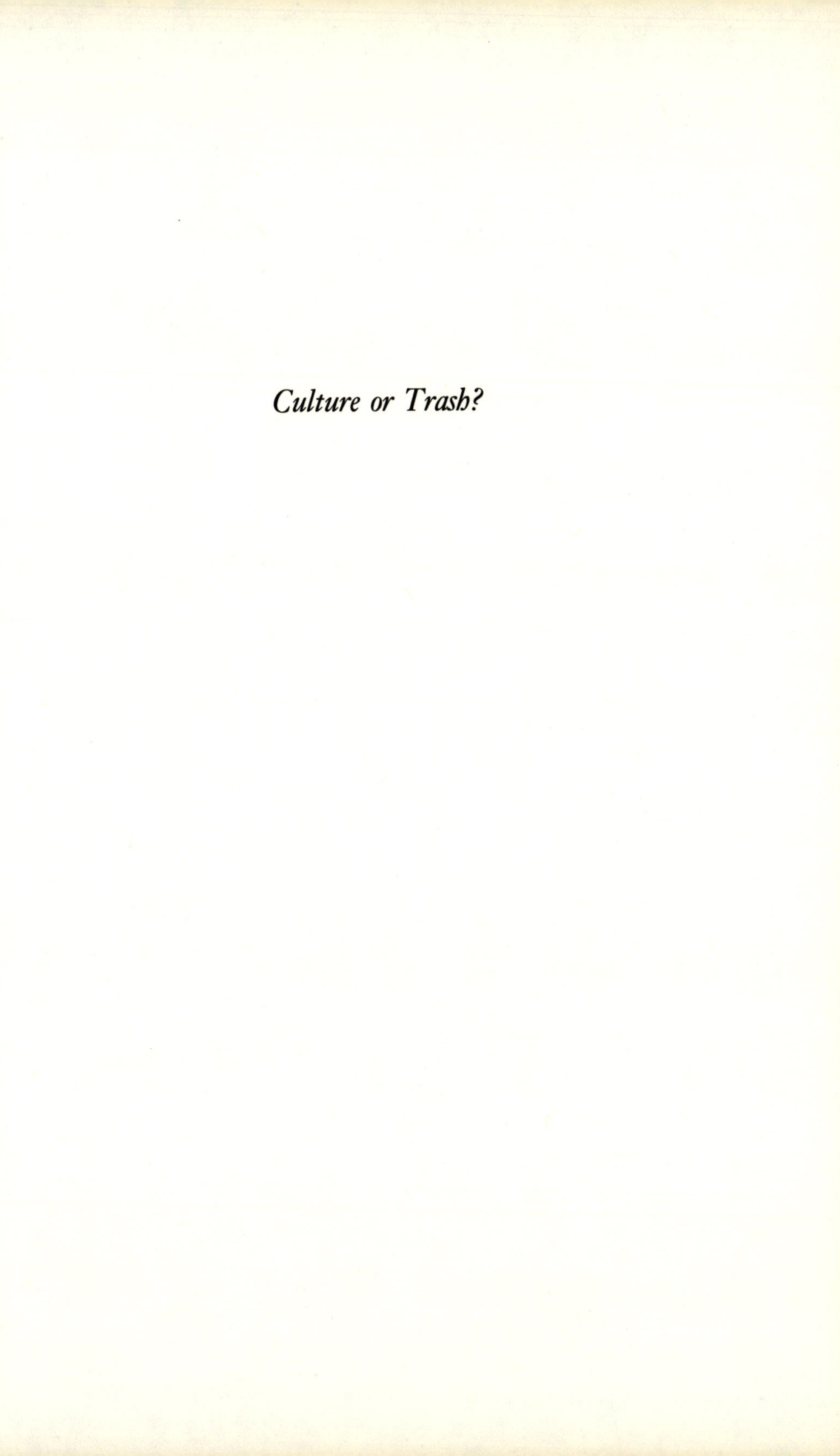

Culture or Trash?

CULTURE
or
TRASH?

A Provocative View of Contemporary Painting, Sculpture, and Other Costly Commodities

by James Gardner

A BIRCH LANE PRESS BOOK
Published by Carol Publishing Group

This book is dedicated to my parents.

A Birch Lane Press Book
Published by Carol Publishing Group
Birch Lane Press is a registered trademark of Carol Communications, Inc.
Editorial Offices: 600 Madison Avenue, New York, N.Y. 10022
Sales & Distribution Offices: 120 Enterprise Avenue, Secaucus, N.J. 07094
In Canada: Canadian Manda Group, P.O. Box 920 Station U, Toronto, Ontario M8Z 5P9
Queries regarding rights and permissions should be addressed to Carol Publishing Group, 600 Madison Avenue, New York, N.Y. 10022

Carol Publishing Group books are available at special discounts for bulk purchases, for sales promotions, fund-raising, or educational purposes. Special editions can be created to specifications. For details contact: Special Sales Department, Carol Publishing Group, 120 Enterprise Avenue, Secaucus, N.J. 07094

Manufactured in the United States of America
10 9 8 7 6 5 4 3 2 1

Library of Congress Cataloging-in-Publication Data

Gardner, James, 1918?–
Culture or trash? : a provocative view of contemporary painting, sculpture, and other costly commodities / by James Gardner.
p cm.
ISBN 1–55972–208–8
1. Art, Modern—20th century—Marketing. 2. Art, Modern—20th century—Economic aspects. 3. Art criticism—History—20th century. I. Title.
N6493 1980.G37 1993
709'.04'5—dc20 93–2518
CIP

Contents

	Preface	vii
	Acknowledgments	ix
1.	The Age of Art	1
2.	The Art World	22
3.	The Chattering Class	48
4.	Modernists and Postmodernists	68
5.	High and Low	85
6.	The Reborn Figure	104
7.	The Remains of Abstraction	129
8.	The Radical in the Studio	147
9.	The Art of the Body	170
10.	Art Art	195
	Epilogue: The Art of the Future	213

PREFACE

This book is founded on the intuition that there is something called contemporary art. It might seem silly ever to have doubted a fact that appears so self-evident. But when you think about it, it is not self-evident. For when shall we say it begins, and whom shall we include in the discussion, and, more significantly, whom shall we leave out? The present book is about those artists whom the art world—that alliance of museums, dealers, and critics—has decided to take seriously. It examines and judges what they have been doing for the past fifteen or so years, since the emergence of what is known as postmodernism.

The work of these artists represents a small portion of what is actually being made today. Most art is unambitious and, to be frank, unimportant. I have not dealt with this art. The art I have dealt with is mostly ambitious and unimportant. And it is unimportant, I argue, because its ambitions are not the ambitions of art, but those of politics or psychology or pornography or something else.

There is art being made today that is very good, but which I have not discussed because it is content to remain within the older forms of artistic ambition. Painters like Esteban Vincente, Brice Marden and Agnes Martin are making beautiful paintings; just as Richard Serra and Mark di Suvero are making beautiful sculptures. Because they are older artists working in an older and more conservative style, it is not be necessary to make the case for them. Then there are some older artists like Alice Neel and Eva Hesse, both deceased, who nevertheless presaged or influenced what younger artists are doing, and so they have been included in the discussion.

There are other more recent artists who have achieved memorable results in the new style, like Anish Kapoor and Pat Steir, whom I praise very highly indeed. I am only sorry that there were not more such artists. Nevertheless, such were the spatial constraints of the book, and such is the immensity of contemporary art, that I have had to leave out of the discussion many excellent artists, as well as many artists deserving of a far less reverent treatment than they usually receive.

In chapters five through ten, which discuss the art itself, I have assembled the artists around certain general themes. I don't deny that there is frequent interpenetration between the themes to which the chapters are devoted or that several artists could have been discussed in the context of more than one chapter. Nor would I insist that this is the definitive schema for discussing contemporary art. But some sort of structure had to be found for the welter of objects and personalities under consideration, and the one I adopted seemed to me convenient and clear.

ACKNOWLEDGMENTS

There are more people to whom I am indebted in writing this book than I can name. But I should like first to thank my friend and former editor at *National Review*, Brad Miner, for giving me the idea for this book and for his helpful advice along the way. I also want to thank David Klinghoffer, Bruce Wolmer, and Suzanne Ramuljak for reading portions of the manuscript before publication and giving me their opinions and advice. I am especially grateful to my agents Jake Elwell and Larry Gershel at Wieser and Wieser for their confidence in me and for their exertions in my behalf. Thanks as well to Hillel Black, my unusually respectful and sensitive editor at Birch Lane, and also to Ellen Jaffe for her care in copyediting the manuscript. Finally, I owe a considerable debt to the staffs of both the Watson Library at the Metropolitan Museum and the Whitney Museum Library.

ONE

The Age of Art

"Painting is a work and a labor of the body rather than of the mind, and is, more often than not, exercised by the ignorant." You are unlikely to meet one person in a million who will share this sentiment. And yet, when it was expressed by Mario Equicola, a contemporary of Leonardo da Vinci and Raphael, he had every reason to feel confident that he was voicing the consensus of his age. Compared with poetry and music, painting was thought to be vulgar to its very roots: It was a servile art rather than a liberal art, and thus it did not befit the dignity of a free man. A century later, Peter Paul Rubens was turned down for an important diplomatic post under the king of Spain for the very same reasons. "The reputation of this monarch will necessarily suffer if a man of so slight importance is to be approached by ambassadors" because "he practices an art that is in the end base and done by hand."

Sculptors were held in even lower esteem. Leonardo, passionate though he was in defense of painting, compared his mallet-wielding brethren to bakers. Had he needed the support of antiquity, he could have found it in Lucian and in Plutarch, who observed that many might admire the sculptures of the great Phidias, but no decent person could ever want to be Phidias, since he was essentially just a stonecutter.

These opinions seem ludicrous to us because they are totally at variance with the prevailing notions of our time. So completely have we reversed the judgment of our forebears that now, for the first time in Western culture, visual art has not merely achieved parity with poetry and music, but to all appearances has overtaken them. This is not to deny the achievements of our novelists, poets, and composers nor to contend that today's best or most interesting cultural artifacts are paintings rather than novels or symphonies. And yet, at this moment in our culture, art and the artist generate an intensity of interest that other provinces of the imagination rarely command.

The artist is glamorized in films, plays and novels. He is profiled in *Vanity Fair* and in *Harper's Bazaar*, in *Vogue* and in *Mirabella*. Hundreds of art periodicals, with no precise equivalent in the fields of music and literature, regularly treat the artist to prolonged critical adulation. Dozens of publishing companies bring before the public, in sumptuous volumes, the works of even second-tier artists. Meanwhile art schools spew out thirty-five thousand students a year; new art museums open across America every other week; forty million people visit them each year; and in the midst of it all, there has emerged a dazzling three-ring circus of art galleries, art lawyers, art critics, art historians, art restorers, and auction houses that we sum up in a single, incomparably grandiose term: The art world.

Like *democracy* and *freedom*, the very word is shibboleth. Whereas music and literature are essentially neutral terms that refer to certain cultural activities and their products, the word *art* is dense with glamour and lofty purpose. Art is the aroma of four course meals at Le Cirque and the swank of duplexes along Park Avenue. Art is the crack corps of gallerists in Soho and the ten million rebellious geniuses living in the splendid penury of Alphabet City. In museums, Art is the solace of the middle class. In private hands, Art is the bulwark of established wealth and the first recourse of new money. For many, Art is the highest, the finest thing to which we can now aspire or give a name.

And yet, does it not sometimes seem that we go too far? Is it not possible that, in compensating for the ignorance of our forebears, we have at times allowed this new love of ours to verge on idolatry? Consider a case in point. In August 1976 visitors to the Hanson Fuller Gallery in San Francisco were greeted at the door by a young man in a waiter's outfit. Very politely, he offered them coffee while they looked at the art. If they accepted his offer, as many did, he served them the coffee in a simple white cup, with cream from a simple white pitcher. While the visitors drank, they looked briefly at the group exhibition that was up on the walls and then they left. What they did not know, what most would never learn, is that they themselves were part of an artistic act, a performance piece titled *Garçon!* by the conceptual artist Chris Burden. As it turns out, the polite young man in question was none other than this semifamous artist. And that was the entire piece: Burden serving coffee to people in an art gallery (roughly three hundred cups in the space of a week). Maybe the banality of the exercise was the whole point. Maybe it wasn't. More important is the fact that, since the entirely unremarkable cream pitcher was part of an artistic performance, it had ceased to be a mere utensil: It had been transubstantiated into a "relic," to use Burden's own word. And as a relic it was labeled and encased in glass and was recently selling on the secondary market for $24,000.

Burden's cream pitcher is less important for what it is, or what Burden thinks it is, than for what it represents, what it says about us. Is it not a kind of grail for our secular age, a potent symbol of that special, bizarre reverence in which we have come to hold the visual arts? Whatever each of us individually may think of Burden's audacious act of marketing, we must live with the fact that ours is the age in which someone would consider paying $24,000 for a plain white cream pitcher so long as he could have it in writing that Chris Burden had used it for a performance piece. Even if most collectors would admit that $24,000 was a bit steep, how many more customers could have been found if it had been offered at $500. It would have seemed a bargain, given Burden's comparative fame in the right artistic circles. Of course, Chris Burden is hardly a celebrity on the order of Andy Warhol or Pablo Picasso. Yet even if he were, on what basis could we impart to a small cream pitcher any value beyond a few dollars and change? What emotions, what cultural or economic referents, are being invoked in this odd transaction?

Some might argue that *Garçon!* and its relic are a powerful indictment of the master-servant relationship in late capitalist society, a parody of the valorized commodity, a *mise-en-cause* of bourgeois cultural icons, and so on. But even if this were a valid interpretation, and we have no reason to believe it is, would that make the pitcher worth $24,000? Others might contend that the encased relic has a sculptural quality. They might even claim to see beauty in it, as in such found objects as Marcel Duchamp's inverted urinal. Whatever one might think of their judgment, it should suffice that Burden himself has rejected this reading. He would insist that the pitcher is just a pitcher, not some vanguardist sculpture. The work of art is the performance itself: The rest is ancillary.

Compare Burden's cream pitcher with the wedding gown that Madonna wore on the cover of her *Like a Virgin* album and that was sold not long ago at Sotheby's. The dress might reasonably have been expected to make a lot of money. After all, Madonna is for the moment just about the most famous person on the planet. Thus, somebody might plausibly want the thing for whatever sentimental reasons, just as one might wish to own Dorothy's ruby slippers, or the sequined jacket that Elvis wore the last time he played Vegas.

Now you might think that if Burden's cream pitcher can sell for $24,000, then Madonna's wedding dress should sell for at least several trillion dollars. Why then did it go for a niggardly

$11,000? Why, at a still more recent auction in Paris, did a relic said to contain fragments of the very cross on which Jesus Christ was crucified, a relic whose authenticity was presumably accepted by the bidders, go for a mere $18,000, far less than what was being asked for a serving utensil touched by a semifamous artist.

You could ponder and analyze and dissect the issue for years, but in the end it will all come down to a single word, and that word is *art*. Burden's pitcher is the relic of an act of art, the performance piece *Garçon!*. Thus it exists not merely at the bald, material level of a serving utensil, but in the higher, almost supersensible realm of "art history." It is in some small sense the incarnation, the reification (to use a trendier word) of a moment in art history. And for this reason it confounds the calculations of our otherwise too practical world.

For those who have followed Burden's career for the past twenty years, however, there was nothing especially remarkable about *Garçon!*, except perhaps for its relative modesty. Burden first garnered recognition through an intriguing publicity stunt in 1976, the same year as *Garçon!* Titled *Chris Burden Promo*, it consisted of his buying a thirty-second commercial slot on network television (during "Saturday Night Live"), in which he flashed before the eyes of a confused nation the names (which were also read aloud by a voice-over): Leonardo da Vinci, Michelangelo, Rembrandt, Vincent Van Gogh, Pablo Picasso, Chris Burden. And that was it. It all seems pretty shallow and transparent, doesn't it? The sleazy parvenu pawing his way toward money and fifteen paltry minutes of fame. And yet, whether out of aggravated masochism or mental instability, Burden, in his performances, has inflicted so much physical and psychological damage on himself in the name of his art that he is clearly sincere about something.

On April 23, 1974, for example, in a piece titled *Transfixed*, he was crucified by being nailed to the back of a Volkswagen Beetle. Photographs survive showing the young man nailed to the spreading hood. To this day Burden's palms are marked with the stigmatical welts that remain where the nails entered his hands.

Of another performance, *Five Day Locker Piece*, held from April 26 to April 30, 1971, at the University of California at Irvine, he writes: "I was locked in locker number 5 for five consecutive days and did not leave the locker during this time. The locker measured two feet high, two feet wide, and three feet deep. I stopped eating several days prior to entry. The locker directly above me contained five gallons of bottled water; the locker below me contained an empty five-gallon bottle [to urinate into]."

Equally famous was *Kunst Kick*, performed on June 19, 1974: "At the public opening of the Art Fair in Basel, Switzerland, at twelve noon, I lay down at the top of two flights of concrete stairs in the Mustermesse. Charles Hill repeatedly kicked my body down the stairs, two or three steps at a time."

On more than one occasion Burden has risked his life for art. The circumstances were controlled, but that does not greatly mitigate the sense of danger. In *Doorway to Heaven*, at 6 P.M., on November 15, 1973, "I stood in the doorway of my studio [in Venice, California] facing the boardwalk. A few spectators watched as I pushed two live electric wires into my chest. The wires crossed and exploded, burning me, but saving me from electrocution." In *Velvet Water*, on May 7, 1974, "I repeatedly submerged my face in the sink and attempted to breathe water. After about five minutes, I collapsed, choking." But the most famous of all Burden's performances has to be *Shoot*, held at the F Space in Santa Ana, on November 19, 1971. "At 7:45 P.M. I was shot in the left arm by a friend. The bullet was a copper-jacket 22 long rifle. My friend was standing about fifteen feet from me." The bullet survives as a relic.

Though I don't believe that Burden anywhere refers explicitly to the Christian martyrs, there are curious parallels between his performances and the theatrical ordeals of the early church. They exhibit the same delight in extremity, in testing the limits of human endurance. One thinks of Saint Simeon Stylites standing atop a pillar in Syria for sixty-eight years, descending only twice to move to a taller pillar. As with Saint Simeon, the educational and spiritual point of Burden's performances consists in their appeal to our imaginations. For a thousand years the mind of Europe was fascinated by what it must have felt like to be Saint Sebastian riddled with arrows, or Saint Catherine stretched upon her wheel, or Saint Steven stoned to death, or Saint Lawrence lying stoically on the fiery grill. For us there is a similar fascination in the idea, more than in the visible act, of Chris Burden inhaling water or being kicked down a flight of stairs or being shot at from fifteen feet away.

Both the acts of the martyrs and the performances of Chris Burden have an abrupt, epigramatic brevity. They are cosmic one-liners. At the same time, Burden has isolated himself from the rest of society. His theatrical self-denial, his flamboyant rejection of normal human behavior (by lying in bed without speaking for three weeks, by stuffing himself into a luggage locker for five days) represents an aggression against society that is less protracted, perhaps, but scarcely less arduous than the hermitage of Saint Anthony or the Carthusian monks.

But in the name of what god, in the service of what religion are these ostensibly religious acts performed? In the absence of any direct spiritual reference, Burden is left with no center of homing other than Art itself, that abstract, gaseous entity arising out of the mass of artifacts created, and acts committed, in its name. This idea of art must never be confused, however, with "art for art's sake." What that vague and superannuated phrase really meant was "art for beauty's sake." Beauty was the end of aestheticism and art was the means. Most people, when they say they like art, really mean that they like beauty through art, or truth through art. Only a phony or a fool would admire a Cézanne landscape because it was art. Surely the fact of its being great, dramatic, authoritative art is what commands our attention. In contrast, Burden's cream pitcher has been stripped of any value or interest beyond the bald, naked fact of its identity as an art object. It is a kind of martyrial affirmation of the idea, the word *art*.

Burden's performances can be seen as a terminal point in the ancient interrelation of art and religion. For most of its existence art seems to have been in the service of one divinity or another. Even at its inception in the caves of Lascaux and Altamira, as some scholars now believe, art's very identity was subsumed in a spiritual act of magic. By painting a dead bison onto the moist limestone walls of Altamira, you propitiated the lord of the hunt and made the next day's forays more profitable. And long after art emerged from the shadow of religion, long after it was conceived of as a separate entity, there remained an indissoluble link with the deity that inspired everything from the statue of Zeus at Olympus to the shimmering windows of Chartres and the Madonnas of Murillo. Only in the last century was there a definite rupture. The secular element that had been gathering strength since the 1700s came to a flowering in the work of realists like Gustave Courbet. These artists might depict a peasant in prayer, but they made no claim for the piety of the painting, only for the factuality of the subject.

And yet, because the relationship of art and religion is so close, this severance proved to be astonishingly short-lived. In the art of symbolists like Gustave Moreau and Paul Gauguin something quite unprecedented begins to happen. The religious element comes surging back with a fervor that had not been seen in centuries; but it returns in a new and entirely unexpected form. Now the ancient religious sense begins to claim art as its end rather than as its means.

Listen to Moreau describing the creation of a work of art: "At every moment when the most intense emotions fuse in the depths of one's being, at the very moment when they burst forth and issue like lava from a volcano, is there not something like the blossoming of the suddenly created work, a brutal work if you wish, yet great, and superhuman in appearance?"

No artist had ever spoken that way before. Yet the same

intensity inspires this odd comment by Wassily Kandinsky: "The unbounded warmth of red has not the irresponsible appeal of yellow but rings inwardly with a determined and powerful intensity. The artist must train not only his eye but also his soul." As a number of writers have observed in recent years, art, which started out as the conduit of religion, has now become its substitute. But unlike traditional religion, which distinguished means from ends and process from fulfillment, art is at once the inspiration for this religious sense, its conduit, and its goal.

By creating art through his mere thaumaturgic touch, by engendering value through a simple act of nomination, Chris Burden becomes emblematic of art's new status in our society. Yet he is hardly unique in this regard. Like Burden, the Austrian artist Hermann Nitsch began as an abstract painter, and some of his early works, with their dramatic dribblings in scarlet and ultramarine, are among the more memorable abstractions of the early sixties.

But formalist preoccupations came to seem too constraining to a man of Nitsch's special temperament and by the late sixties he had fallen in with the Aktionen artists, a group of Austrians who pioneered body art. Nitsch founded the *Orgien, Mysterien Theater*, or "Orgies, Mysteries Theater," whose performances continue to be held annually amid the hills and vineyards of his castle in Prinzendorf. These elaborate ceremonies usually entail the slaughter of animals and, quite literally, a bloodbath in which young Austrians slosh around in the intestinal muck of livestock.

Nitsch's reasons for doing what he does are none too specific. "Everything that exists should be worshipped," he has said, not very helpfully. He elaborated to the Viennese police: "The concentrated aesthetic liturgy of the O. M. Theater can expand itself over a lifetime and can transform the process of living into a positive, life-enhancing aesthetic ritual."

If there is a Dadaist exuberance in all of this, the one element of Dada that is missing is its imperishable sense of fun. Nitsch is as solemn and severe as a bishop presiding over the eucharist. The ceremony itself, however arbitrary its cause or inspiration, is carried out as punctiliously as a mass. For a typical performance Nitsch requires an energized audience of several hundred spectators, a butcher, a pair of skinned lambs, two actors, two stagehands, a chorus of fourteen, and a noise-orchestra of cymbals, ocarinas, pan lids, flutes, violins, rattles, and cowbells to generate "the ecstasy created by the loudest possible created noise."

To the riotous, rhythmical clapping of the audience and the full blare of the orchestra, a desquamated lamb is strung up and crucified, hoisted to a great height and then dropped, so that it comes crashing against the ground. A few participants cover the carcass in a white cloth. Then, with metal hooks and their heels, they smash in the skull. With each blow, the chorus and orchestra let out an ecstatic clamor until the sheet is finally ripped away and the participants begin to tear the carcass limb from limb.

Now the stagehands bring out a large wooden vat filled with lukewarm water and floating entrails. After the audience members pass in solemn review of the vat and stick their hands in, the stagehands gather all the entrails into a bag and walk three times around the right half of the audience and three times around the left. They set the sack down in the center of the theater. All at once, members of the audience leap forward and rip open the bag, and soon are slipping around in the muck and innards. Throughout this activity they are being doused with buckets of egg-yolk, cow's urine, ether, cow's meat, overripe peaches, black bread, and hair from a thirty-two--year old woman. Suddenly an actor is being chased around the room. After a while, he is caught and a mock-crucifixion takes place.

Thereupon, yet another desquamated lamb is hauled out, followed by the cowled figure of the artist himself. "Holding the lamb by the hind feet," he says, "I beat the dead lamb ecstatically [against the walls of the cellar], throw the animal to the ground, beat it with my fists, kick it, trample about on it, begin to tear up the body, put my hand into the bloody cavity of the breast, press my knee in and bite into the raw flesh of the carcass. . . . The excitement generated by these actions has broken through to the extent of ecstasy."

As with Chris Burden's performances, those of Hermann Nitsch leave relics behind. Signed photographs of the performances could be bought recently at the Luhring, Augustine Gallery in New York for $2000 a piece. Bloodstained chasubles and sheets, naturally, went for rather more.

But even this inspired act of marketing pales in comparison with the posthumous industry in the remains of Joseph Beuys, sometime leader of the Fluxus movement. Not since the crafty Venetians spirited the corpse of Saint Mark out of Alexandria in 824 have the remains of a dead man been proved so lucrative to the living. In December 1989, three years after this inscrutable German died at age sixty-four, no fewer than four Beuys exhibitions were running concurrently in Manhattan. Most spectacular was Bits and Pieces at the Ronald Feldman Gallery on Mercer Street. Assembled across the spacious gallery were some twenty vitrines, raised glass boxes containing an astonishing multitude and variety of objects: lumps of peat, a pine cone, bits of string, an old *Wall Street Journal*, a clutch of grass, some old boots, a pair of stag skulls, several chunks of quartz, and two of the great man's toenail clippings.

These objects, which the artist had given to Caroline Tisdall over a period of a decade, were now being sold as is and en bloc for $3 million. Though some drawings were also thrown in, these objects were in no sense intended as art, nor were they part of any performance, as had been the case with Burden and Nitsch. They had merely belonged to the artist, and he had passed them on to Ms. Tisdall. Though ultimately the Feldman Gallery failed to sell the work, no one in the art world publicly found the asking price outlandish.

There was an almost Apollonian noblesse in the way Beuys gave these things away, in his confidence that the recipient would be delighted to have them, as she surely was. Nor was she the only one whom he so honored. A number of similar collections exist, and they too, we may fairly speculate, are growing more valuable by the week. The idea behind it all was summed up in Beuys's millenarian battle cry: "Every man an artist!" What he meant was that each of us, in our lives, accumulates knickknacks, furballs, and whatnots, all of which, assembled, constitute a single, unified work of art. The idea is charmingly egalitarian in its way. Yet you don't need to be a wizard to figure out that no one is going to pay *you* $3 million for your furballs and crumpled Kleenex. Why? Because Beuys was an artist, and not just any artist, but a charismatic, messianic artist. And, therefore, if he touched it, whatever it is, it is worth top dollar.

Clearly we have come a long way since the days of Equicola, who deemed painting and sculpture unworthy of free men, and who scoffed at any notion of art's nobility. Indeed, we have reached the point where an artist's toenail clippings, a pair of boots he once wore, a piece of paper he discarded, are endowed with something very nigh to holiness. It will be argued that the three artists discussed thus far are highly exceptional, that most of what is made and bought and admired today is far more conventional than the objects sold under their name. Undoubtedly this is true. But Burden, Beuys, and Nitsch are representative, if nothing else, of a kind of honor that is regularly bestowed on the visual arts, a shift for which nothing in the earlier history of art prepared us.

What inspires this enthusiasm remains unclear. A cynic might find the secret of art's success in the fact that it is the most easily assimilated culture around. Whereas literature and music exist in time and must be sat through, the visual arts provide instant gratification: A thousand objects can be seen in an afternoon. Like the ancient pagans, we seem to prefer any golden calf to the disembodied Jehovah. We want our deity to live, not like music on the air, nor like poetry on the printed page, but out there in the world, where we can see it and feel it and caress it with our hands. Art's tactility, its objecthood, its conspicuous ownability is irresistible. It can be possessed on postcards, posters, and even on postage stamps, in lavishly illustrated books or, if one has the wealth, in the very flesh. It is almost promiscuously reproducible.

But surely there are other reasons for art's ascendancy over literature and music. Art is the only cultural enterprise which, in recent years, has not fallen prey to a kind of aesthetic conservatism. Until the late sixties all the arts, as though in concert, seemed to be striving to extend the boundaries of their respective media, castigating them unto their final perfection, purging them of all that was superfluous or arbitrary. Whether in the brothels of Emile Zola's naturalism, or the quilted landscapes of Virginia Woolf's reveries, or the urban sprawl of the the *nouveau roman*, there was a distinct sense that the novel had some definite destination, and that it was getting there through the exertions of these doughty pioneers. At the same time there was often a moral dimension to this quest, and many would have shared James Joyce's ambition "to forge in the smithy of my soul the uncreated conscience of my race."

If this dream is never explicitly rejected today, that is only because it has been so thoroughly discredited and forgotten. If anyone talked like that now he would sound ridiculous. In poetry as well, whom do we look to for cultural guidance, for formal innovation, as earlier generations turned to Ezra Pound and William Carlos Williams and Wallace Stevens? Who strives with T. S. Eliot to "purify the language of the tribe"? No one, of course. Even to pose the question sounds massively out of touch with reality. As regards composers of contemporary "art music," is there really anyone alive today, with the exception of Philip Glass or Ned Rorem, whom the generally well-educated public can even name? There is a feeling abroad, in every art other than the visual arts, that private individuals are trying to create cultural artifacts as best they can. There is no more militancy, there are no more battle cries, there is no united cultural front: only tenured professionals earning an honest living.

How different things are in the art world! Once you eliminate quality from your thinking, you cannot help but be impressed by the powerful variety of forms, the palpable aggression, the raw energy that characterizes the visual arts at this time. So what if much of the art is idiotic? There is clearly the sense that these people have not retreated into complacency. They alone seem to enshrine, with almost neurotic eagerness, what Ezra Pound required of all the arts: Make it new! Despite the art world's trendy chatter about the death of the avant-garde, artists are still flattered to believe that they are remaking the world, seeking and finding unheard of revolutionary forms of expression and sensation, going that one final step beyond which it is impossible to go.

Isn't this, in a sense, the artist's birthright? Wasn't it artists who created the whole vanguardist idea in the first place, an idea that once proved so enabling to culture? And isn't it artists whom we have to thank for our inbred receptivity to movements and stylistic changes: all those slogans and manifestos, all those buzzwords and cycles of taste? Quick, name a contemporary literary movement! Are there any? While the other arts appear to have sunk into quiescence, of visual art has served up to an eager market everything from Neoexpressionism and Neo-Geo to Scatter Art, Sots Art and the East Village Scene. Postmodernism itself, a word that applies to an entire phase of our culture, was first popularized through the visual arts.

There is the concomitant sense that artists are the ones who are pushing forward the boundaries of free expression, calling into question the important issues, examining, vexing, debating. In recent years no other province of culture has dealt so insistently or so polemically with political issues. Visual art has never been more overtly activist than at this moment. It is rare to enter one of the major SoHo galleries these days without finding art that is partially or fully saturated with issues of race relations, U.S. foreign policy, date rape, AIDS, or homelessness. The ongoing controversy over the National Endowment for the Arts has been so uniformly concerned with visual artists like Robert Mapplethorpe, Andres Serrano, and Karen Finley that you could forget that the NEA gives funding to music, literature and dance in addition to visual art.

The furor over the novel *American Psycho* by Bret Easton Ellis and over the opera *Klinghoffer* by John Adams was purely political rather than artistic: Should publishers bring out books that appear to be phallocentric? Should one stage an opera in which there is the suspicion of anti-Semitism? One had no sense with these flops as one had with the uproar regarding Mapplethorpe and Serrano, that nothing less than free speech, indeed the free state, hung in the balance.

Symptomatic of visual art's prestige and domination of contemporary culture is the way it has imperiously assimilated to itself all the other arts. The works of Glenn Ligon and Jenny Holzer are rarely more than pages of words, yet they are conceived of and praised as paintings rather than as literature, even though they are admired more for what they say than for any graphic sense. Though the performance pieces of Holly Hughes are really little more than monologues, they are judged not as theater but as visual art. Karen Finley's performances are often undistinguished dance, yet they are seen not as choreography but as art. Video artists regularly arrogate to themselves the powers of music and cinema without forsaking for one second their claim to being visual artists like painters and sculptors. Somehow, it is all important that what they do be designated as art.

An objection may have occurred to many readers early on: Even if the visual arts should prove more popular than literature or opera, what are we to make of popular music, of movies, of pulp fiction? Surely, it can be argued, the audience for these is far greater than the audience for visual art. Obviously, this is true. But what if I should say that the culture we are discussing is high culture; that popular culture does not concern us? It would, of course, require astonishing innocence not to anticipate some response to the effect that distinctions between high culture and popular culture are arbitrary and elitist. Isn't this what artists themselves have been telling us for the past decade? It surely is. And yet, popular culture and elite culture are as divided as they ever were, and nowhere more so than in the works of the very artists who have most aggressively attacked the idea of the cultural elite.

It would be disingenuous in the extreme to claim that your basic janitor looks at Brillo boxes in the same way that people with degrees in art history look at Andy Warhol's famous sculpture. Or that there is anything in Jeff Koons's floating basketballs, or in Jean Michel Basquiat's grafitti images, that is meant to appeal to inner-city youths. The art establishment has merely co-opted elements of popular culture for its own elitist ends: In its perennial process of sanctioned revolution, it has chosen the one thing, popular culture, that was most unpalatable to the older generation. Yet not everyone will have read the relevant chapters in such fashionable French thinkers as Baudrillard and Lacan and thus they will miss the point. Or perhaps that is the point.

More interesting than any standoff between elite and populace is the unprecedented nature and demographics of the new and expanded elite that frequents museums and enthuses over the visual arts. In the early years of the century, Ezra Pound claimed that you needed only five hundred people to constitute a functioning civilization, provided they were sufficiently well educated. He meant that, in his pessimistic opinion, there were only about that many people in the world who were really alive to the most advanced forms of expression.

But clearly something unprecedented is happening when forty million people visit American art museums a year and almost a million of them stood in interminable lines and paid $12 to study the chromatic values of Henri Matisse, as they did in 1992 at the Museum of Modern Art in New York. This is nothing less than mass elitism, a truly democratic miracle! Situated somewhere between those few thousand men and women who actively alter our cultural attitudes and the beer-guzzling football fans of proverbial lore, this new mass elite, consisting of perhaps fifteen million souls in all, has been primarily responsible for the unprecedented growth of the American art scene in recent years. Through mass education and mass communications, they have become, on the whole, much more sensitive to art than their grandparents were. They truly know and truly love a good painting when they see it.

If art is a religion, these people are not, like Burden and Beuys, the zealots and martyrs of the new faith, but rather its staid parishioners. Their devotion is obedient and respectful, occasionally betraying the pharisee, but all the same sincere. It is possible, of course, to exaggerate the cultic nature of art: to make artists into saints and sometimes gods; critics and curators into priestly go-betweens.

But if there is any truth in the analogy, then maybe it is more than coincidence that, according to figures provided by the Metropolitan Museum in New York, more people go to see art on Sundays than on any other day of the week, during the very hours when their forebears were singing hymns in church. Like the cathedrals of the past, to use André Malraux's analogy, the museum is the stateliest building most of them will ever enter. No wonder many dress for the occasion, as they once put on their Sunday best. No wonder they speak a little more softly, a little more reverently, as they pass through its spacious halls. Only in a museum will they stand within arm's length of some object worth a hundred or a thousand times more than they will ever earn. The thought is daunting indeed!

And in large part they frequent museums for the same reasons that their forebears went to church: for consolation, guidance, spiritual renewal. It does their souls good. It grants them a reprieve from the workaday world and access to a realm that is somehow nobler, somehow loftier, than the one they inhabit all the other days of their lives.

And yet a paradox presents itself. The reader will pardon my bluntness, I hope, but if it is true, as it is often confidently asserted, that a receptive, open-minded public is essential for art's well-being, why is it that in this, the most open-minded, the most respectful, the most indulgent period in the history of art, the labors of our artists are no better than they are. Since artists are now more thoroughly adulated than at any earlier moment in our culture you might expect that art would flourish accordingly; that these days would bring forth a richer, more manifold harvest of genius than we have seen before. Consider too Robert Hughes's telling calculation that more people are graduated from American art schools every two years than there were citizens in the city of Florence during the last quarter of the fifteenth century. The sense of fairness seems to require, the law of averages seems to demand, that we too should have our artistic geniuses, and plenty of them.

Why then does art seem so much less impressive now than in the days when artists were scorned by men like Mario Equicola, when they bowed to the power of princes, the wealth of the bourgeoisie, the rod of the Inquisition? I pose the question not, of course, to advocate a return to those times, but to suggest, contrary to the common opinion, that the poverty of so much contemporary art is nothing more or less than the price it must pay for the freedom it so conspicuously enjoys.

If my assessment of contemporary art sounds unduly severe, consider that not even its most engaged supporters claim otherwise. More insidiously, they reject notions of quality as outmoded and elitist; they praise the artist for humor, good intentions, political insight, everything other than mere artistic excellence. And yet, however loudly some deny it, the more sensitive critics of the younger generation assuredly envy their elders with all their hearts: for they had Jackson Pollock and Mark Rothko to discover and to call to the world's attention; they were the ones to whom we looked for guidance through the works of Jasper Johns and Frank Stella. Younger critics have to exert all their historical imagination to conceive what it must have felt like to encounter art at once revolutionary and great.

Who are the artists about whom it is now possible to be energetically enthusiastic? The art that is revolutionary is not very good, and the art that is good is certainly not great. There are good enough artists around—that is not the issue or the point. There are artists to amuse us for a moment or intrigue us for an hour, to make us see things in some clever light. But where are the great ones, the deep ones, the obscenely gifted ones?

In part, what we have been witnessing these past twenty years has been a sense of depletion that is periodically visited upon a civilization's powers of creativity. Such moments are a little like economic recessions, except that they strike far less frequently and are far more entrenched when they do. This was true of the last quarter of the fourteenth century; the last quarter of the seventeenth century; and the fourth, fifth, and sixth decades of the nineteenth century. Not every age can or must bring forth works of genius. And it may be that our century, having nurtured so many splendid monuments to the imagination, has, in its closing decades, earned the right to rest.

But whatever turns out to be the final cause of our artistic recession, the immediate cause is nothing other than the pervasive and unchecked reverence in which art is held by critics and public alike. The most striking feature of recent artistic discourse, the quality that sets it apart from all earlier discussions, has been its chronic unwillingness to address the weaknesses inherent in what our artists do.

For example, in a recent Weekend section of the *New York Times*, which probably devotes more space to art than any other nonspecialist publication, all ten gallery reviews were favorable, even though the praise tended to be of the tepid, hedging, irresolute variety. It is hard to imagine the book, film, theater, music, or even food critics of the *New York Times* succumbing to such a degree of chinlessness. Yet this is fairly typical of art criticism in our day. Somehow critics have gotten it into their heads that, as midwives of the artistic process, they are to encourage artists and respectfully offer suggestions. To sit in judgment is not their job.

This timidity begins to make sense when you consider that critics have traditionally missed the point about the best art of their generation. Remember the outcries against Courbet, Monet, Van Gogh, Picasso, and Pollock, whom most contemporary critics savaged with remorseless merriment. In a sense, we can distinguish two main types of art critic: John Ruskin, the angry reactionary, and Baudelaire, the sensitive, forward-looking friend of art. Because the Baudelaires of the world have been right far more often than the Ruskins, today, with only the rarest exceptions, everyone wants to be Baudelaire. Never again, critics are resolved, will they miss the boat as embarrassingly as their forbears did when confronted with Impressionism and Cubism. Better that a thousand nonentities should be heralded as the new Picasso than that the new Picasso should meet with scorn or neglect!

This same attitude has spread to the public, at least those fifteen million who have an interest in art. Who is to decide what is good art and bad art, they will ask. Isn't it true that Van Gogh sold only one painting in his lifetime? Like the critics, they are absolutely resolved not to be part of the philistine majority that once claimed that a seven-year-old could paint a Picasso, that mocked Pollock as Jack the Dripper. No, this generation of art lovers, all fifteen million of them, must be in the select group that gets the point. As a result, the more fervid their interest in art becomes, the less disposed they are to view it with the necessary standard of detachment. And so the free fall of art continues, with no immediate end in sight.

As H. G. Wells is said to have remarked on first seeing the Manhattan skyline: "What great ruins these will make!" In the realm of culture, every era produces certain artifacts that seem imposing as long as they are current and unconscionably awful the second they cease to be current. Our cultural landscape has always been blighted by these disfigured traces of what were once its proudest and tallest towers, but it takes a strong stomach to consider with equanimity what future generations will make of what we have loved, all those floating basketballs and burping cathodes and morbidly solemn pronouncements posing as art. Indeed, what will we ourselves think of this art once it has been shorn of its preeminent grace, the fact of its newness? Only by reclaiming the right to criticize art, to call the makers to account and insist that they do better, shall we be free of the lugubrious cycle that, for almost two decades now, has sapped most of the vitality out of the visual arts. If revival is inevitable in our lifetime, it can be hastened by our words and our convictions. If it is not inevitable, and we cannot be sure that it is, then it is not only important that we speak up, it is imperative.

Though we may love the art of the past, in a very real sense we may not claim it as our own. Only this art that is being made here and now, while we are alive, while we are present, can properly be called our art. And so we are right to see it with something of parental or filial solicitude and right to think that it may be worth fighting for.

T W O

The Art World

Artcards come fifteen to a pack. They look, feel, even smell like baseball cards. The only thing missing is the frangible slab of pink bubble gum that always accompanies those mainstays of American boyhood. Surely Todd Alden's Artcards are among the cheekier send-ups of today's art world. As with real baseball cards, you never know which fifteen art-world players you will get out of a possible one hundred twenty-six. That's part of the fun, of course, as is the quest to own every last one of them. "Buy 'em, collect 'em, trade 'em . . . auction 'em!" says the jaunty inscription on the back.

As parodies go, the Artcards work admirably. David Salle's card, for example, shows the artist in a vaguely menacing, muscular pose. His name appears above his head. Below his waist is written "Gagosian," the name of the gallery that represents him and, by implication, the team he plays for. To show that he is a painter (rather than a critic, dealer, collector, or curator such as also appear in the cards), at his left is a fifties-style cartoon head of a beatnik with a goatee, dark glasses, and a beret, the emblem of the artist. On the back are his date of birth, where he was educated, and where he lives.

"Before becoming one of the most commerically successful painters of the eighties," the caption reads, getting the breezy tone just right, "David worked as a paste-up artist laying out spreads for the porno magazine *Stag*. In fact, many of his graphic female nudes were 'appropriated' from its pages." Equally good are the cards for artists Robert Gober, Cindy Sherman, and Marcel Broodthaers; Whitney curator Lisa Phillips; critic Robert Pincus-Witten; and collector Agnes Gund.

Few art-world figures objected to being included in the cards, and one suspects that most were flattered. Which just goes to prove that everyone scoffs at the art world, not least the people who, by any sane reckoning, are its very bastions. What is the art world? It is everything having to do with art minus the art itself. It is the corporation that sponsors the blockbuster exhibitions; the critic who puffs the work; the expert who authenticates it; the leisured class that buys it; the company that insures it; the man who frames and installs it. There is room as well for the groupies and hangers-on, for snobs and philistines, for true intellectuals and phonies. In the elaborate pecking order of the art world, there are, however, punctilious protocols of success, mediocrity, and failure. "I can walk into the Odeon or Barocco or the other places that artists go," the sculptor Judy Pfaff recently told the *New York Times*, "and speed-read my place in the art world. If you're not hot, there's a lull when you pass through the door."

All of this is admirably lampooned by Todd Alden's Artcards. And yet something about them doesn't quite ring true. One is reminded of nothing so much as Robert Altman's *The Player*, and the eagerness with which all those Hollywood heavies clamored for cameos. In both cases, the result was to demonstrate their emancipation from the system that feeds them, through an ironic distancing that nevertheless underscored their enviable centrality. Merely by appearing in these cards as an art-world player one transcends that status. So what is the art world? The art world is the others. It is those who cannot view it with the necessary irony, those who, through a curious paradox, want to break into it but cannot.

Because of all the vocal and sometimes sincere dissatisfaction inspired by the art world, many people believe that things have never been as bad as they are now. This is a mistake. In *The Development of Modern Art*, the distinguished and disgruntled critic Julius Meier-Graefe asserted almost a century ago that, "The amount of talking and writing about art in our day exceeds that in all other epochs put together.... Art has become like caviar—everyone wants to have it, whether they like it or not.... It has become the feudal cognisance of the aspiring bourgeoisie, as necessary to the well-educated as some indispensable garment.... The popularization of art is rendered thoroughly impossible by the extravagant prices commanded by recognized works of art and demanded by those that are not so recognized, in a frantic, absurd, and, unhappily, thoroughly dishonest traffic."

A generation ago, Robert Morris, one of the noisiest and most gifted artists of the sixties and seventies, went so far as to assert that, "Artists' lives are bound within the repressive structure of the art world: the iron triangle is made up of museums, galleries, and the media."

The art world as we know it is several centuries old. For Alberti and his fifteenth century contemporaries it didn't exist, since art as yet was the province of sovereigns, princes of the church, and captains of finance. Only on the streets of Rome in the 1600s did art finally become that portable, barterable object of our longing, the sport of hawkers and the furniture of the bourgeoisie. By the eighteenth century, with Holland's ascendancy over Italy in the mainstream of Western art and with the bourgeoisie's ascendancy over church and aristocracy, there emerged a new art world structurally akin to our own. Museums, as public institutions, first came into being with the opening of the Louvre in 1793. Special exhibitions were still far in the future, but the Parisian Salon, founded in 1737, was annually thrown open to the public for praise and ridicule. The modern notion of the art school started in 1635 with the Ecole des Beaux-Arts in Paris and in 1768 with London's Royal Academy. Meanwhile, dealers like Gersaint, the friend of Watteau, trafficked in the latest merchandise as well as in what might be called the secondary market of older works. There even existed an emerging press in the pages of *Le Figaro* and *Le Mercure de France*, and for a more elite audience, in Grimm's *Correspondence Littéraire* and Goethe's *Propylaen*.

This was the tiny embryo from which the present octopus would grow. Yet only very recently did it assume the dimensions it has today. Once the art world was so sparsely inhabited that you could live to an old age without ever meeting anyone who called himself an artist, let alone a dealer or critic. Curators, restorers, and art lawyers hardly even existed. Scarcely more than a generation ago you could have seen, in the space of a single afternoon, most of the contemporary galleries in New York. Had you visited a downtown gallery, you might have seen in a single room most of the advanced artists of the age, shabby, anonymous, and broke. Of course, back then most of the people who now would kill for one of their discarded drawings would not have crossed the street, let alone taken a cab, to see those ornery and unwashed demimondaines.

For as yet no glamour accrued to them. They were not the tanned and fatted darlings of the society pages. In her book *The Art Biz*, Alice Goldfarb Marquis relates how Robert Rauschenberg sold only one painting at his first one-man show at Leo Castelli's. And the woman who bought it was so abashed by the ridicule of her friends, when they saw it in her living room, that she promptly returned it. This was a time when, few though the galleries were, the artists seemed to be fewer still. Provided you had anything at all in the way of talent or appeal, it wasn't too difficult to find a place to exhibit. When Andy Warhol walked into Castelli's soon after that dealer's exhibitions of Johns and Rauschenberg, the dapper Italian was unimpressed by his work, finding it too reminiscent of Roy Lichtenstein. Castelli suggested Warhol try the Stable Gallery. He did so, and was picked up, with no especial eagerness. Thus his career began.

The greatest change that the art world has undergone since then has been a change of size rather than of structure. Now in the throes of a Malthusian nightmare, the art world is overpopulated to the point of bursting. For every artist who gets into a SoHo gallery, two hundred more seem to be pounding at the doors, and for each of these hopefuls, a dozen others are spilling annually out of the master-of-fine-arts programs of the West, waiting for their chance at the honey pot. According to the most recent census, 900,000 Americans consider themselves professional artists. According to a prospectus issued by the School of Visual Arts, ninety thousand of them live in the New York area alone. Even though the recession has battered the Manhattan art market, the fact that it has closed seventy galleries over the past two years is less impressive than that six times that number have remained open.

This giddy expansion is visible throughout the art world. The days are long gone when an aspiring young art historian could approach his subject like Columbus sailing into a new world, where little was known and all was to be discovered. Now his dissertation reads like the footnote to the dissertation someone wrote a generation ago, and the footnote to a footnote of someone writing a generation before that. The days are long gone as well when nice young men wound up in museum work, though they were often equipped with nothing more than a good name and a gentleman's C. No training was required because no training existed.

Now, when everything exists in order to end up as a course at an accredited institution, when classes are taught not only in the history of art but in curatorship as well, the crush to become part of the museum world is so great that institutions like the Whitney offer degrees in curatorship itself. Aspiring young men and women, armed with the relevant texts of Derrida and Lacan, set up exhibitions that "interrogate" the very notion of the exhibition. When they get out they count themselves lucky to find work as interns. If this option fails, many of the young turn to the auction houses. Here as well, the major firms have initiated courses for those who want to be auctioneers or "experts," and their graduates too are willing to wait in the wings for years as interns.

It has become so easy to carp about the art world that it is almost an intellectual challenge to find anything nice to say about it. In fact, the only thing really wrong with the art world is all the extravagant and entirely unwarranted expectations that we seem to have for it. If we applied to it the same standards of acquisitiveness and greed, of ambition and labor, that we apply to say the meat-packing industry, we should find that it is in no way inferior to meat packing, though obviously no better. It possesses the same shrewdness and the same gritty integrity. Only when we labor under the illusion that so vast a network of human beings will congregate for any other purpose than their own profit and preferment do we run into difficulties. Granted, this myth is fostered by curators, dealers, critics, and artists themselves, and buttressed by some eminent exceptions to the rule. But those in the art world who cannot see through this calculated myth either do not last long or do not go far.

And yet, it is truly astounding how much of that energy and rampant careerism, how much of that shrewdness and expertise, is pressed into the pursuit of an object of almost acrobatic impracticality. For rarely in human endeavor are whim and fashion, dreams, misprisions, and cant brewed into a costlier concoction than in the art world.

Consider, for example, the Panza deal. With an abundance of fanfare and some nervousness the Guggenheim Museum announced in February 1990 that it had purchased from Count Giuseppe Panza di Biumo, an Italian industrialist, some three hundred works of art by American minimalists of the sixties and seventies. Donald Judd, Carl Andre, and Dan Flavin, the sort of artists who quicken the pulse of the international market, were only among the more prominent artists included. To sweeten the deal even further, the count's perfectly pleasant villa in Varese had been thrown in at no extra cost.

The transaction, organized by the museum's new director, Thomas Krens, was almost ten years in the making. The amount they finally agreed upon, though never disclosed, is generally reckoned at about $35 million. What is known is that, in order to make payment, the museum had to unload Marc Chagall's much-loved *Birthday* painted in 1923, Wassily Kandinsky's *Fugue* from 1914, and Amedeu Modigliani's *Boy in a Blue Suit* of two years later, and that these three paintings sold at Sotheby's in May 1990 for $47 million.

Now minimalism is not to everyone's taste. Even its strongest adherents must admit that its drastic maceration of form, its chromatic abstinence, and the glacial coolness of its message can take you only so far. Yet it is surely a serious, fastidious, and demanding art, which, at its best, has enriched our visual culture. And it must also be said, first, that there was probably no finer collection of this art in all the world, and second, that in 1990, when a single Van Gogh sold for $82.5 million, the prospect of getting three hundred of the best works of some of our best artists at less than half that price sounded extremely reasonable.

The provocativeness of the purchase lay elsewhere. It lay in the fact that much of the sculpture that had been bought did not exactly exist. That is, the work existed on paper but had never actually been constructed. The count had preferred to purchase it in this condition, since, as he pointed out with no apparent irony, the fact of its having no material existence exempted it from some rather steep Italian import taxes. Instead he got blue prints, together with that all-important signed certificate attesting to his total ownership of the commodity in question.

In one sense, you do not really own something until you have the legal right to destroy it. In the movie *The Magic Christian* there is a truly horrific scene in which David Niven buys a Rembrandt at auction for a million dollars, and, without even removing the totemic object from the premises, pulls out a pair of scissors and starts cutting it into confetti. In default of this power, possession is no better than a lifetime loan and the hardly satisfying privilege of leaving it to anyone you like.

But to Panza's surprise and dismay, his ownership proved to be not nearly as total as could be wished. The problems began when he tried to construct the art. As is usual with such works, this had to be done at Panza's expense, without the artists' assistance. He hired workmen to build objects as close to the sculptors' specifications as possible, and only afterward did some of the artists decide to visit the premises and give their blessings to the result.

But a few of the artists, most vociferously Donald Judd, complained that the results were not at all up to their finical demands. Judd charged that Panza had rushed the facture of his works and, in his hurry, had resorted to an inferior form of plywood. For this reason, Judd refused to cooperate anymore with the count, and because he had created the works specifically to meet the dimensions of the count's villa, he denied that they could be transferred to the Guggenheim.

As Michael Torvan, an assistant curator at the museum, explained to the *New York Times*, "Minimalism fought against walls and galleries. As part of its meaning it posed a challenge to what museum and exhibition spaces were. . . . When an artist makes work that has instructions attached, you get into a serious debate about what comprises the work. . . . There is no real precedent for these questions and no real precedent for this many of these objects going into a public institution."

The implications were immediately apparent. "As far as I'm concerned," Judd declared, "the Guggenheim has bought a pig in a poke." In other words, although the museum had paid all that money, without the artist's imprimatur all it had really acquired were some sheets of paper with scribblings that vaguely alluded to a still-born, if not aborted, object. Things could not get much worse than this. For an instituition like the Guggenheim, the authenticity of the object is an idea of almost religious power. If artists refused to acknowledge the work as their own, all of its aura vanished away, leaving the museum with some useless pieces of string or wood, a length of plexiglas, perhaps, and a disincarnated idea.

One of the works that Panza did not sell, but loaned to the Guggenheim, was a conceptual piece by Lawrence Weiner, a work that raises more questions than perhaps it intended. I propose to the reader an experiment. I seek his or her complicity in the commission of a crime: the theft of a work of art. For I will give the reader—quite literally—a work by Lawrence Weiner, as it appeared on the walls of the Guggenheim SoHo:

LOUDLY MADE NOISE (forte) AND/OR MODERATELY LOUDLY (mezzoforte)
SOFTLY MADE NOISE (piano) AND/OR MODERATELY SOFTLY (mezzopiano)
NOISE MADE VERY LOUDLY (fortissimo) AND/OR MODERATELY LOUDLY (mezzoforte)
NOISE MADE VERY SOFTLY (pianissimo) AND/OR MODERATELY SOFTLY (mezzopiano)

No, this is not a poem. This is Art, and all that that implies. There you have the artist's conceptual statement, exactly as it appeared on the walls of the museum, with no alteration except that at the museum the parentheses were painted blue. Even if we accept the premises of conceptual art and of concrete poetry this does not get very far. In fact, it is really quite astonishingly tedious for something so brief, and it is hard to imagine how anything like this could be made much more interesting. Yet I have another point in mind. This is what the artist has to say about such works of art: "I am politically a socialist. . . . Here I [was] working everyday, fully participating in my culture, yet everything I [was] making could be owned by anyone who read it. It was not necessary to buy it."

Not ten years after making that statement, in February 1993, Mr. Weiner placed on walls of the Marian Goodman Gallery four conceptual pieces, which I shall also give the reader: BREAD

CAST UPON THE WATER, WINE POURED INTO THE SEA, STONES PLACED UPON EACH OTHER, WOOD THRUST INTO BRINE. Mr. Weiner, with all best vanguardist and socialist intentions in the world, seems to have reconciled himself to selling each of these works at $40,000. The happy few who have purchased them cannot take the walls of the gallery home, of course, nor would it make any sense to peel off the paint, as is sometimes done with Renaissance frescoes. For the material is the language itself. Thus, what they got, besides the language, was a signed certificate registering the words of the piece and the understanding that the work would not be sold to anyone else. It was in the fullest sense of the term theirs: They owned it.

And yet, if as Mr. Weiner has said, these works can belong to everyone, why would anyone want to pay $40,000 for them? If $40,000 gives you some special title to them, how can those other beneficiaries of his socialism be said to own it? Although I saw these works at the gallery, I also had them communicated to me over the telephone by one of the gallerists, the first time, perhaps, that a work of art was so transmitted. It all comes down to a question of charisma, of annointing, for which some people are willing to pay $40,000. In what is almost a parody of this process, a member of the Guggenheim staff told me that although the work they had displayed did not belong to the museum and although it has now been painted over and thus ceases to exist, still they were excited at the possibility that Count Panza might decide to offer it to them as a gift.

This curious alchemy of rampant acquisition and neurotic restraint is new to our culture, and only recently has it taken on the character of an obsession. Surely, high prices were paid in the past for the works of famous painters, and some reputable artists even tried to sell their own works as the labors of more illustrious contemporaries: Sebastian Bourdon painted some very nice Claude Lorrains; Bellotto was a dab hand at Canaletto's Venetian cityscapes. Good art was always valued and, as a commodity, it had been sought after at least since the seventeenth century. But the insistence that it be not merely good but authentic, that it be not merely attributable but documented, took hold only in the middle of the eighteenth century and became widespread at the end of the nineteenth.

For most of the period known as the "old masters," authenticity was largely irrelevant. Rubens, it is true, drew up for the king of England a price list relative to the percentage of a canvas to be painted by him as opposed to his studio. Yet the king sought Rubens's participation not because he was Rubens, but because he was great, and because the more evidence there was of his hand, the better the work was likely to be. But now authenticity is sought for its own sake and is often more highly valued than excellence. In practice this means that anything by Rubens, no matter how weak, is better than anything by Theodor Rombouts, no matter how fine.

Today, prices stand or fall on the basis of this perceived authenticity. The only thing that distinguishes Weiner's work from an exact copy is our knowledge that this charismatic biological entity has sanctioned one work and not another. And yet, why is it that, at the very moment when this authenticity is all important, it is being so widely and vociferously challenged, usually by the very people who crave it most? In her hugely influential book, *The Originality of the Avant-Garde and Other Modernist Myths*, Rosalind Krauss has called into question the unique and authentic artifact, which she defines as quintessentially modernist. By valorizing the copy, she contends, we create "a demythologizing criticism and a truly postmodernist art, both of them acting now to void the basic propositions of modernism, to liquidate them by exposing their fictitious condition."

For Krauss and others of her school, authenticity and originality are the two bugbears of the older criticism. Not only do they smell vaguely undemocratic and elitist: more grievously, they're modernist, and modernism is old and establishmentarian, and everyone, naturally, wants to be new and postmodern.

In a similar spirit Thomas Krens, the Guggenheim director and architect of the Panza deal, recently inaugurated the Osmosis Series as "an alternative to the museum's more traditional one-person and thematic group exhibitions. These conventional formats tend to underscore the ingenuity of one artist's achievements or the singularity of a particular aesthetic movement. As a challenge to such notions, which perpetuate modernism's faith in the concept of originality, Osmosis encourages artists to work collaboratively, winning new aesthetic territory." Was this the same man who only three years before was happy to pay many millions of dollars for the prestige of some disembodied ideas as long as a few blue-chip artists were willing to put their authorship in writing?

These and similar notions can be traced to one famous essay, "The Work of Art in the Age of Mechanical Reproduction," written by the German philosopher Walter Benjamin in 1936. Krauss has called this essay "the most important statement yet made about the vocation of photography." In it Benjamin announced that, with the coming of photography and its ability to reproduce works of art ad infinitum, the mystique of the individual, unique artifact must vanish. "What is really jeopardized [by photography]," Benjamin writes, "is the authority of the object.... That which whithers in the age of mechanical reproduction is the aura of the work of art."

Doubtless it will profit the doctoral candidates of the future, scavenging the annals of art for any unclaimed dissertation topics, to calculate how often this essay has been quoted, alluded to, pillaged, adulated, and misread in the art writing of the eighties and nineties. The doctrinal authority and prestige of its author have been invoked to validate everything from the combines of Rauschenberg and the multiples of Warhol, to Mike Bidlo's sophomoric performances and the plagiarisms of Sherrie Levine. The death knell of the individual object and of originality itself rings like catechism through the turgid pages of contemporary criticism.

And yet, no one seems to have noticed or cared much that Benjamin's thesis is palpably wrong. We have now lived with mechanical reproduction, as he calls it, for over 150 years.

Reproduction of art has reached such a degree of perfection that technology now exists that would make it impossible, except under a microscope, to distinguish an original from a copy. It may even be that greater pleasure can be had from seeing the latest, magnificent photographs of the newly restored Sistine ceiling, than from actually standing in the airless chamber, straining to view the distant and ill-lit surface, while five hundred over-excited, over-heated tourists jostle you from behind. Furthermore, the unaided eye cannot take in the whole ceiling at once, though the camera can, and it can also lift you to within inches of the ceiling's surface.

But the result of photography's success is not, as Benjamin predicted, that the art object has lost its value, but that its value has been hugely enhanced. Benjamin's argument makes as much sense as to say that with the advent of film and television, theater must cease to exist and actors themselves, those living, physical entities, must cease to be the object of anyone's affection. Recordings, by the same logic, must empty the concert halls; televised sports events must empty the stadiums. But the univeral experience of modern times gives the lie to this prediction. If anything, the ability to reproduce an object a millionfold has caused the original to seem more holy than ever. The excitement of standing in front of the Mona Lisa itself, seeing it perhaps through the eye of a camera, with a blizzard of bulbs flashing around you, is very like the excitement of meeting a real celebrity, previously known secondhand, but now encountered in the flesh.

Nowhere, however, was Benjamin more wrong than when he spoke of the art of photography itself: "From a photographic negative for example, one can make any number of prints; to ask for the authentic print makes no sense." And yet, any connoisseur of Edward Weston's photographs will covet a print made by the master himself, and one person at least was recently willing to pay $190,000 for one. Later versions that his son Bret made under his supervision might sell for a tenth of that sum, while posthumous prints made by another son, Cole, might go for a hundredth. In fact, auction catalogs often reproduce photographs at their actual size and these reproductions are worth nothing.

It is this aura of the authenticated object, nothing more and nothing less, that is the art world's true stock-in-trade. It is this aura that gives meaning to Chris Burden's $24,000 cream pitcher and prices a Lawrence Weiner at $10,000 a word. If some alchemist could bottle this quintessence the way we bottle the waters of Evian or Saratoga Springs, perhaps we should have no further use for the work of art itself. Indeed, this spurious adulation has already turned us away from the object of our reputed love, causing us to praise mediocrities of illustrious authorship and to overlook true excellence to which no great name can be attached. To that degree, it has become the enemy of art.

How shall we counter this creeping contagion? Perhaps the only way is to devise an aesthetics of forgeries, of copies, studio works, and all the other corrupt acts of beauty that harrow the soul, and perhaps even menace the existence, of the art world. Anyone who is not prepared to love a forgery or a copy is not prepared honestly to love the real thing either. Anyone who will withdraw his admiration from Rembrandt's *Polish Rider* if it turns out, as some Dutch experts now contend, to be by a student of the master, can never have truly loved it at all. Such a viewer has been enamored of a name, nothing more. Usually, of course, life is made easier by the manifest inferiority of the copy. But this fact must not distract us from the principle of the thing.

All of these issues were brought to a head a few years back when a group of British scholars decided to prove, to no one's satisfaction but their own, that a painting known as *The Fortune Teller*, which the Metropolitan Museum had bought in 1960 as by the seventeenth-century Georges de la Tour, was, in fact, a fake. The implications were: "Now that you know that the work isn't by de la Tour, you will naturally get it off your wall." But, if in fact it had not been created by de la Tour (though surely it was), it would have been by someone as good as that artist, if not better, since it clearly stood out among the fine works attributed to him already. And if the work had been painted in the 1940s, as the British contended, we should be delighted to know that such fine art in this manner was still possible.

The only honest way to admire a work of art, at least at the initial stages of our experiencing it, is to disregard its date, provenance, and authorship and to admit that, in theory, a forgery could be better and more interesting than the authentic object. This view does not deny that an imitation by definition lacks originality and that originality can be a part of art's excellence. Nor can we deny the satisfaction that we humans, sentimental as we are, take in the knowledge that the divine Michelangelo once touched that sheet of paper. But we must admit that this is very different from objectively admiring the visible object before our eyes. It is the aesthetics of autograph collecting, not the aesthetics of art. It is no great exaggeration to say that the art world has been transformed into a massive, glorified autograph market.

Money, the measure of this market, has become the fourth dimension of art. Once ancillary to the appreciation of art, price now lodges itself like a reflex at the center of our aesthetic faculty. We can no longer think about art without glancing down the long perspectival price tunnel whose brightly lit foreground features all $82.5-million worth of Vincent Van Gogh's *Dr. Gachet*, with the rest of human artifice receding by degrees into less remunerative twilight.

In the days of Pliny, Vasari, and Ruskin, people used to rank artists. Everyone knew that Michelangelo and Raphael occupied the summit of art, and there was little disagreement as to where other artists stood in relation to them. But in our own age of dogmatic relativism, when the very idea of rank seems foolhardy and irrelevant, if not worse, the old urge has merely been translated into monetary terms. We know that Vincent Van Gogh is the *ne plus ultra* of art, because his paintings make more at auction than the works of other artists. Relativists by reflex, we are perversely in love with calibration, and there is nothing quite like a price tag to expunge from criticism its irritating vagueness.

Price is to aesthetic judgment what digital clocks, exact to the nanosecond, are to hourglasses. Amid the fragile incertitude of the critical act, price is a fixed and unerring point. Every auction held at Sotheby's and Christie's is furnished with a massive electronic board that records each bid as it is called out by the auctioneer. A shiver of metallic plates on the screen gives us, in no time at all, the exact price, hence the exact value down to the dollar, pound, lira, mark, French franc, Swiss franc, and yen. Here is the new truth about the object. Here is all you need to know.

I have no intention, however, of repeating the hackneyed laments about filthy lucre. Not to consider money in the causation of Florence in the 1400s or Rome two centuries later or Paris two centuries after that, would be as foolish as to reduce all of that art to money, as certain Marxists now try to do. In a city in which Giotto, the greatest painter of the fourteenth century and not the least of its usurers, could write a hymn praising money and mocking poverty, only a fool would have expressed any dismay over the commercializing of art. The later Medici might pretend to loftier things, but in general patrons and artists knew very well where they stood with one another. Their precisely drawn out contracts were the result of a shrewd tug of war, with each side pulling for its own advantage.

In *Painting and Experience in Fifteenth Century Italy*, Michael Baxandall cites a contract signed by Giovanni d'Angelo de' Bardi and Sandro Botticelli for what would become the latter's ethereal *Virgin and Child*, now in Berlin: "Wednesday 3 August 1485: At the chapel of S. Spirito seventy-eight florins fifteen soldi in payment of seventy-five gold florins of gold, paid to Sandro Botticelli on his reckoning, as follows—two florins for ultramarine, thirty-eight florins for gold and preparation of the panel, and thirty-five florins for his brush [i.e. his personal skill]."

In the same spirit, Borso d'Este commissioned the beautiful frescoes in the Palazzo Schifanoia, that crowning glory of the

Emilian quattrocento, at ten Bolognese lire a square foot. It was a neat transaction, like any other, and there was little talk of inspiration, infinity, or the interrogation of tradition. A rare bird like Alberti might, as a hobby, amuse himself with architecture and perspective, or sully his hands with sculpting bronze medallions, but to most artists, born as they were into the artisan class, this would have made about as much sense as aspiring to be an amateur cobbler or bricklayer.

There is nothing wrong with the desire to make a buck. It may even be that the art world's frantic desire to do so is the nicest thing we can say about it. It provides a healthy ballast for their hot-air balloon, which otherwise might go sailing off into the stratosphere. Less healthy, however, is the fact that this acquisitiveness is never expressed as the point behind most of what the art world does, but as a merely incidental detail. True, almost every modern movement was lauched by doughty pioneers who were confident that they would never see a penny from their revolt, and who were more astonished than anyone when, as often seemed to happen, the money started pouring in. But this does not justify the art world in its perennial charade that money doesn't exist, or that it is only others who are concerned with it, or that one's fascination with it, like that of Jeff Koons's, is glamorously ironic and postmodern.

The best that can be said for many dealers and artists is that if they deceive others, they do so because, in all the sincerity of their hearts, they have first succeeded in deceiving themselves. A friend and independent dealer whose integrity I respect tried to reason with me. He tried to show me why Lawrence Weiner's work was worth every penny of the $40,000 that the gallery was seeking. I was given to understand that I did not understand what conceptualism was all about. I answered that I fully appreciated what the conceptualists were trying to do, but that it was not clear to me why a few disincarnated words, and rather tedious words at that, should sell for so much when the complete works of Shakespeare could be had, in some cases, for less than the price of admission to see those rather tedious words. To be brutally philistine about it, what, after all, was one getting for one's money? Why, even if we accepted the premises of this art, should we want to own it at all. Why, if we were willing to pay $40,000, would we not pay $400,000, or $4 million, or $4 trillion?

My friend's answer would have seemed like the height of cynicism were he not so obviously sincere. How different was this transaction from purchasing a Van Gogh and keeping it in a vault? In either case all one really had was the abstract knowledge of possessing the thing. I asserted that the work had no more visual merit than if you emblazoned a wall with ten words picked at random from the corpus of tort law in the state of Utah. He rejoined that many collectors and museums had been perfectly content to buy works for much more even though these had no esthetic merit whatever, and I had to concede that this was certainly true. And besides, he said, what was the ultimate value of art, anyway? I had expected this response, of course, and saw little point in pursuing that line of discussion too much further. Yet it struck me that from this dealer's point of view, the purchase of a work of art was no longer an exchange of cash for a commodity. It was infinitely more abstract. It was a gesture as philosophical as Weiner's language art. It was a $40,000 beau geste, a gratuitous act, which, like ex votos in an earlier age, accrued to the virtue and public standing of the donor.

The problem with paying $40,000 for a Weiner, or assigning a price to any work of art, is that from that moment forth there can be no further recourse to vagueness. From that moment forth we have clipped the wings of art's fabled infinity, even though in many cases it is that vague infinity, and nothing else, that we are paying for. "You invest in the immortality of the masterpiece," reads the legend on one of Barbara Kruger's provocative images, the words superimposed on the almost touching hands of the Sistine Chapel's Adam and God. In most transactions, there is a measurable correspondence between a thing and its price tag. Petrolium, wallpaper, European travel, pornography, snorkels, and dog food are all rooted in a world of shared experience and shared values. Only in art, it seems, has the object been finally freed from its moorings in the world of real things.

But how is this aura created and where does it come from? What in Koons's floating basketballs makes them so desirable that at least two buyers were recently willing to bid over $100,000 for them at Christie's? Most people, after all, on first seeing them, found them ugly, tawdry, inartistic. Indeed, Koons had chosen them precisely for their inaesthetic qualities. And yet, as Lucy Lippard shrewdly remarked years ago, "[Nothing] stays ugly for long in today's art scene." Or, as Roy Lichtenstein said of his reasons for choosing comic book art back in the late fifties, "It was hard to get a painting that was despicable enough so that no one would hang it—everybody was hanging everything. . . . The one thing everyone hated was commercial art; apparently they didn't hate that enough either."

There comes a magic moment when certain works by certain artists suddenly shed their explosive newness, their arrogant unprecedentedness, and, entering the halls of art history, take on the appearance of having always been there. They have been before our eyes for so long (five years should do it) that they become fixtures of our vision. They have appeared in the press, in galleries, and exhibitions; they have found their way into the track-lighted living rooms of the wealthy and the perfumed chambers of the great; they have made the headlines of the auction world, and figured in someone's book, and been parodied in a *New Yorker* cartoon, and plagiarized in a vodka ad, and suddenly they become Art As We Know It. At this point they subtly begin to alter vision itself: whenever we see a Brillo box in the wild, or a regulation Spalding's basketball dribbled across the Felt Forum, we suddenly find it—artistic.

This appetite for art knows neither stint nor limit, whether the art is stashed in a safe or glimpsed in museums or reproduced in books. Any form of art, whatever its age or origin, suddenly becomes relevant to the collector as soon as the more established avenues of acquisition are priced out of the market, and to the scholar when nothing remains to be said about some more popular field. Thus there is no longer any art in existence that we are permitted not to take seriously, no matter how old or new or high or low, no matter who made it or where it came from. All art is relevant and all art is expensive. There is, we may fairly surmise, not a second in the long continuum of art history, stretching all the way from the Gravettian earth mothers of the Upper Paleolithic to the still moist canvases of Spring Street, that is not being marketed and written about by someone, somewhere in the art world.

A century ago, fifty years ago, there were huge lacunae in the market, and huge pockets of inattention in the study of art history. It has been the work of this century systematically, if unconsciously, to fill each crack and bubble until everything is spoken for. Short of some unimaginable cataclysm, a reversal is improbable. Unlike the past, the future of taste will consist in a differential not of the quick and the dead, but of the incandescently hot and the lukewarm. The latter will be invested with a punctuated or rotating immortality, whereby everything will always be taken seriously, and every other generation fifteen months of overexposure will force its prices upward. Never again will it be possible for any artist to fall as precipitously from grace as did Guido Reni, whom the eminent French classicist Nicolas Poussin thought one of the three greatest painters in history, but whose works, as late as the 1950s, could be had at auction for $300.

All art is cherished and studied, but no art is more avidly cherished or more assiduously studied than the art of our own time and culture. You might think, because the art of the past is rarer and more fragile, that it would be more fervently sought. But it doesn't happen that way. Whereas in the nineteenth century, art lovers might besmear a new canvas to give it the venerable look they liked, now we love contemporaneity; we love art that reflects ourselves. It is perhaps a little like the idiotic thrill of seeing oneself on closed-circuit TV. It answers to the same deep-seated layers of personal and collective vanity. This love spills over into a general love of modernism because our art is presaged in that art, and it also favors those forebears, like Piero della Francesca and Caravaggio, who seem to mirror our concerns, rather than artists like Raphael and Botticelli, who do not.

Clearly we have witnessed a revolution in taste when a painting by a living artist, Jasper Johns, sells for over $17.7 million. In Peter Watson's *From Manet to Manhattan*, two charts tell the whole fascinating story. Of the ten most expensive paintings auctioned in 1959–60, from £275,000 down to £48,000, only one, the least expensive, was the work of an artist of this century, Picasso. The rest, with a single eighteenth-century exception, dated from the seventeenth century. One generation later, the ten most expensive paintings of 1987–1990 (that it is four years instead of two is not important), sold from between $82.5 and $26.4 million, and dated from the twentieth century or the end of the nineteenth, with only one sixteenth-century exception at the very bottom.

These high prices reveal more than simply a taste for modernity. They point up the entrenched paradox of art in our time. For contemporary art was born of modernism's revolt against the establishment in the middle of the last century. However at odds modern and postmodern art have been, or have seemed to be, one ineradicable constant, running through both like a genetic code, has been that art must challenge order, disrupt complacency, disturb the peace.

"To be at odds with his times—there lies the raison d'être of the artist," André Gide told painters and sculptors, and they believed him. Then Herbert Read told them, "Art . . . is eternally disturbing, permanently revolutionary," and they believed that too.

Such sentiments as these formed the cultural model that galvanized creative people for six generations, and that has now become the flattest of platitudes. Not the least reason for the astonishing saleability of the art of the modern tradition, is that revolution and rebelliousness are now cherished for their own sake, as pleasant adornments to the human condition.

Turn anywhere you want in the art world and you see signs of this conviction: "An artist can be both diplomat and revolutionary," a smiling, tanned Robert Rauschenberg said in a recent *New York Times* ad that solicited upper-middle-class money for a worthy cause.

Introducing the 1993 Biennial at the Whitney, director David Ross wrote: "Inherent to a museum of American art is the responsibility to question as we celebrate, to provoke as well as to conciliate. The museum may indeed be a place of sanctuary for a war-weary world, yet its greatness lies in its ability to function simultaneously as a site for the contest of values and ideas."

We have come to the point were rebelliousness is offered as a college course. During its 1993 spring semester, Parson's School of Design, one of the largest art schools in the country, offered something called "Artist as Activist in the 90s." The catalog described the course as being offered "for those students who want to be activists in their lives and in their art.... It's important to unite to set our own agendas rather than conforming to those of others. Topics include: Performance and Street Art, Wheatpaste Art and Effectiveness of Postering... Affirmative Action and The Call for Diversity in the Art World. We will finish the semester by creating our own action.... Bring to the first class: A blank sketchbook which will become your activist journal and an article or piece of artwork about an issue that you feel affects you directly."

Other courses, by the way, included Development of the Corporate Image, for aspiring graphic designers, and Flower Drawing.

Yet rebels need reactionaries or they have no reason to exist. Here is where the engaged artist runs into difficulties. For how can he prove his manhood against an enemy that keeps caving in without a fight? The bourgeoisie was puzzled at first by Impressionism, Cubism, and Abstract Expressionism. But after a while it came to cherish these art forms so much that the rebelliousness that characterized each movement in differing degrees began to seem inseperable from great art, and finally to be indistinguishable from it. Thus, there was no brickbat that the fractious artist could hurl at the bourgeoisie that the bourgeoisie wasn't able to catch, indeed collect. If we liked Edouard Manet, the theory goes, maybe we will like this artist too. Since Manet has become valuable, maybe this painter as well will one day be valuable.

Clearly the revolution is over and the revolutionists have won. But most artists, like most revolutionists, never caught on that the act of revolt was different from the act of governance, that the forces that seized power could not sustain that power without themselves undergoing fundamental change. The thrill of rebellion is so intoxicating to the artists, so appealing to the bourgeoisie, and so lucrative to the market that they are all naturally loath to give it up. In the circumstances, the embattled artist, trying to separate himself from the bourgeoisie that sustains him, reminds one of that Japanese general who still will not accept that World War II ended half a century ago and who spends his time parading about in dress uniform on his desert island, cursing all who come near.

This sham battle is the real cause of the controversy between Senator Jesse Helms and the art world. Few people realized that each side needed the other for its own ends, and that both sides splendidly achieved what they wanted: The far right gained legitimacy in the eyes of its constituency, and the art world was allowed to continue dreaming of the barricades a little longer. For them, this was a kind of low-fat, low-tar, lite and user-friendly rebellion, with all the high drama and none of the sacrifice of real revolt. In a culture in which, according to *Spy* magazine, the abrasive Ron Baechler's $15,000 NEA grant went to paying a quarter of his 1990 taxes, the kind of abnegation required of earlier rebels is ludicrously beside the point. Not that artists should feel the pinch of penury; but, since the loudest opponents of the NEA usually do not, it would be nice if they dropped the pretense.

It is not that the government should not give grants either: but surely it is strange when certain artists, in their revolt against the establishment, not only expect to be bankrolled, but demand their subsidy from the very institutions for whose destruction they seem to cry out. Wasn't the government justified in balking at a grant that would have subsidized, and implicitly have endorsed, David Wojnarowicz's advocating that Senator Helms be doused with gasoline and set on fire, and that Representative Dannemeyer be thrown off the Empire State Building. That Wojnarowicz had the right to make these statements is not at issue. At issue is the right of the Congress not to reward him for doing so.

Of course, the only thing more pleasant than getting an NEA grant is being refused one; or, having received one, turning it down in protest; or having accepted it, leaking to the press that you have given it to some other applicant who was denied. Karen Finley, the performance artist who rubs chocolate over her body in simulation of excrement, can say what she wants about iron-fisted censors and white-male oligarchies, or about the psychological and professional fallout she suffered on being refused a grant. But at this point, the only thing that keeps her from reaching her audience is the price of her tickets and the speed with which they sell out, thanks to all the free publicity from which, to her credit, she has shrewdly profited.

Likewise, Andres Serrano, to whose work federal money was awarded and then retracted because of his photograph of a crucifix steeped in urine, recently sold out his entire show at the Paula Cooper Gallery, consisting of artsy images of victims of violent death, photographed close up in a morgue. In fact, if memory serves, there was not a single artist touched by the NEA controversy who did not emerge wealthier and savvier for this apparent brush with authority. It would be naive to express, let alone to feel, surprise at this. For it is rebellion itself that the contemporary art world cherishes most. People will pay for it.

But does everyone want it? There is a growing sense of the falseness of it all, a desire to return to some sanctum in which sincerity, if not excellence, can be found. In seeking to free themselves from the centripetal pull of the art world, many have headed for that last frontier of visual culture: outsider art. This is the art created by nonprofessionals either hostile to the mainstream or, more often, totally ignorant of it. Scholars quibble, as they always will, over what distinction, if any, should be drawn between outsider art and art brut. In essence, the term is a big tent that encompasses the art of the homeless, mentally ill, handicapped, self-taught, illiterate, or criminal. These works are admired for being free of the stale conventions of the art world, as well as for the poignancy of their being forged from real experiences far more disturbing than anything known to the narrow world of SoHo and 57th Street.

To see this work is to understand in a hurry what so much mainstream art has been faking for the past eighty years. The works of Beuys and Burden and Nitsch suddenly start looking very pale next to the real thing. Among the outsider artists who have achieved prominence are Clementine Moore, a 101-year-old black woman who spent all of her life on a plantation; Harry Lieberman, who started painting his quaint scenes of Jewish life at age 76, and continued to do so up until his death at age 103; Ken Grimes, a Connecticut artist who has depicted his encounters with extraterrestrials; Greg Pellner, an autistic obsessive-cumpulsive; and Ken Barnes, a convicted murderer. The art thus produced is rarely good and never great, yet it is indisputably fascinating as a record of the extraordinary circumstances in which it was created. And some of this art, like the watercolored architectural capriccios of an eighty-year-old recluse who called himself Rizzoli, has true distinction.

Outsider art was of interest to serious men like Paul Klee and Jean Dubuffet for many years. But only in the last five years or so has the trend approached what could be called critical mass. This was reached at a recent fair at the Puck Building in Lower Manhattan, the first ever devoted to outsider artists. Almost five thousand people paid $10 each to see their works, and total sales were estimated at between $2 and $3 million, with one work selling for $60,000. What was strange was that, although everyone had come to escape the art world, to savor the fresher air of artistic realness and sincerity, in fact, most of the people who showed up looked very like the people you see at any SoHo opening. They were not merely *of* the art world, they *were* the art world! One sensed it in the cut of the clothes and the coif of the beard, the musky undertones of expensive aftershaves and the fruity bouquet of the perfumes.

And as you walked among the hundreds of serried stalls, you began to notice that many dealers had works by the same artists, either because they had bought them at good prices on the already emerging secondary market, or because they, and a hundred other dealers, had descended on the humble dwelling, institutional or otherwise, of the afflicted, demon-ridden artist, and had borne away all they could carry. Of course, each one was at pains to assure you that, since many of the artists had representatives, there was no possibility of exploitation. There was also an effort to demonstrate sympathy and understanding for the artist. One dealer, a soft-spoken chap in gray serge and tassled loafers, gingerly held a pretty wooden box, selling for $4,000, between manicured fingers. It had been made out of glue and matchsticks by a convicted murderer and rapist. "He's doing time down in Mississipi," the dealer said with a bland smile. "And only forty years to go!"

With some exaggeration, admittedly, but not too much, we can see the outsider fair at the Puck Building as the art world's finest hour. For this was the moment when the last and most remote outposts of human artifice were finally enfranchised by the center. Henceforth, we are unlikely to discover or even to conceive of any artistic domain in which scholarship and the market have not already begun to stake their claim. Now that the art world has assimilated artists who were so marginal that they never even realized they were artists at all, there is no longer art in any country, from any time, or by any group, that is not being feverishly bought, sold, and discussed by collectors, dealers, and critics. And so, unless some obliging extraterrestrials start producing something very soon, the art world must weep like Alexander the Great at the lugubrious prospect that there is nothing left to conquer.

THREE

The Chattering Class

On February 26, 1961, the art world finally did something about John Canaday, the art critic of the *New York Times.* A letter was written to the editor that began thus: "Reading Mr. Canaday's columns on contemporary art, we regard as offensive his consistent practice of going beyond discussions of exhibitions in order to impute to living artists en masse, as well as to critics, collectors, and scholars of present-day American art, dishonorable motives, those of cheats, greedy lackeys, or senseless dupes."

The letter then gave numerous instances of Canaday's aggressions, among them this one from September 26, 1959: "As for the freaks, the charlatans, and the misled who surround this handful of serious and talented artists, let us admit that the nature of abstract expressionism allows exceptional tolerance for incompetence and deception."

And this from July 24, 1960: "The chaotic, haphazard, and bizarre nature of modern art is easily explained. The painter finally settles for whatever satisfaction may be involved in working not as an independent member of a society that needs him, but as a retainer for a small group of people who as a profession or as a hobby are interested in the game of comparing one mutation with another."

The letter was signed by fifty prominent American intellectuals, among them Robert Motherwell, Willem de Kooning, Meyer Schapiro, Harold Rosenberg, and John Cage. But the response to the letter must have astonished its writers no less than Canaday himself. On the two following Sundays fifty additional letters appeared for and against the critic. In one of them Edward Hopper described him as "the best and most outspoken art critic the *Times* has ever had." And yet, the opposition to Canaday had its effect. Even if we accept his claim that he received an additional 600 letters, of which 550 were favorable, the future belonged to his adversaries. Henceforth, he was on the wrong side of art history.

The Canaday Affair is a milestone in the collective attitude toward modern art. Although he continued for many years to express his doubts about much, but not all, of the art of his contemporaries, still the art world's attempt to silence him demonstrated where the real muscle of the new order resided. A decade earlier, John Canaday would have been holding the fort against a few pesky Apaches. Now, for all his supporters, he had become a reactionary outsider tilting against the Pentagon of the art world.

The rear guard had made its heroic last stand a few years before, when The New American Painting, a massive exhibit of the New York School, toured eight European countries in 1958 and 1959. In their excellent anthology, *Abstract Expressionism, A Critical Record*, David and Cecile Shapiro have excerpted reviews from each of the cities to which the show traveled. Many sensitive and welcoming comments were included, but the reviews that linger longest in the mind came from critics who clearly did not like the exhibit one bit.

"It is not new. It is not painting," declared the acidulated critic of the *Corriere della Sera*. "This is not art—it's a joke in bad taste," a London paper asserted. The critic of *Le Figaro* was moved to ask, "Why do they think they are painters? We . . . [must] deplore the terrible danger which the publicity given to such examples offers, as well as the imprudence of the combined national museums in offering support all too generously to such contagious heresies."

But even as these dissenters proclaimed their choleric critiques, they and their criticism were going out of fashion. The tone, the energy, and the conviction of their words were about to pass out of the diapason of art writing. With few exceptions abroad and almost none in America, critics from now on stood shoulder to shoulder with artists in their heroic struggle against an enemy that had almost entirely ceased to exist.

For abstract expressionism was to be the last movement in the history of art to encounter the old style of contempt, that gauntlet of bludgeons and brass knuckles that greeted earlier vanguards like impressionism and cubism. By the time Warhol's *Brillo Boxes* went on display at the Stable Gallery in 1964, criticism had given in, and the public had become inured to the increasingly homogenized outrage that the art world continued to create just for them. If they doubted this art, as was very likely, nice people now were more apt to worry about themselves than about the artists. A few years later, they would know better than to express their doubts in public. Today, perhaps, they will not even admit those doubts to themselves.

In the February 1993 issues of *Art in America*, *ArtForum*, and *Flash Art*, three of the most prominent periodicals in the field of contemporary art, there appeared 108 reviews, of which 101 were favorable, 4 were mixed, and 3 were unfavorable. This being so, one may legitimately wonder about the function of the critic at the present time. Given this virtually unanimous endorsement, the critical act seems about as interesting as whether, in his next election, Saddam Hussein will garner 99.7 percent or 99.8 percent of the Iraqi vote.

In the past, people read gallery reviews with the same keen interest they still bring to reviews of movies, concerts, and restaurants, an eagerness to know if the work will be praised or panned. Today, the only people who read such reviews have some professional interest in the art world. I doubt there is any critic alive who is able materially to increase—or decrease—attendance of an exhibition, aside from the simple fact of giving it publicity. Though there are some very good critics writing today, it is hard to see how any one of them ever caused people to see what they would otherwise miss, or to avoid what otherwise they might have seen.

In the circumstances, there can be little difference between a good review and a bad one. The earlier differential between praise and blame has been translated into degrees of hype or silence. The mere fact of being written about at all is an endorsement. Some stirring of criticism's older function can, it is true, be found in reviews of museum exhibitions, in which, without incurring the displeasure of the art world, the critic may vent his spleen against curators and corporate sponsors. The reception of the 1993 Whitney Biennial proves this to be so. But as regards the art itself, faint praise is the most terrible weapon in the critic's arsenal of dissent.

Though there are more art periodicals today than ever before, the critic exists to fill the spaces between their illustrations, which themselves exist to fill the gaps between the ads. The articles themselves are little more than ad copy for the galleries, which indirectly pay for them through a tacit understanding that the purchase of ads outright will increase their chances of being written up. In turn, the authors of these articles are often the same critics who write the largely unreadable and entirely unread catalogue essays for the same galleries' exhibitions, a conflict of interest that seems to bother no one, standards for this sort of thing never having been high. The Gagosian Gallery actually employs a full-time critic to praise it in the pages of its own catalogs. To talk of having sold out misses the point. This critic doesn't write differently from before; he doesn't write differently from other critics; he just gets paid more.

Such being the case, a word of explanation, if not an apology, is needed for devoting a whole chapter to the critic. After all, I imagine some irate reader saying, artists, even when they aren't successful, at least try to bring something beautiful or important into the world. All critics do is sit around talking about what they themselves can't create. To this ancient complaint I offer a new answer: Artists surely create art, but critics, increasingly, create artists. Indeed, the less artists want to create art, the more urgently we critics seem to want to create them.

For the days are long past when art existed on its own terms as paint on canvas or figures in the round, easily legible artifacts that critics might interpret and judge, but whose status as art objects they could not really question. The anxious object, as Harold Rosenberg memorably called it, has become the art object par excellence. A work of art like Duchamp's famous urinal is "anxious" because it no longer affords us any assurance that it is a work of art at all. Duchamp said of this and similar works, that art was what he or anyone else decided to call art. He was wrong. That the artist says it is art does not count for much of anything until the critic decides that the artist himself counts for something. Here again, the critic accomplishes this not by praising or attacking the object, but by paying attention to it or by ignoring it. The critic alone elevates a receptacle for bodily fluids to the existential status of a work of art. He is like a *masgiach* in a kosher restaurant, examining the food and declaring it edible, indeed delicious, for the faithful.

Close to two decades ago, Tom Wolfe's *The Painted Word* attacked the then regnant order of High Modernist Abstraction. His title well summarized the thesis of the book, that all the verbiage and all the theories surrounding Abstract Expressionism and its successors were more striking than the works themselves, which merely illustrated the arid obsessions of a few postwar New York intellectuals. Criticism, he contended, no longer merely preceded art: It had begun to supplant it.

This view is overbold, of course. Surely there was a lot of rot spoken and written back then about Jackson Pollock, Barnett Newman, and the rest of the New York School, some of which they even took seriously. But the essential fact about that movement is that it was just about the most sincerely ocular art ever made. You didn't need to go beyond your own retina to appreciate it fully, and any loftier musings imputed to the paintings were usually a distraction. It is ironic, therefore, that the tendency to which Wolfe referred, the need to intellectualize art to the detriment of its physical competence and beauty, should be far truer of the art that was coming into being just when *The Painted Word* appeared, the art that was destined, with stunning swiftness, to topple the empire of the New York School. I refer to that various and elusive thing called postmodernism.

It was apparent that words were the fastest, easiest route to rebellion against the old order of high modernism, whose austere formalism had seemed to void art of reference to anything beyond the object itself. Representing the United States in the 1990 Venice Bienniale, Jenny Holzer's slogans were blurted from filamented tubes, engraved into marble, and strewn across the demure, federalist walls of the American Pavilion. From the basement of the Museum of Modern Art, a talking head in a TV bellowed, "Feed me, eat me, help me, hurt me," in Bruce Nauman's *Anthro/Socio*, part of the 1991 Dislocations exhibition. While the paintings of Glenn Ligon and Christopher Wool are nothing more than words stenciled onto canvas, Group Material's AIDS Timeline at the 1991 Whitney Biennial used words on the wall, videos, and printed handouts to inform their audience of everything it already knew about the AIDS epidemic. Words even appear in paintings by relative formalists like Julian Schnabel, such is their momentary glamour.

Surely these words are largely gratuitous, like the words contemporary designers sew on jackets and jeans. But words are more than mere typography. And since meaning of one sort or other must attach to them, these ideas become the defining difference between contemporary and older art. But what if these ideas were themselves gratuitous? No one is saying this, of course, at least not for the time being. Too much is at stake. The artists want you to believe that their commitment to larger intellectual programs has compelled them to reintroduce the ideas that the modernists banished: they want you to know what they think of racism, abortion, and the Middle East. But, in fact, it is really the idea of ideas that charms them. And the critics, who once discussed "significant form," now talk of ideas and politics, so officiously, in fact, that they sometimes find in a work of art more ideas than are even there. But I believe you will seek in vain for any artist who has objected to their doing so.

Now these ideas, like all ideas, are wedded to their age. No one who has glanced even superficially at the history of art, politics, and philosophy will have failed to see how consistently the doctrines of an age fit the mood and even the look of that age. The tumultuous paragraphs of Thomas Hobbes fit perfectly into an age that had witnessed the wholesale slaughter of the Thirty Years War, the extravagance of Cervantes, the brooding chiaroscuro of Caravaggio. One hundred years later, the enlightenment of Montesquieu and Voltaire found its match in the lucid, sun-drenched images of Boucher and Canaletto, as well as in the neatly pitched battles of the ancien régime. Existentialism, a mere generation ago, was allied to the grim abstractions of Franz Klein, the anguished testimonials of the *nouveau roman* and the threat of nuclear annihilation. Is there any good reason to believe that there will be less of an affinity in our own time?

Philosophy and criticism have traditionally aspired to be above the age, to answer only to the single and sovereign claim of reason and of truth. And in some ages, surely, they have come closer than in others. To deny this fact would be to indulge in cynicism and scepticism. But only look at the long history of ideas and what you are seeing, more often than not, is a history of fashion rather than a history of reason. A bright child in junior high, given the mystifying words of Plotinus or Marsilio Ficio, could poke holes in their neo-Platonic reveries without too much difficulty. And he could do this because he exists outside the web of fascination that they once exerted and that they exert no longer. Now a different fashion holds him and his contemporaries, and so it will be until the fashion changes.

There is a startlingly honest passage in Irving Sandler's *American Art of the 1960s*, in which he, one of the foremost writers of the New York School, an art of passionate self-expression, describes his initial encounter with the new generation of cool, geometric artists who were coming of age at the end of the fifties. "Fewer and fewer young artists seemed to care what we said or even to listen to us. . . . Worse than that, a number challenged not only our beliefs but their very pertinence to art. What in painting, they demanded to know, represented, symbolized, or signified seriousness or honesty or crisis, existential or any other kind? Point to it, they said. We once could, and could communicate it, or thought we could, but the sensibility, the intellectual climate, had so changed that our kind of art talk was no longer convincing or at least intelligible even to ourselves."

Even in his brief précis of the argument, written thirty years after the fact, Sandler's language is imbedded with the buzzwords of an earlier time. *Seriousness*, *honesty*, *crisis*, these are verbal dividers between the generations. They are the words of those who lived through the Depression, even only as children, who fought in the Second World War, who saw and perhaps profited from the emergence of America as the foremost power of the earth. Their words and ideas could go out of fashion because, in one sense, they had been fashion all along.

Perhaps Pascal, that most lucid of thinkers, had this thought in mind when he wrote that opinion was "the Queen of the World." There is a will to opinion in human culture, to have opinions and to heed the opinions of others, often at the expense of expediency, personal comfort, even reason itself. The legitimacy of governments, the allure of fashion, the volatility of the marketplace are shot through with the stuff of opinion. Politics is opinion converted into action. Literature is opinion converted into words. But art, only art, is opinion made flesh, blazed into the very molecules of pigment and stone.

And just as in politics, opinion and pragmatism are always present, but each to a greater or lesser degree at different times and places, so all art mixes formal considerations and opinion, but will tend more toward one than toward the other at different times. In the quattrocento, the age of Masaccio and Piero, formal considerations predominated, as they would with Michelangelo and Titian in the 1500s, and with Caravaggio and Bernini in the century after that. But at the close of the 1500s, in the Mannerist works of Federico Zuccari and the younger Palma, opinion gained the ascendancy of form, as it did again in the late baroque paintings of Lebrun and Maratta, and in the works of Mengs, the Nazarenes, and the Pre-Raphaelites.

The art of our time is overwhelmingly the art of opinion. Indeed, at no earlier moment in the history of art has opinion presumed so insistently upon the province of form. Though competent formal work is still being done, the collective attention of the age is directed elsewhere. Thus it is not especially difficult to be an art critic these days. Formally speaking, in terms of mastery of color, line, and composition, most of this art is an easy call. Entire provinces of contemporary art can be accepted or rejected wholesale, and there is rarely if ever the need for the kind of trained eye that earlier art demanded.

Some will say that Julian Schnabel and Erich Fischl excel as painters in a traditional sense, and these claims will be considered in a later chapter. But most contemporary art aspires to do nothing of the sort. To speak of Koons's basketballs floating in a tank of water in terms of formal beauty, of spheres and rectangulations, would clearly be idiotic. I am quite sure the artist would agree. In looking at his art, in accounting for it, you must deal primarily with the ideas, the doctrines, the attitudes, the opinions that are being promulgated.

But how shall we examine these ideas? By my reckoning, there are four ways. The first supposes them to be either right or wrong, and is prepared to test them to determine their status. In general this has been the job of contemporaries. There are always some critics like Samuel Johnson and John Ruskin for whom no horse is so dead that it will not profit from at least one more well-directed kick. But after a certain time has passed, ideas enter the realm of history, and a less passionate and partisan approach seems called for, that of historians like Lovejoy and Panofsky, who are mainly content to describe and explain.

Lately, however, a third aproach, dear to writers like Umberto Eco and Jacques Derrida, has gained popularity, whereby it is not sufficient to describe these doctrines: they must be actively endorsed. For the writers of this school, there is no doctrine so feeble or superannuated but is ripe for resurrection. Typical of this trend is the dustjacket of newly edited work by Giordano Bruno, that hare-brained sixteenth-century neo-Platonist. It advertises the book thus: "Today, when visual thinking and creative association are competing with, if not overtaking, traditional logic and rationality, *On the Composition of Images, Signs, and Ideas* becomes an opportunity to rethink the whole notion of mental process."

Finally, in response to all of the above, there is that great moment in Wagner's opera *Siegfried*, in which the eponymous hero, having tasted of the dragon's blood, is suddenly endowed with a rare and wonderful power: when people speak to him, he does not hear what they are actually saying, but rather what they really mean. Mime, the misshapen dwarf, wants to kill Siegfried and take his sword, but the more he tries to wheedle the young hero with flattering words, the more clearly Mime is heard to say, "I intend to kill you and take your sword." So Siegfried unsheathes the terrible weapon and slays him with one thrust.

This insight of Siegfried's is what all criticism should aspire to: the ability to see through the posturings of the artist to the truth of the object; to develop such an instinct for what rings true or false that, however hard words may try, the real meaning behind them cannot be shut out for long. The faculty that Siegfried acquires by magic is as valuable to the critic as broad visual memory or refinement of vision. All areas of criticism could profit from this virtue, but none cries out for it more than the criticism of the fine arts, which at the present time have become a disheartening spectacle of cant and humbug.

A case in point: At the 1993 Whitney Biennial, the admission buttons that Daniel Martinez designed as one of his works of art, contained the words *I can't imagine ever wanting to be white.* Each person entering the exhibition was required to wear one. Martinez, who is black, presumably intended his work to indict white values, traditions, and hierarchies. And so it was dutifully understood by most of the critics who saw it. Yet to some of us it rang false. Most of the people who were in a position to receive the button were white, and rather than being challenged by it, they seemed to wear it in the smug confidence that they, at least, were above its implicit reproach. By way of demonstration, they claimed to admire the boldness and cleverness of the work, and this appreciation, it seems, is what the artist wanted all along. Thus both parties came away from this transaction having gotten what they came for, Martinez, credit for cleverness; attendees, credit for an open mind. This state of affairs goes beyond preaching to the choir: It is a fragile ecosystem of cant. Contemporary art, which calls so much into question, would prefer not to question this. Before such issues as this, it seems, the restless, querulous mind of the art world is stunned into paralysis.

Usually the buzzwords and beliefs that saturate an age are invisible to the people they most affect. But once the fashion changes, as it always will, nothing becomes so quickly or so embarrassingly obvious. The very people who spoke those words in all solemnity now feel ashamed of having ever said them. They feel they have finally shaken off a foolish dream. In fact, they have merely exchanged one dream for another. Nowhere does this seem more obvious than in art writing. To see superannuation in action, to feel the very texture of outmoded style, look to the criticism of an earlier age. It is a veritable wax museum of quaint costumes, outmoded words and sentiments, and a thousand odd "period" details such as you'd find in Franco Zefirelli's production of *Rigoletto*, or Merchant and Ivory's tributes to the Edwardian age, or Oliver Stone's archeological forays into the sixties.

"The painter should be a good man and versed in literature," Alberti tells us in 1437. He should "show himself well behaved, and especially polite and good-natured.... I like a painter to be as learned as he can be in all the liberal arts, but primarily I desire him to know geometry.... We should always take what we want to paint from nature, and always pick out the most beautiful things." So much of Florence in 1437 is refracted through the prism of this passage. It states what would have been inconceivable a century earlier and unlikely a century later: the civic pride of the free cities of Tuscany; a sunny confidence in the benefits of humanist education, a sublime certainty that art is noble and ennobling, that it seeks the good and sometimes finds it.

We'll have none of that. We know, or think we know, that the best artists are often the worst citizens. More to our taste perhaps is Joris-Karl Huysmans's famous description of the *Isenheim Altarpiece*, by Matthias Grünewald: "No other painter had so magnificently exalted loftiness or so resolutely leapt from the height of his soul into the depths of heaven.... Here was a masterpiece of art on the ropes, that depicted the tangible and the invisible, that manifested the body's putridity and sublimed the infinite anguish of the soul." Listen closely and you can hear the philosophy of Schopenhauer and the operatics of Gounod echoing down the boulevards of Baron Haussmann's Paris. Huysmans was one of the finest critics of his age, but also one of the most typical. The swooning theatricality of the passage charms our postmodern age, as do the intimations of perversity. Only the talk of the soul makes us uneasy. It suggests religion, and thus is not our way.

So we turn with some relief to a more secular piece of writing: "The white stripe is like the rest of the white but it's underneath it and yet forward of it. The whole surface has to come forward.

If this didn't occur the black lines would lie slightly in front of the canvas, as most marks do, and the areas would stand back slightly.... This description may have been dry reading but that is what's there." This is Donald Judd describing a work by Barnett Newman. The mood is as mod as geodesic domes, JFK, and lava lamps. Notice the restless aggression in the words, a workmanly directness that in nineties-speak would be called in-your-face. It is from the sixties, naturally. A critic from the Fifties would have given it more warmth; a critic from the seventies would have made it lighter in mood and might have qualified it with a dab of extra-artistic matters. We of the nineties like the sullen truculence of this passage. Still, we can never (at least not for the time being) condone the author's arrogantly judgmental formalism, which seems to purge art of all social and political issues. Now we know better.

But when the art historians of the future return to look at the writing of own our day, how will it sound to them? What will stand out as its most salient features? First of all, they will probably be impressed by the abundance of sexual references, usually in a form that the critics themselves deem to be twisted and perverse. Flipping through the reviews in the February 1993 *Artforum*, one reads: "It is this sense of sexuality, sometimes sinister, sometimes not, that saves Watson's paintings from repeating the same old song and dance." "Zlamany shows beauty itself, or its enjoyment, as a kind of decomposition. If she continues to move away from the direct depiction of dead things, her point could become even more subtle, seductive, and cruel."

Even when the work is not sexual, the idea of seduction obsesses these writers. In the same issue, four different critics have written on three consecutive pages: "The viewer is alternately challenged to read the words, and seduced by the pattern they create." "Each photo [of seascapes!] is startlingly sensual, seductive." "What, finally, Conelly so clearly reveals...is the power of oil on canvas to dazzle and seduce." "Pearlstein guides the eye into and around the patterned crevices of his picture's screwy planes, seducing the viewer with the pleasure of looking."

Those same future historians will detect a marked increase in political references compared with earlier criticism and, I would guess, with their own. In the February 1993 issue of *Flash Art*, artist-critic Adrian Piper exemplifies the breathless stridency of such writing: "The ideology of Greenbergian formalism undergirded the threat of McCarthyism to render politically and socially impotent a powerful instrument of social change—visual culture—whose potential government censors have always seen far more clearly than artists do and rationalized that impotence to the castrati." Another critic writes of the sculptor Kiki Smith, "She kindles an almost primitive self-consciousness about the corporeal apparatus as a subset of social symbolism. Her political agenda positions the female body as a biological servomechanism for the irascible patriarchy."

Finally, who among the historians of the future could fail to be impressed and perhaps baffled by the bizarre idiom that derives from French semiotics. Jimmie Durham, according to one critic, "speaks in what Delueze and Guattari defined as a 'minor language,' and at times, when he drops the textual play acting, lets out the raw 'nomos,' the cry from the groundless state under even the minor in language." Or as Arthur Kroker and David Cook wrote in *The Postmodern Scene:* "This is a discourse on the disembodied eye of the dead power at the center of Western Experience, and the convergence of the trinity/sign as the essential locus of the Western episteme." Or as Norman Bryson said with rather more charm and intelligibility, "P^1 TS EE P^2 ."

That is the way they used to write, the way they used to think, the way they used to talk in the nineties. In the catalog to the 1993 Whitney Biennial, the most highly political exhibit of its kind ever held, one curator wrote with surprising candor that, "Today everybody's talking about gender, identity, and power the way they talked about the grid in the late sixties and early seventies." And if we could transplant their souls into the bodies of nineteenth-century artists, we would find them talking of manliness and civic duty. Back three hundred years and they would chew your ear off about *disegno* as opposed to *colorito;* another three hundred years back and they would be talking themselves hoarse about God.

In response to all that chatter, Barbara Rose has said it very well when she noted, "The act of criticism is the value judgment. The rest is art writing." The truth is that critics no longer criticize, except in the sense that, publicly, they praise everything. The thought of publishing a dissent makes most of them uneasy. In other circumstances, this would be an admirable and humane compunction. But for those who seek their livelihood, such as it is, in judging art, it represents a dereliction in their duties to their readers and to the truth. It is likewise perfectly understandable that most people would disrelish the thought of being chased by a furious bull. But in that case they should not become matadors.

In one important sense, the value of all art, and thus of all criticism, is relative—relative, that is, to the claim being made for the object in question. Show me a drawing by a six year old child, and I will praise the drawing and the child. But tell me that it is a great work of art, that it propels human artifice to its next stage of evolution, and I despise both the child and the art. Perhaps the main problem with contemporary art is the absurdly inflated claim that is constantly being made for it. There is nothing really wrong with Jeff Koons's silly basketballs, or his stupid sculpture of the Pink Panther, or the lifesized porcelain simulacrum of the artist straddling his porn-star wife, Cicciolina. In other circumstances, one could admit that it was the sort of goofy, well-intentioned trash that might look great in someone's dorm room—not our cup of tea, perhaps, but good-humored and innocuous enough.

But no—we are to call it a pivotal expression of postmodernist irony,a wry commentary on the falseness of American values in the late twentieth century, etc.... Only then does it become truly intolerable. Ultimately, it is not quite true that quality and judgment have been expelled from art criticism. They are as much in force as ever before, but the quality that is sought today is not formal excellence so much as it is the originality, real or presumed, of the statement.

Among the old masters, from the seventeenth century on, there was a precise hierarchy of the genres of painting. At the top you had historical and religious paintings, generally rather large. Beneath them was portraiture and beneath that tavern scenes, still lifes, and landscapes which were generally smaller and less ambitious. It all sounds pretty idiotic these days, as it probably should. But is it not possible that we have erred in the other direction? With a few misgivings, we accept the seemingly elitist idea that some works of art are better than others and some worse. But every work of art is to be seen as competing in the same arena, for the same laurels, and under the same terms.

It is unacceptable that Koons's *Pink Panther* should merely be some silly sculpture that someone decided to make. It must be existentially on a par with the Pieta of Michelangelo: That is what they made then. This is what we make now. Even if we accept that it is not as good as the earlier work, still it is seen as occupying the same arena of influence and prestige. We are prepared to admit, perhaps unfairly, that illustration and decorative art are inferior to the fine arts, but anything that enters the magic circle of the fine arts is in contention with the Sistine ceiling. Despite all the talk about high art versus low art, this is one distinction that no one in the art world wants to go near.

Though it aspires to assail the conventions of high art, contemporary art preserves intact what was most typical of the older tradition: the idea of the Work of Art, that totemic object, laden with tradition and honors. Contemporary art is ready to throw so much away, to transform and subvert so many things, but it is not quite ready to dispose of this notion just yet. That is because the entire structure of contemporary art, from the highest academy to the grungiest gallery, is riding on its preservation.

The origins of our contemporary dislike of the word "quality" are sometimes traced to Baudelaire. In his criticism, according to one reading, enthusiasm took the place of taste and judgment. It was along these lines that Robert Storr, a curator at the Museum of Modern Art, recently attacked Clement Greenberg, who once held almost papal status among art critics. Amid much ad hominem attack, Storr criticizes Greenberg's arrogant confidence in his own opinions. The curator denies that art is about taste, by which is meant an accurate discernment of what is good and what is bad. "We must acknowledge and surrender to the complete, if sometimes tragic, fascination with contemporary life that Baudelaire first demonstrated," Storr writes. "More than 'taste' in this regard, the basic credential of the critic is disciplined but childlike avidity."

Of course, the fact that Baudelaire had both taste and avidity should not justify those who have neither from enlisting his prestige in their war on quality. Admittedly, there are powerful reasons for wanting to abolish taste. Taste is difficult to come by. It requires intelligence, learning, and humility before the object. Above all, it requires an innate sense of judgment that either can be developed or not, but that has to be there in some measure in the first place or it can never be there at all.

Here is where I part company with certain of my contemporaries. For I believe that not everyone is born with an innate sense that can be developed into this sensitivity. Some who possess it never develop it because the circumstances of their lives do not permit it, and that is very sad. But others, with all the wealth and position and degrees in the world, lack that innate sensitivity, and hard as they try, no power can endow them with it. Usually their ambitions end in farce. This fact has nothing to do with social or political conditions, though surely it would be convenient to think so. Rather, it is a question of indwelling temperament. And the best that a society can do is to place its citizens in the way of culture so that, if they want it and if they can respond to it, it will be there for them. To believe, because not everyone can or would respond, that the whole idea must be abandoned, is a parody of what democracy is about.

Now, I will agree with Mr. Storr to this extent, that the experience of culture should be about enthusiastic affinity as well as taste. The two are different but not mutually exclusive. There is a great deal of art that I am ready to enjoy though I cannot wholly respect it. There is pleasure to be found in the sixteenth-century paintings of Pomerancio in Rome and in the work of the followers of the younger Palma in Venice, which proceeds from nothing other than the silly, ham-handed mediocrity with which they abuse the mainstream tradition that I love.

But this pleasure must in no way be confused with the far greater pleasure of standing before a real Titian or Barocci. Titian occupies my eye in a way that seems, yes, timeless—timeless not in any trite, poetic sense of the term, but in the very real sense that, formally, the lived-in weight of his figures, the richness of his colors, and the perfection of many of his compositions, have as much (if not more) vitality, by which I mean living visual power, as the best work of the last one hundred years, or, for that matter, of the next one hundred years.

Because my judgment, or taste, has inspired in me this great admiration for Titian, I have as well an enthusiasm, or affinity, that overflows the confines of his own career and extends to the circumstances in which he lived. Anything from sixteenth-century Venice shares in this fascination, whether in literature, music, painting, or architecture, because it comes to us from the time of Titian.

In contemporary art, aside from some few artists of genuine achievement, there are a great many more who can give pleasure as long as our criterion is not so much art as something else. Speaking as an enthusiast rather than as a critic, I find that what appeals most in the art of my contemporaries is, strangely, its smell. It is all so new that as you enter a gallery or a space, the freshness of the acrylic on the canvas, of the newly unfurled rubber or hewn wood or molded Plexiglas rises into the nostrils almost before it reaches the eyes. In a matter of time, sooner perhaps than anyone now cares to admit, this smell will vanish with the freshness of the work, and most of its aura will fade like an exhalation. But for the time being, it is the art of the Now. It fits hand in glove with this moment when we live. It is our art, and so it is not wrong that we should respond to it with Mr. Storr's enthusiasm. But how shall we respond to it when it loses its babyhood? This is the point at which taste or judgment properly takes over from enthusiasm or affinity.

But how can we ever say for sure which work or which artist is better, I imagine the reader asking. Surely it is all relative. Isn't that what we are taught in college? If someone demanded of me why Raphael's drawings were better than those of his contemporary Giovanni Penni, I would try to prove this opinion by placing their works side by side and comparing them. I could point to the energy of one line compared to the inert flaccidity of the other; the grace of one man's shading against the dullness of the other's; the acute observation with which one man poses his figures compared with the other's starched and stereotyped banality.

But if I were pressed further as to the basis for claiming that Raphael was a better artist than Penni, or that any one work was better than any other, I would answer thus: It is well known that when the philosopher Descartes was plagued with doubts, and was seeking some way of establishing a basis for certainty, he hit upon the formula "I think, therefore I am," from which cornerstone he set out to erect an entire edifice of belief. What is the cornerstone of my belief? The knowledge, which no one may contravene, that Raphael was a better painter than I am. This I know to be the case, beyond controversy. I know this not only because I see and admire his works, but also because I know that I cannot draw to save my life, that I have no power to create a convincing sense of volume, that I have no gift for coordinating colors. Once this is accepted, everything else follows.

Ultimately, there is no way around the subjectivity of criticism, which does not mean that we should abandon criticism, but rather abandon the foolish hope or the unscrupulous demand for mathematical proof. One of the beauties of baseball is its serene, statistical accuracy. Who is the best hitter in the league?

The one with the highest average. Now you might say that player A, batting .350, is really better than player B, with .360, but that player A had marital troubles or encountered more formidable pitchers. But if player C, batting .110, said he was better than players A and B put together, he would be laughed off the field. Clearly we can never have, and we should never seek, such accuracy in cultural matters. But it might be nice if we began greeting certain artists in the same way.

Ultimately, there is nothing quite like great art for clarifying the issue of quality. On the third floor of the Whitney, the very floor which, as I write this, is being defiled by Sue Williams's puddle of plastic vomit, the same museum mounted, a few months ago, what was perhaps the most perfectly beautiful exhibition of a modern artist that we shall ever see. The artist was the Canadian-born Agnes Martin, whose paintings, pale silver-pointed grids on canvas, mainly from the sixties and seventies, were among the purest and most moving works of Minimalism.

For once the Whitney rose memorably to the occasion, creating an environment of such luminous, silent excitement, that it filled one with sadness to think that there was a time, which no younger critic or artist can now recall, when everyone aspired to be this good. There was nothing ambiguous about the immensely nuanced subtlety of Ms. Martin's paintings: Clearly we were in the presence of a noble and prodigiously gifted artist. Beyond all the cant generated by contemporary artists and their critics, if painters of this seriousness could ever again become the majority, or even a plurality, it would signal the regeneration of art.

F O U R

Modernists and Postmodernists

Few periods in art ever began as punctually or as emphatically as the eighties seemed to do. The nineteenth century was ushered in with Gericault's *Raft of the Medusa* in 1819; the present century started with Picasso's *Demoiselles D'Avignon* of 1907; and the sixties got under way only in 1964, with Andy Warhol's *Brillo Boxes.* But we were a matter of months into a new decade when, in June 1980, the Times Square Show invented Art As We Know It. Throughout the seventies, a vague, irresolute and self-referential eclecticism had seemed to dominate an art world in stagnation. At the Times Square Show, however, something very different indeed was starting to take place. As Jeffrey Deitch wrote in that September's *Art in America*, its artists were "committed to social change, approaching art as a radical communications medium rather than as a circular dialogue with the past." That translated into a lot of graffiti, neo-pop allusions to mass culture, representation rather than abstraction, homoerotic art, and art by minorities. In cultural terms, it was like storming the Bastille.

For an entire month the abandoned four-story bus depot and massage parlor was filled with downtown SoHoites, uptown socialites, and such prostitutes, pimps, homeless people, tourists, and scandalmongers as might pass by. One of the first things to catch the eye was the eight-foot blowup of a Kung Fu Amazon, borrowed from a nearby movie theatre. Also on view were Kathleen Thomas's spiked rubber-skinned dildo machine, Samo's graffiti scribblings, and Kenny Sharf's customized air conditioner with Star Trek motifs. Out of several hundred works, fewer than a dozen were abstract and none of them would have pleased the elders of the New York School. If modernism was dead, this was its wake.

And yet, to say that the eighties started with the Times Square Show, indeed, to say that anything started with the Times Square Show, is a lie; useful perhaps, but a lie all the same. For there was little in the Times Square Show that could not be traced back in a continuous sequence to what had been painted and sculpted in the generation before. But what is called art history is really the history of what interests art historians. More representational art was made in the 1950s, during the reign of abstract expression, than ever before, just as more abstract paintings are probably being made at this moment than at any point in the past. But these abstractions are ignored because the collective attention of the art world is elsewhere. Yet, one day, when nonrepresentational art returns to favor, those thousands of abstract artists now toiling in total obscurity will come crawling out of the woodwork, and the entire art world will sigh collectively at the folly of an earlier taste that ignored such genius, a taste in which they could not possibly have shared.

The Times Square Show was important because it forced us to look at what had been going on at the margins of modernism for at least a decade, and to see that a great change was taking place in contemporary art. Nowadays, people like to talk about critical mass in relation to culture, the moment when, for whatever reason, all the filiations of a trend fuse into a movement. Until that moment, everything seems to be waiting in a state of tense readiness, and suddenly it all pours forth, perfect and complete. In retrospect, this is what happened at the Times Square Show. Here was the first jubilantly public declaration of what the art world was starting to call postmodernism. It was surely not the first tremor of that movement, but many perceived it as such, which amounted to the same thing.

Few people will go on record in praise of "postmodernism." Most artists and critics will tell you that it is an imprecise label for many widely differing forms of artistic expression, a crude approximation of what is really taking place. But since we have to use words, and since no one has come up with a better term, postmodernism will be used in the following pages to denote the art that succeeds modernism and usually attacks it.

By 1980, we were clearly post-something, but no one quite knew what. There was talk of postminimalism, postperformance, postmovement, post-logical positivism, postcivilisation. But none of it seemed to serve. The term *Postmodernism* had been in the air for some time, though seemingly in application to everything other than art. As early as 1934 *postmodernismo* appeared in discussions of Spanish poetry, and Arnold Toynbee was using the term in 1947. By the late fifties and early sixties, literary critics like Irving Howe and Harry Levin had applied it to Salinger, Mailer, and Kerouac.

But as Charles Jencks writes, "It wasn't until 1971 and Ihab Hassan's essay 'POSTmodernISM: A Paracritical Bibliography' that the movement was actually christened and a pedigree provided, although, even then, the term, like its inconsistent capitalization, wasn't clearly defined." That would come about a decade later, largely through Mr. Jencks's own energetic pamphleteering for the movement.

To understand postmodernism, you have to know what modernism was. The term refers to the century of art from realism to minimalism, from Manet's *Olympia* in 1863 to Ad Reinhardt's black-on-black canvases exactly one hundred years later. In what is perhaps the classic statement of modernism, Clement Greenberg, its foremost theoretician, wrote:

> The essence of modernism lies, as I see it, in the use of the characteristic methods of a discipline to criticize the discipline itself—not in order to subvert it, but to entrench it more firmly in the area of its competence.... Each art, as it [turned] out, had to effect this demonstration on its own account. What had to be exhibited and made explicit was that which was unique and irreducible not only in art in general, but also in each particular art. Each art had to determine, through the operations peculiar to itself, the effects peculiar and exclusive to itself. By doing this each art would, to be sure, narrow its area of competence, but at the same time it would make its possession of this area all the more secure.

The logical consequence of this quest was that architecture must purge itself of all ornament and superfluity of design, refining itself down to the strict rigidity of wall and orifice, glass, brick, and steel; music must consecrate itself to examining tone and tempo; and painting must become form and color on a flat canvas. All art, Greenberg believed, was marching in step to this preordained rendezvous with destiny, when the pure, artistic essence would be distilled once and for all. Though Greenberg, as a young man, had been a confirmed Trotskyite, this radical reduction of the artistic process left no room for distractions like class warfare, race relations, kitsch, or didacticism. All of it would have to go.

Greenberg's position, however, was twofold: it described and prescribed, though it did not determine with any precision when it was doing one or the other. Surely Greenberg's idea was not spun out of whole cloth. There was ample evidence in modernism to justify the general thrust of his argument. The notion of art for art's sake had figured prominently in Baudelaire's criticism, and Maurice Denis had argued, as early as 1890, that painting was really only colors and forms on a flat surface. And what Denis had prescribed in theory, painters like Kandinsky, Mondrian, and Hoffman were soon creating in practice. But Greenberg went further than description, challenging and exhorting artists to be equal to his austere ideal, and going so far as to suggest that any who fell short of it were ipso facto not modern, or not modern enough.

But Greenberg's doctrine turned out to be more prescription than description, editorial writing posing as reportage. Thus it is more important for the art it justified and inspired than for the accuracy of its explanation. In order to preserve a coherent thesis, Greenberg had to ignore fairly systematically the rowdyism of dada, the muscular posturings of futurism, and the transfigured moonshine of the surrealists.

Though all were part of the modernist project, they played little if any role in Greenberg's tidy March of Art History. In fact, even the art he held up as exemplary was rooted in styles and movements whose underpinnings were antithetical to what he advocated. Would Picasso have painted *Les Saltimbanques* without the example of Puvis de Chavannes's languid symbolism? Could Pollock have hit on his authentic style without Matta's surrealist automatism? The very soil that had nourished Picasso and the abstract expressionists was thus marred by extra-artistic elements: the pranks of Duchamp no less than spiritualism of Kandinsky, the faux-naive works of Rousseau no less than the pseudo-psychoses of Dubuffet. Far from being a unified movement, modernism was so multifarious that the fabled diversity of postmodernism pales in comparison.

Despite the flaws in Greenberg's view of things, the power which, for more than a generation, it exerted over the minds of intelligent people was almost incredible. Though there was never a moment during the heyday of its hegemony, from about

1950 to 1975, when other kinds of art were not being made, his ideas soon became the dogma of the schools. Even when, by the early sixties, younger critics like Barbara Rose, Michael Fried, and Sidney Tillim put Greenberg to the proof, they were playing his game by his rules. To this day, a painter like Frank Stella implicitly accepts Greenberg's teleology: Painting is going somewhere specific, and Stella means to take it there. For many others, Greenberg occupies the collective semiconscious of the art world like an exalted father figure hurled hourly from his throne.

Put another way, Greenberg presided for a long time over the game of modernism like a grandmaster over a chess board. Along came some bright young things, Rose, Fried, and Tillim, who thought, not always wrongly, that they could play the game just as well if not better, but who, though they might quibble over a few gambits or seek to rewrite a few regulations, still accepted the basic rules of the game. Then one day, around 1980, someone came along and knocked off all the pieces and decided to use the thing as a dart board. It is an entirely different game requiring entirely different skills. It is the game we are playing today.

But postmodernism never really engaged modernism in debate. Rather, it turned its back on the older styles and decided to do something else. The simple truth, as it appeared to the upstarts of the eighties, was that all these establishmentarian chaps were starting to look very middle-aged, that they had been doing what seemed like the same thing forever. And then there were all these younger people, bristling with youth, and yearning for something completely different, anything in fact, as long is it was new and as long as it was theirs. What they wanted turned out to be something quite specific: whatever was not modernism. Modernism, they felt, had abolished politics: so they brought it back. Modernism had suppressed eroticism, so they brought us Mapplethorpe. At no point was modernism intellectually discredited; it just went out of fashion.

At the same time, postmodernism never effected a true or total severance from the older art. Indeed the new artists couldn't keep away from it. Postmodernism became a sustained if perverted act of homage to the modern movement. Mike Bidlo, with all the postmodern irony in the world, created an imitation of Pollock so exact that we now know how Pollock would have painted if he had been merely mediocre. Bidlo even went to the length of staging a performance piece in which he urinated into a fireplace, thus repeating Pollock's imperishable tinkle in Peggy Guggenheim's hearth. Similarly, Sherrie Levine imitated Kasimir Malevich's monochromatic paintings with a painstaking accuracy which, in a less complicated age than our own, would be called forgery. Less directly, but with equal conviction, the late Jean-Michel Basquiat derived most of his paintery turns from mainstream modernists like Dubuffet and Masson, while Ross Bleckner's ideas of size, like Kenny Sharf's, derive from the abstract expressionist scale.

By the same token, what is most representative about contemporary art had been in place long before 1980 and was hardly underground, some of it was represented by prestigious galleries and exhibited in respected museums. Performance art, video art, and conceptualism were all born in the citadel of Greenbergian formalism. The installations of Ed Kienholz and George Segal presaged almost every refinement of the genre known to the eighties and nineties. You can even see a distinctly New Age sentiment, a lightening of the palate and a giggling quality, in the abstractions of Larry Poons and Jules Olitski.

Meanwhile, Pop Art had already broken down the wall dividing high and low culture; photorealism, among other movements, had reintroduced into painting the representation of the real world; and conceptualism, with its elegantly printed words, was the progenitor of today's art of verbosity. There was even a considerable amount of political art created in protest of the war in Vietnam, art that closely resembled what is being done today, except that even its creators tended to view these works as parerga, rather than as the serious business of their lives.

The paradox of postmodernism is that it remains far more

concerned with modernism than the modernists ever were. Most modernists never wanted to be modernists at all: they wanted to make art the way they wanted to make art, and then someone informed them that they were making modernist art. By contrast, it is crucially important to the average postmodern artist that he be postmodern, and to insure this he must define himself in relation to modernism. Postmodernism, to use a buzzword, is pure "negativity." With few exceptions, the premise and the contents of most postmodern works are their rejection of modernism. Each of them seems to be informing you, with a little voice within it, that this is precisely what it is doing.

When Julian Schnabel first displayed his plate paintings in the early eighties, their message was, The artists of the older generation are going to hate this. Its crude images, willfully crude, naturally, fly in the face of everything they stand for. David Ligare's exorbitantly classical image of *Hercules Protecting the Balance Between Pleasure and Virtue* seems to say, Fifteen years ago, who painted like this? No one, that's who! And Sue Williams's puddle of plastic vomit at the most recent Whitney Biennial announced, Here I am, a puddle of plastic vomit, in Marcel Breuer's high modernist building no less, home to Pollock and other dead white males!

Each artist laboring under the banner of postmodernism seems to be in a state of perpetual revolt against the immediate past, as though he had just gotten it into his head to attack modernism's oppressive heritage, as though this were still greatly needing to be done, as though no one had thought to do this before. Protocol seems to require that critics respect this illusion, which most of them are happy to do, especially when they don't see that it is an illusion.

And yet it is hard to imagine how anyone could fail to notice that postmodernism, though not yet fifteen years old, has become the established order of the art world. Postmodernism wins grants, is praised in the press, taught in the schools, bought by collectors, and exhibited in museums. For all its newness, postmodernism has passed with vertiginous speed from infancy to midlife crisis. At fifteen it is what modernism became only after a hundred years. But the myth of the underdog rebelling against the oppressive power structure of the art world shows no signs of weakening. This is the myth of origin from which all the prestige, authority, and, ultimately, all the marketability of postmodernism proceed. Too much is at stake for it to be shelved just yet.

In fact, there are deep structural similarities between modernism and postmodernism. The word modernism derives from the medieval Latin *modernus* which refers to that which belongs to the present. Most earlier art had existed in a kind of temporal vacuum. For the artists of the Middle Ages and the Renaissance, the notion that art should seem old or seem new was nonexistent, certainly not in any form like that of recent years. The important thing was that it be good. Caravaggio, in the early years of the baroque may have been a rebel, but the art he made in Rome was not intended to be new, only to be more powerful than the enfeebled mannerism of the artistic mainstream. If anything, he saw himself as reviving Titian and Raphael, after the corruption of painting at the hands of Federico Zuccari and the Cavaliere D'Arpino.

Time starts to infiltrate art in odd ways only in the nineteenth century in the academicism of the Ecole des Beaux-Arts. Painters like Bougereau and Couture actively sought an art that was not merely derived from the past but that recreated it. Thus Couture and a sixteenth-century Venetian might pose a figure in the same way, but the Venetian would have done so because it looked right that way, whereas Couture would have done so because he wanted to look "sixteenth century." Modernism is in one sense academicism in reverse, stood on its head. Almost from its inception it was to be the art of the new, as academicism had been the art of the old. We recall Daumier's battle cry: *Il faut etre de son temps.* You have to be of your own time.

But eventually time turned against modernism, and its assault took two forms. Look at the clear white spaces of Mondrian's geometric essays and notice how they have turned a dull sharkskin grey. Likewise, the steel and glass of modern architecture have been scarred and ravaged by years of smog and use. Modern art and architecture, like all human artifacts, have grown old, but unlike the castles of the Rhine and the Virgilian landscapes of Claude Lorrain, they have gained no grace or charm in compensation for their loss of youth. Modern art, like modern man, can no longer age gracefully: The best it can hope for is to retain as long as possible the appearance of being young.

But time was determined to ravage modernism in still more insidious ways. Much of modernism, as we saw, aspired to create an art of the eternal Now. The art of the Bauhaus, that stripped the ornaments off buildings and took the curves out of Mondrian, had hoped to discover a style so obedient to the eternal laws of geometry, that it could never grow old, any more than could a theorem of Euclid. Later, the architecture of Louis Kahn and the paintings of Ad Reinhardt, like the prose of Jack Kerouac and the music of Pierre Boulez, aspired to be, if not eternal, at least so new, so now, that they could never go out of date. It was ornament that seemed to carry the weight of age and style. But how could the idea of a bare wall or a straight line grow old? No one had ever seen that happen before. It didn't make sense.

And yet, gradually, while no one was watching, the modernist movements grew old, just as the rococco and the Pre-Raphaelites had grown old. Looking at Pollock's *Blue Poles*, one can't help thinking, That's how they used to paint in the fifties, when Eisenhower was president and a steak cost you a dollar. In the same way, Reinhardt's black-on-black paintings conjure up Sputnik and JFK. By the seventies, the tone and style of modernism, the artists who created it, and the critics who defended it were all aging or old.

At the inception of the new decade, this fact could no longer be ignored. Modernism, that noble if flawed enterprise that had inspired so many masterpieces, suddenly became hideously senescent. It was like certain people who seem miraculously ageless, until one day we see them after an absence, and their real age has caught up with them. Modernism was doomed to fall by the very sword it had lived by. An art whose preeminent charm, for many, was its contemporaneity must perish the second it ceases to be contemporary. An art obsessed by novelty and youth, as modernism seemed to be, must one day become old, so old that by 1980 the very desire for the New, what Harold Rosenberg called the Tradition of the New, had come to seem old.

In addition to time there was one other factor in the fall of modernism. Modernism had become stalwart and beribboned and no more inclined to revolution than some epauletted commissar reviewing the troops on May Day. But since much of modernism's appeal was precisely in its rebelliousness, it must lose that appeal on winning general acceptance. Like the church militant placing its sackcloth and crowns of martyrdom on the porphyry altars of the church triumphant, the modern movement was eventually compelled to admit that it had ceased to be rebellious, that it had become the force of order. As early as 1959, according to Irving Sandler, abstract expressionism "was avant-garde only in the sense that it was in advance of the taste of the general public: in fact, it had not been extended in any radical manner for some half dozen years. Moreover, its premises had become so familiar that it had attracted followers in numbers that seemed more like a main army than a vanguard."

Modernism was much more than newness and revolt, and many of its greatest figures were not interested in these things at all. But modernism was seen as the rebellious art par excellence, and by 1980 it could no longer deliver on that promise.

In morphological terms, as biologists say, there is a clear evolutionary link between postmodernism and what it supplanted: both desire to be the art of the moment and to be somehow rebellious. The energy with which postmodernism pursues these two main goals is what entitles us to see the entire movement less as a challenge to modernism than as a continuation. Postmodernism aspires, according to some, to be postmovement art, the art which, according to one writer, exists at the end of art history. In fact, it is a movement like any other, with fairly legible spatial and temporal coordinates. And for all its fabled diversity, it assembles itself into a circumscribed canon of formal and intellectual terms. One day people will look back on Anselm Kiefer and Jeff Koons, and say to themselves "That was the way they made art back in the 1990's, in the days of Madonna and Bill Clinton."

In one sense, postmodernism is more rebellious than modernism ever was, because rebelliousness, which had been a means to an end in modernism, has now become an end in itself. To ignore this fact is to misunderstand the seemingly contradictory nature of much that we call "postmodern." How else can we reconcile artifacts that at one moment are bristling with engaged, populist fervor, and given over in the next to rarefied semiotical elucubrations? How can we square the overtly pornographic images of David Salle and the antipornographic crusade of a feminist artist like Sue Williams? The very proliferation of styles leads to the conviction that there are no styles. The lack of any single dominant motif, like pointillist jabs or cubist facets or the parabolic swirls of gestural abstraction, suggests that the lockstep of earlier decades has come to a halt, leaving us free-floating through the end of the history of art.

Yet postmodernism, like modernism before it, aspires to call violently into question established traditions and practices. Both converge upon the center from equal if opposite angles of assault. Postmodernism in this sense is modernism reborn. Having sloughed its old skin and old habits, postmodernism carries on the assault against the center, even though that center is now defined as modernism itself. In algebraic terms, $p = non\text{-}q$. Postmodernism is determined to be that which modernism was not and not to be that which modernism was. It is this fact that gives the movement its unity and coherence.

Because of this rebelliousness, postmodernism can be assimilated into Greenburg's view of things more easily than one might expect. Greenberg, as we saw, understood the history of art to be a search for the most essential principles of a process. He found the summation of the process, the end of art history, roughly in abstract expressionism. But those who came after naturally disliked the idea that there was nothing left for them to do but rework what Pollock and Rothko had already done. The minimalists, inspired by the hard-edge abstractions of Barnett Newman and Ad Reinhardt, were convinced that art had a little way to go, so they created a cool, glacial art, inert to the point of paralysis. "I'm just making the last pictures which anyone can make," Reinhardt said. And, indeed, he did seem to reach the zero degree of human artifice, than which you simply could go no further. Until someone did. The conceptualists pushed Greenberg's teleology so far that it voided art of its material existence, leaving an object so reduced, chastened, and rarefied that by the seventies it had quite literally ceased to exist.

This was the point at which the modernist universe began to implode. And as science fiction writers believe will happen when the big bang starts to reverse itself, the newest artists encountered at each station of their recessional the very things that had been discarded along the path of modernism's ascent. After conceptualism, the very teleology of Greenberg required its negation. There was nowhere else to go but back. Artists like Carlo Maria Mariani found inspiration in the exuberantly figural art of eighteenth-century Rome. Others, like Sue Coe, rediscovered political artists like Ben Shahn and the social realists, whom Greenberg had bulldozed away. Still others sought inspiration not only in folk art and symbolism, but in the Pre-Raphaelites, the Renaissance, classical antiquity, and prehistory.

But several key elements of modernism, as we saw, were enshrined in postmodernism. The rebellious freedom of form and content, the aggressive individualism of personal style, the overt sexuality, and the defiantly antinomian politics—all of this had been modernism's stock in trade, and all of it has been reconstituted in the most recent art. Postmodernists like Rosalind Krauss might challenge modernism's quest for originality, but in doing so they preserve modernism's timeworn tradition of calling their predecessors to account. Likewise, because vanguardism was associated with modernism, and because modernism had become a bedrock of tradition, artists of the eighties found it necessary to strike modernism where it lived, by challenging the very notion of the avant-garde, for no other reason than that it seemed essential to modernism's existence. In reality, however, rejecting the avant-garde is the preferred vanguardist posture of the present age. And so it goes with that other sham battle that discredits originality and the desire for newness because both were dear to modernism. But what is the appeal of history and all those revived styles in contemporary art, if not the fact that, relative to modernism's frumpy "nowness," postmodernism's glamorous "thenness" looks new and exciting? Postmodernism, far from denying modernist vanguardism and newness, has given them a new lease on life.

But there is one very important sense, the only sense, in which postmodernism has severed its links with modernism. There is such a thing as a postmodernist mood, a postmodern condition, or more exactly, the reigning attitude of the last quarter of the twentieth century. Postmodernism in art is a gaudy sideshow to a far deeper commotion that pervades every particle of contemporary life. Having passed out of the industrial age, which lasted from about 1800 to 1975, Western culture has entered, or is entering, the age of information. Postmodern art objectifies this change.

What is the postmodern mood? Unlike what it supplanted, postmodernism is often querulous, but never brooding. In the same way that rococco art tended to be light and sportive compared with the sullen immensity of the baroque, so postmodernism is lighter in spirit than modernism, retaining little of its existential baggage or high seriousness. Postmodernism is far more eager to please and entertain and it makes fewer demands on us. It is viewer-friendly. For all its agitation, it is the collective sigh of relief of a world that suddenly understood that it was not likely to be blown to bits in a nuclear holocaust.

In one of the most famous utterances in art criticism, Emile Zola referred to Impressionism as "a corner of creation viewed through a temperament." Postmodernism is that same corner of creation glimpsed through an attitude. It is the attitude of a civilization grown old and weary of itself, of an Alexandrian age that has seen everything twice before. In politics, Reagan's charm consisted in emanating the calm assurance of a Hollywood B-movie. Clinton appealed to voters through his studious emulation of JFK and the implicit promise of a new Camelot. Ross Perot seemed like a digitalized version of Harry Truman. In culture, the music of John Corigliano repeats Mozart; the narratives of John Hawkes and Erica Jong recall eighteenth-century novels; the architecture of Ricardo Bofill reenacts Bernini; and the fashions of Mark Jacobs cannibalize the sixties.

This feeling of déjà vu, and the attendant sense of having lived a little too long, finds expression in a collective irony stronger than anything we have seen before. Our speech is studded with scare quotes around every second word. Our politics is not the politics of despair but of lost illusions. And our illusions have been lost not because our generation is more immoral than earlier ones—if anything we are a little more scrupulous than they were—but because the mass media have removed almost all the barriers that distance or privacy had thrown up between people. Where everything is knowable there is nowhere to hide. It is impossible to believe in royalty, which is sustainable only through a certain resonant mystery, when bugging apparatus can pick up and broadcast the most private bickerings of the Prince and Princess of Wales. And how can we believe in great men when a polyp in their colon becomes common knowledge, when every lapse of speech and every facial blemish is transmitted immediately to a mocking world?

In the 1992 presidential election many people seemed incapable of endorsing any of the candidates. We voted for "the lesser of three evils." In this way, we freed ourselves from the embarrassment of seeming to believe in anything, let alone feeling enthusiasm for it. This attitude has left nothing untouched. Children's television replays fifties programming for a young audience that tunes in not to be diverted by its wholesome stupidity, but rather to be fortified in the conviction that they could not possibly be as nerdy as the Beaver. During the commercial breaks, a brand of bubblegum is advertised as being distasteful to policemen and librarians and squares generally, but as the gum of choice of those who are pubescent, gifted, and rebellious. Fifty years ago, even twenty-five years ago such an ad campaign would have been unthinkable. Everything, having been seen before, can thus be seen through. Doubt, once a proof of intelligence, has become its substitute. And the best thing about this doubt is that it can be adopted wholesale and ready to use, like faux worn-out jeans, predistressed for your comfort and wearing pleasure.

Surely one cause of this irony is the relative prosperity of those who practice it. When nuclear annihilation seemed not only possible but likely, there was little room for the irony we feel today. Only when this threat began to retreat did irony become possible on such a scale. Where pain is real and present, ideals spring up out of nowhere. There was nothing ironic about the black community's reception of Spike Lee's *X*. There can never be anything ironic about the Holocaust Museum, which is why it seems so incongruous in contemporary experience. In the heat of the Gulf War as well, irony mysteriously disappeared for a few weeks from many, though not all of its habitual haunts, and a kind of patriotism took its place. Only when the war ended with a swiftness that astonished everyone did irony become possible again, and everyone disowned or denied the clumsy sincerity that had inadvertently been revealed.

The principal alternative, perhaps the only one, that postmodernism offers to this irony is a kind of unalloyed lightness, an absolute purity of sensation that is the polar opposite of pessimism and cynicism. If modernism problematized everything, postmodernism offers solutions that seem almost too good to be true. The lucid harmonies of Philip Glass, the anemic, crystalline narratives of Paul Auster, the translucent sculptures of Christopher Wilmarth, and the swimming pools of David Hockney give us "what we want," a pleasure so uncomplicated, so anesthetized, so Californian, that we almost feel guilty or stupid as we succumb to their facile appeal.

The causes of this change are manifold. The epoch of the industrial revolution, which scarred an agrarian planet with pollution and machines, liquid capital and labor disputes, mass communications and totalitarian regimes, is passing away. And something we can only dimly descry begins to take its place. The New Age sentiment in contemporary culture, the taste for lite beers and detarred cigarettes, the reduction of the machine to the microchip and of pigiron to aluminum and aluminum to plastic, all suggests a technology that is reliant in only the most trivial way on the heavy industries of the receding past.

Modern art grew up along that great faultline dividing the industrial age from an agrarian age that fostered aristocratic and sacerdotal art. It was the mission of modernism to express art's ancient vitality in terms of the new realities. And it succeeded brilliantly. The excellence of a Titian nude will be found intact in a Renoir nude, but reconstituted in the idiom of a new age. What is great about the Parthenon is what is great about Mies van der Rohe's Seagram's Building on Park Avenue. But by 1980, people were starting to feel that modernism's language of forms, though it had served the industrial age well, was no longer adequate to the new realities. Of course, most who acted on this impulse did not see it in these terms. They felt moved to attack modernism because it was old and oppressive; because it was the province of dead white males; because it was imperialist or elitist or both.

In fact, without their knowing it, they were and they remain the agents of a much larger and grander human enterprise: the search for a new kind of expression adequate to this transformed condition. Postmodernism aspires to be the expression of this change. It aspires to be for the new order what modernism was for the old. Whether it has succeeded or can succeed will be the subject of the chapters that follow.

FIVE

High and Low

Keith Haring began 1983 underground, enthusiastically scribbling HAPPY NEW YEAR across the walls of the New York City subway system. A decade later, you could walk into Dean & Deluca and find two hundred artists who, alluding to the relevant chapters in Derrida, would soberly encode the signifier *Happy New Year* on the same walls in an arch reference to the sort of person who might sincerely say it. But you would have a hard time finding a single artist who could possibly mean it.

Superficially, Downtown may look as it did ten years ago, but it has changed. SoHo no longer rings with the ebullient vitality it had back then. Gravity weighs more heavily on its citizens, the temperature has fallen several degrees, and reality, with its lawyers and faxes and bills of lading, has shattered their innocence without bringing much in the way of wisdom. Which is why younger artists, if they are at all perceptive, must feel as though they had arrived in town just as the circus was leaving.

It was far otherwise during the early eighties, when lower

Manhattan seemed, at least in retrospect, like the sort of pleasure dome that enlivens, only once in a great while, the tedious continuum of history: Neronian Rome, Paris in the Belle Epoque, Berlin under Weimar. How changed from the days when amazons in hotpants boogied in the cages of the Mudd Club! Where are they now, those oiled torsos that mamba'ed around twenty-foot boxes of Twinkies at Area, or bowed before Keith Haring's graffiti gods on the walls of the Palladium?

Clubs were the academies of the East Village, even if most of them flared up and fizzed out in swift succession. "I used to wonder what it would be like to see art in clubs," Jim Fouratt of the Palladium told Peter Frank and Michael McKenzie (to whose book, *New, Used and Improved*, I am indebted for several of the quotes in this chapter). "Now [in 1987] I wonder what kind of art would be made by artists who didn't go to clubs." But that changed. By 1990, the principal players had all grown up and gone away, some, like Basquiat and Haring, to their eternal reward, others like Ann Magnason and Eric Bagosian, to Hollywood. The rest, having savored their fifteen minutes of fame, have sunk into an anonymity from which neither God nor man nor all the doctoral students of the age to be may yet redeem them.

Like grown-ups confronted with their geeky pictures in a high school yearbook, today's artists and dealers seem embarrassed that the East Village Scene ever existed. What art-type of the nineties, his social conscience revved into overdrive, could speak with the candor of Patti Astor of the Fun Gallery: "We opened the gallery because I got a tax return which was enough to pay the rent for a small store and buy several cases of beer. We had no great pretense or ambitions about fine art or culture. We just showed what we liked and tried to throw as many parties as possible. . . . The name was a pretty good summary of our philosophy."

Or as the painter John Sex said of Kenny Sharf, "Social commentary isn't Kenny's thing. He's into painting and having fun." Fun was the word to conjure with back then, an antidote to

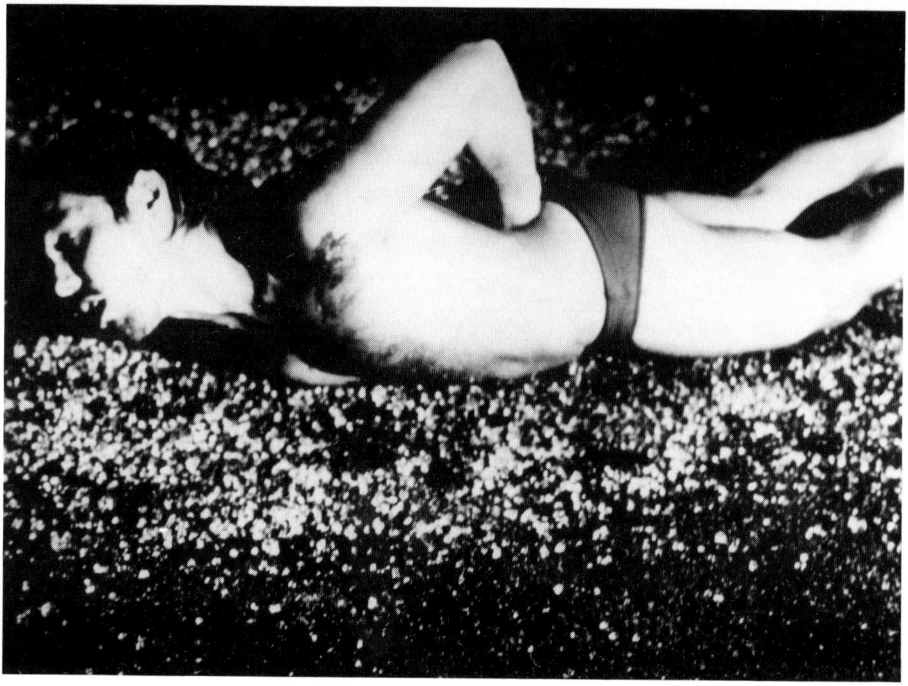

Chris Burden, *Deluxe Book: 1971-1973*, 1974, detail from performance piece *Through the Night Softly*. (Collection of Whitney Museum of American Art)

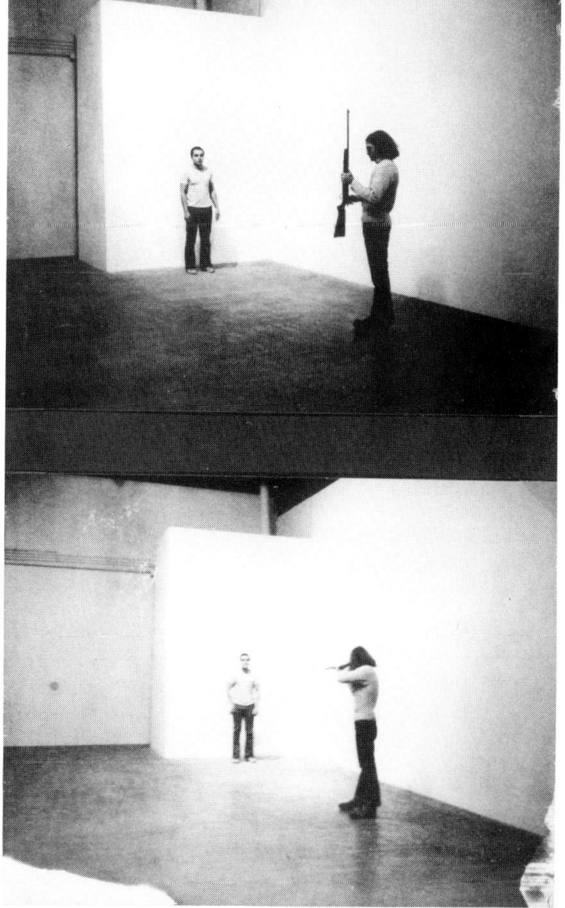

If art has become a religion, Chris Burden is its protomartyr. Among other forms of self-mutilation, this St. Sebastian of SoHo has been shot at and has groveled naked through broken glass, not to mention his inhaling water, being kicked down a flight of stairs, and electrocuting himself.

Chris Burden, *Deluxe Book: 1971-1973*, 1974, detail from performance piece *Shoot*. (Collection of Whitney Museum of American Art)

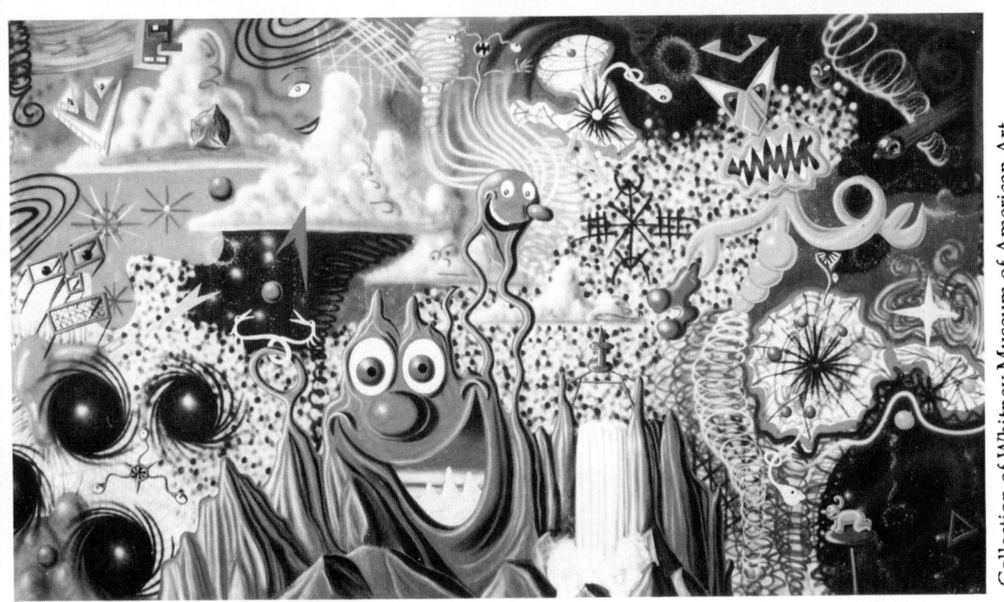

Collection of Whitney Museum of American Art

Kenny Scharf, *When the Worlds Collide*, 1984. Friendly biomorphs, subatomic mutants, and sundry forms of fungoid weirdness typify the graffiti-inspired, fifties retro-madness of Kenny Scharf, one of the more appealing artists to come out of the East Village. In the past ten years, the art world has grown considerably gloomier, and work of such exuberant spiritedness would not be likely today.

Eric Fischl, *A Visit To/ A Visit From/ The Island*, 1983. Few people seemed to care about or even to notice the crudity of this painting when it first appeared, and fewer still seem to care today. Important to note is that it was aggressively figural, in opposition to the rarefied abstraction that generally prevailed in the seventies. Its equally crude division of the world into haves and have-nots and blacks and whites still passes for political insight in some quarters.

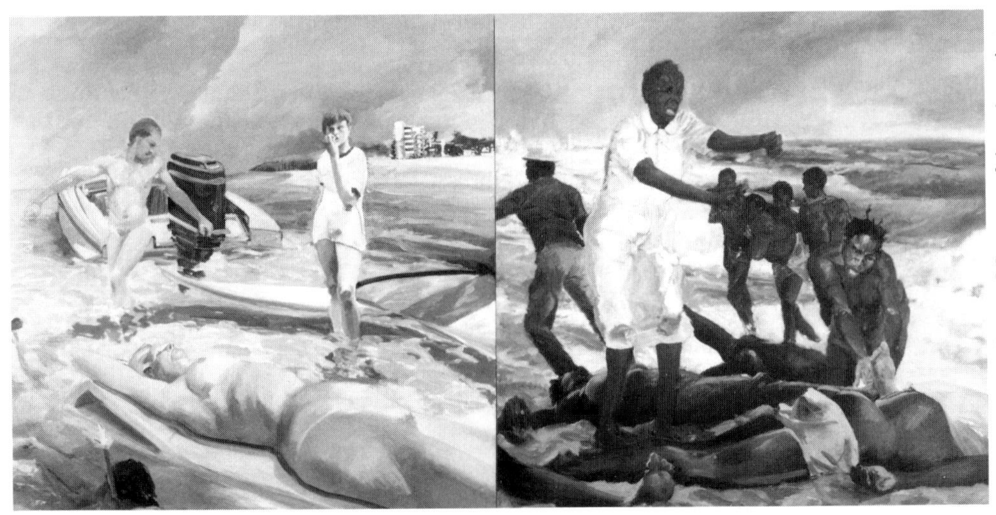

Collection of Whitney Museum of American Art

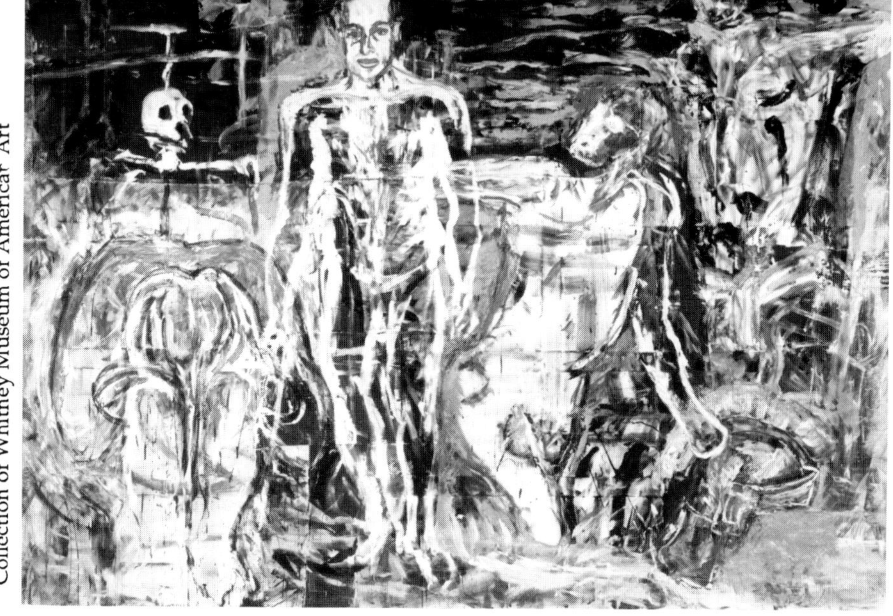

Julian Schnabel, *Hope, The Stages of Man*, 1982. The bright idea here is that the images are painted on velvet, in a "daring" embrace of kitsch and low-brow culture. Schnabel is generally credited with putting passion back into painting in the early eighties. His real genius, however, consists in coming up with snappy titles, like the present one, for essentially inert art.

David Salle, *Sextant in Dogtown*, 1987. This painting has the impacted semiological density of an image bank suffering a seizure. The fact that no conspicuous meaning is generated is explained by arguing that Salle is not actually saying anything, but is questioning meaning itself. At all events, this work, which first looked puzzling, and then looked "classic," now mainly looks expensive.

Collection of Whitney Museum of American Art

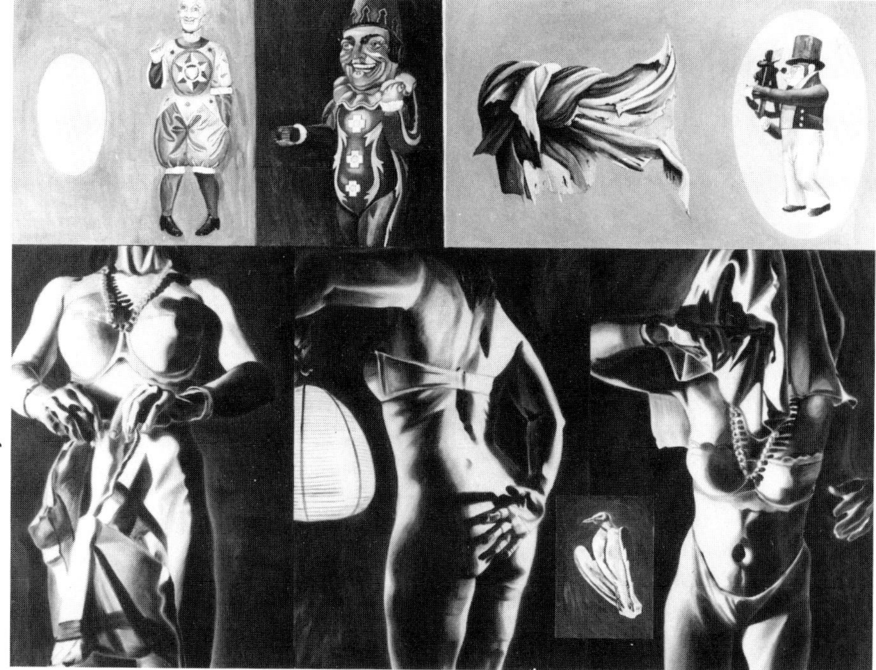

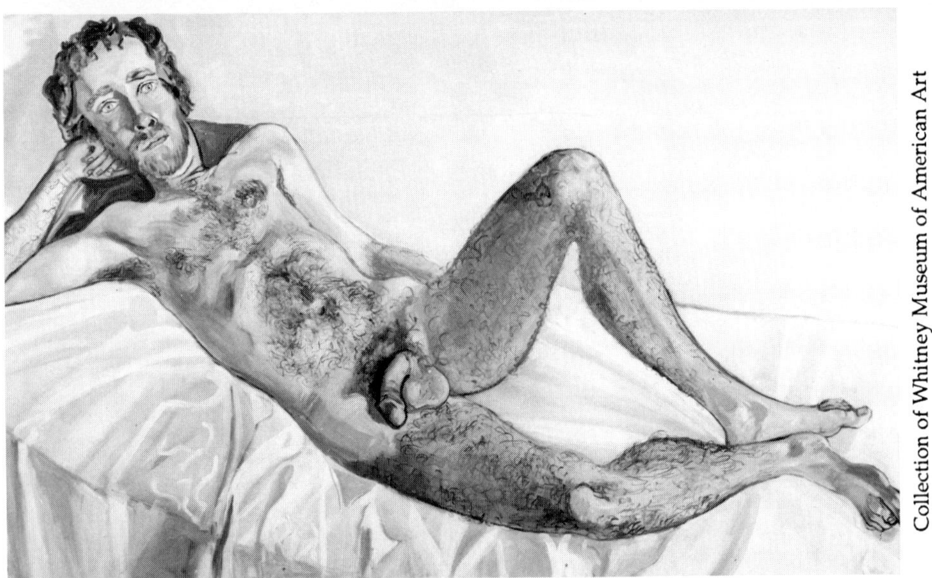

Collection of Whitney Museum of American Art

Alice Neel, *John Perrault*, 1972. This image of a well-known art critic is not what one would ordinarily expect a septuagenarian grandmother to be painting. Nevertheless, with the exception of the gentleman's weakly painted left thigh, it is one of the finest American figure paintings of the past generation, and a striking example of the artist's irrepressible versatility.

Collection of Whitney Museum of American Art

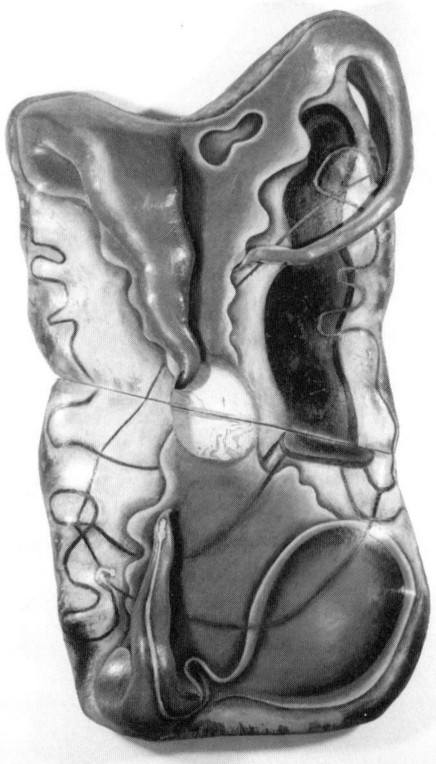

Elizabeth Murray, *Trembling Foot*, 1988. Like many artists of the last fifteen years, Murray has shown a chronic inability to decide whether she were a painter or a sculptor, an abstract artist or a representational one. Though this indeterminacy characterizes the postmodern take on culture in general, Murray has somewhat more respect for modern art than do most of her contemporaries.

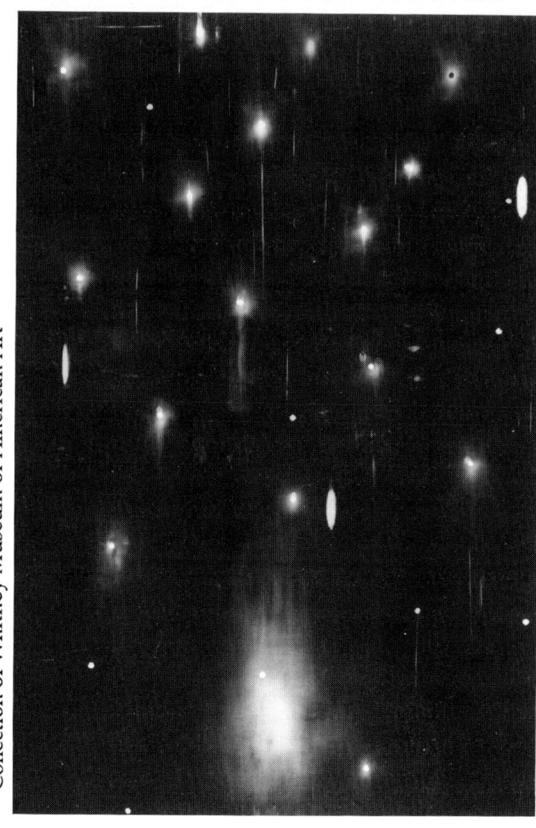

Collection of Whitney Museum of American Art

Ross Bleckner, *Count No Count*, 1989. For the past half-decade, Mr. Bleckner has been making some of the most poetic abstractions in contemporary art. The deep-space, supernoval mysticism of this painting suggests a New Age sentiment that distinguishes the painting from the Modernist abstractions of the postwar period.

Terry Winters, *Good Government*, 1984. Winters is one of the more stalwart proponents of what can only be called Bank Art or Hotel Lobby Art. His two main problems are weak compositions and crusty, lifeless paint textures. His color sense is usually somewhat better.

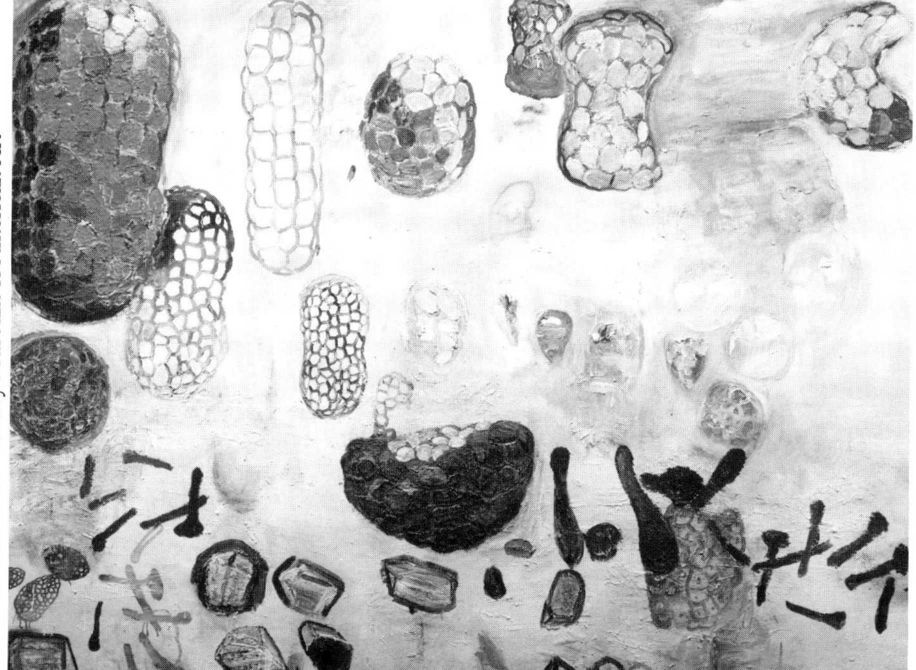

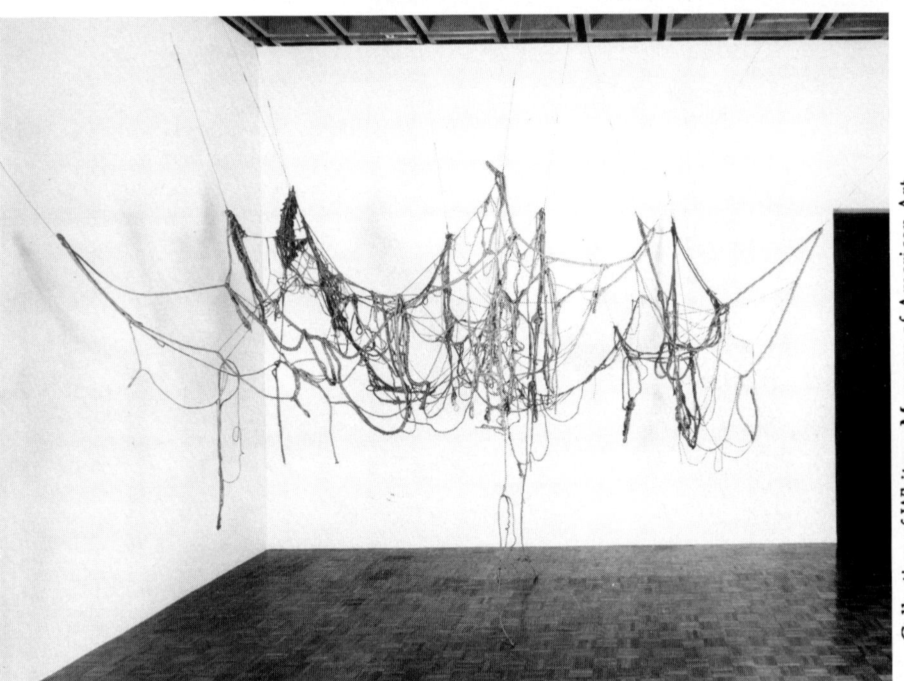

Collection of Whitney Museum of American Art

Eva Hesse, Untitled (Rope Piece), 1970. This highly inventive labor of latex over rope, string, and wire is one of the last works of a tragically short-lived artist. Her Neo-Surrealist feel for the suggestiveness of strange materials, as well as the fact of her being a woman in the male sixties, has caused her to have an immense posthumous influence.

Jenny Holzer, *Unex Sign #1*, 1983. In this Spectrocolor contraption with moving, changing messages, Holzer pushes several of the right, not to mention lucrative, buttons, including populism and political activism. Some of her installations do indeed have a genuine snazziness to them, as this work does not, and suggest that she might devote her attention more usefully to designing discotheques.

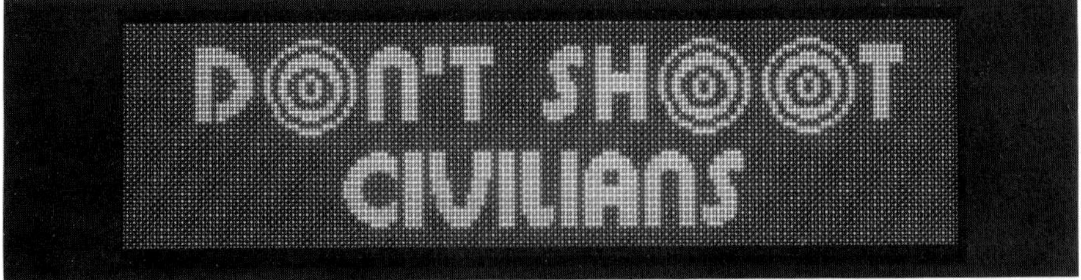

Collection of Whitney Museum of American Art

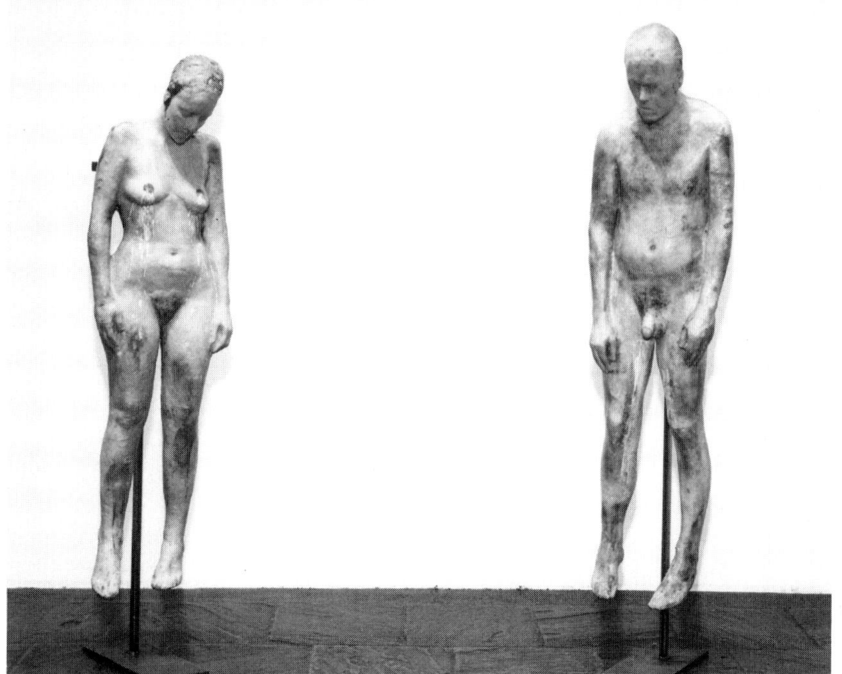

Kiki Smith, Untitled, 1990. These two figures look like George Segal sculptures with a massive attitude problem. Their aborted, lifeless desquamations typify the art world's preoccupation with the body over the past few years. In the age of AIDS and the pro-choice movement, the body is seen as a battleground where the religious right is increasingly gaining the ascendency over the libertarian left.

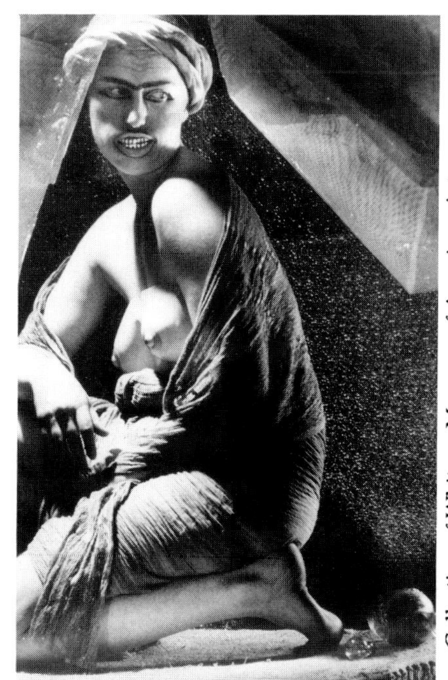

Cindy Sherman, Untitled #146, 1985. In one of her many incarnations, the endlessly protean Sherman recreates herself as an *Arabian Nights* genii. Her prosthetic breasts, mass-produced simulacra, are in keeping with Postmodernism's love of fakery. She was one of the first to exploit photography as a doctored medium to be played with, rather than as a medium through which to record the truth, as it tended to be for Modernist photographers.

Joseph Kosuth, "Titled (Art as Idea as Idea)," 1967. Dispensing useful information as always, Kosuth, in his word art, has been riding the Conceptualist tide for almost thirty years, and embodies a contemporary preoccupation with art itself, with meaning and images. Kosuth was twenty-two when this work was made, which, depending on your perspective, is remarkably young—or old.

red, *n.* [ME. *red, redde*; AS. *read*; akin to G. *rot*, ON. *rauthr*: from same root come also L. *rutilus, rufus, ruber*, Gr. *erythros*, W. *rhwdd*, Ir. and Gael. *ruadh*, also Sans. *rudhira*, blood.]
1. a primary color, or any of a spread of colors at the lower end of the visible spectrum, varying in hue from that of blood to pale rose or pink.
2. a pigment producing this color.
3. [*often* R–] [senses *a* and *b* from the red flag symbolizing revolutionary socialism.] (a) a political radical or revolutionary; especially, a communist; (b) a citizen of the Soviet Union; (c) [*pl.*] North American Indians.

Collection of Whitney Museum of American Art

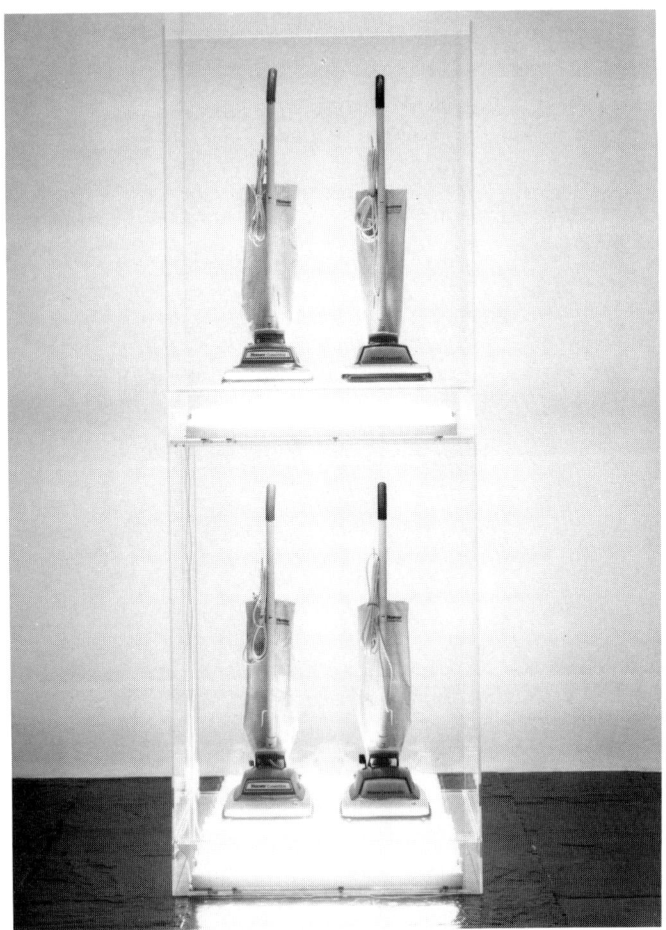

Jeff Koons, *New Hoover Convertibles, Green, Blue; New Hoover Convertibles, Green, Blue; Double-Decker*, 1981-1987. In his displaying of these beauties of consumerism, Koons has boldly gone farther down into the depths of kitsch and banality than anyone else ever has or should.

Collection of Whitney Museum of American Art

the High Seriousness of modernism and the High Mirthlessness of today.

Amid all this celebration, it is astonishing that they created any art at all, and that some of it should even have value. What seemed new and fresh about the East Village Scene was a formal language derived from low or popular culture: cartoons, graffiti, street signs. But what distinguished it from the abstruse aesthetics of pop, and from more recent movements opposed to high culture, was a nostalgia for what these artists, the first to grow up around a TV set, remembered and loved about their own childhoods. They were not opposed to high culture. It just wasn't theirs.

The populism of the East Village was part of that larger questioning of high culture that distinguishes postmodernism from what preceded it. As Adam Gopnik wrote apropos of the Museum of Modern Art's massive High and Low exhibition in 1991: "No period in modern history has seen so many artists involved with so many kinds of popular culture as has the last decade." A new generation of artists coming of age in the early eighties felt that high culture was politically and spiritually dead, an elite corpse to be enlivened only by bracing jolts of the mass media, kitsch, and folk art.

But in this regard, neither the East Village artists nor many others who huddled under the postmodern tent, were quite as daring or innovative as they liked to think. An alliance of high and low had long characterized the modernism of Picasso, Stravinsky, and T.S. Eliot, to name only the foremost icons of the movement. More important, that same alliance had characterized Western culture from its very inception. The temples of classical Greece, high culture incarnate, derived their three famous orders from the trunks of hewn trees and their triglyphs from the crude masonry of Indo-European mud huts. Any classical architecture you will ever see, whether in Athens, Greece or Athens, Georgia, betrays its roots in this primitive tradition.

Dante and Milton, those pillars of the canon, composed in the vernacular even though they wrote with greater ease in Latin and suspected that it was the superior language. The symphonies of Haydn and Beethoven were enriched through the rhythms and melodies of folk music, and Goethe's "Erlkönig" and Coleridge's "Ancient Mariner" were modeled on the lowly ballads of the Middle Ages. Nor is it necessary to point out the equal if not greater influence that high culture exerted on popular culture. This was a fertile symbiosis of long standing.

What really happened in the East Village was much more complicated than generally imagined and strange in the extreme. For it is not true to say that the artists of the East Village forged a link between high and low culture. The divide between the two remained about as great as it had ever been or greater. As popular culture began to take the place of high culture, the art world projected onto it the same nervous seriousness and edgy interest that it had formerly reserved for high art.

Soon, amid ballooning bibliographies and a spiraling inflation of prices, The East Village Scene and its associated movements became part of the dominant taste. In virtually every possible site of privilege and elite art, the SoHo galleries, the Whitney Biennial, the pages of *Art in America* and *Artforum*, popular art succeeded in supplanting high art. This was less a revolution than a dethronement, in which orb and scepter, far from being abolished, merely passed from the anointed to the usurper. Despite what collectors said they did or thought they did, they did not crave this art because it was low culture, but because it was the newest thing to warm the seat of high culture.

Viewed at a higher level of generality, the present battle between high and low rehearses yet once more the age-old struggle of the centrifugal forces of innovation against the more centripetal claims of order and authority. It is the same conflict which, if we may compare greatest with least, distinguished the plays of Euripides from those of Sophocles, and the Song of Solomon from the Book of Job. Down through the centuries it recurs in the debate between Abbot Suger and St. Bernard, the Rubenists and the Poussinists, and the acolytes of Wagner and of

Brahms. At a still higher level of generality, it is the eternal conflict between youth and age, between the conservatism of ossified traditions and the liberal yearning for anything disruptive of the old.

Yet there is something typically American about this preoccupation with high and low. Europeans, having lived with high art much longer, are more at peace with it, and thus less defensive around popular culture. But Americans, who consciously transplanted high culture to these shores, at least before World War II, never overcame the suspicion that it was somehow alien. Furthermore, being the first country to enter the twentieth century, America set the tone and temper of modernity from the very outset. America pioneered billboards and neon signs, comic books and tabloids and all the other trappings of popular culture. Poussin and the Parthenon might be beyond our reach, but these were ours by right of birth.

For the critical record, this high-low debate that has exercised the art world for the past decade is far less important than most people on either side of it are prepared to admit. Both sides seem at their silliest to agree that high and low can be equated with what is good and bad in art, each endearing itself to its adherents for no better reason than that it repels their opponents. But to equate high culture with good art is intellectually remiss; and to equate low culture with kitsch is an unfair, if not a Philistine assumption.

What matters in art is not the source in itself, but rather the use to which it is put. This is why we all would rather be listening to Mozart's folkish *Magic Flute* than to his impeccably inert *Idomeneo;* why many enjoy the poetry of Kipling and no one reads the poetry of Robert Bridges; why I would far rather be standing in front of Hogarth's *Marriage à la Mode* than in front of anything by Sir James Thornhill.

Furthermore, because the high-low debate emerges only late in the eighteenth century, it is irrelevant to some of the finest art ever created. There is no sense in which the *Odyssey* or *Beowulf* or Chartres Cathedral can be called high culture, though surely it is great culture. What made the artists of the East Village distinctive was that they were the first to bring popular culture into the sphere of high culture without any interest in making good art.

Other things interested them. They shared with the socialistic American Scene painters of the thirties a certain humanism, an abstract love of mankind and a hatred for its oppressors. At the same time, they differ from more recent artists, who have exploited the margins of society in their assault against a white, middle-class, heterosexual center. The artists of the East Village reached out to the underclass with a genuine sympathy. Mostly they were middle-American white boys who felt an affinity for the blacks from whom they learned their graffiti, and the Latinos whose gaudy, riotous color sense they had picked up in Spanish Harlem.

Like so much later art, the East Village Scene had a distinctly political element. And yet how different their politics were from what came after. The fear and trembling of contemporary political art was once the language of hope. Instead of the angry nihilism of today's art, you had a kind of intoxicated utopianism. The East Village gang never supposed, like the artists of the Bauhaus or the activists of the sixties, that they could change the world. Rather, the world was not such a bad place if you knew where to look.

It can be argued that they felt a patriotism of sorts, perhaps even something like piety. Explaining why he had painted Woody Woodpecker and Felix the Cat onto an American flag, Ronnie Cutrone said, and may have meant, "It's funny that I got hit with so much abuse about defamation of the flag when what I was trying to do was broadcast myself as a patriotic American artist." He also said and may have believed, "If it weren't for my belief in God and prayer every day, I never could have gotten through the rough phases of being an artist."

Their views on childhood as well form a stark contrast with the art that came after. By the late eighties, childhood had become a scandalous trap in which by no means innocent victims were menaced by dysfunctional adults. Robert Gober's carceral cribs and Ida Applebroog's none-too-ambiguous images of molestation are, for the moment, the received ideas about childhood. It was not so ten years ago. The East Village artists felt a deep and generous affinity for children. All children, because they watched cartoons instead of Bergman films, and preferred doodles to Mondrian, were automatically avant-garde. In an odd way, childhood was for these artists as pure and sunny as it had been for Boucher and Fragonard, though it was lived, not in Arcady or the forests of Fontainebleau, but in the suburbs of the Mid-West.

"A dream I've had for quite a while," Kenny Sharf once said, "is to have a traveling art circus. I'd drive up in my custom Cadillac hooked to a customized trailer with a built-in stage. Every town we played in Keith [Haring] and I could do mural commissions in. We'd show the kids how to make art and document it all on film. Then at the end I'd park it in a cool place and build a giant amusement park." It is typical that both Sharf and Rodney Allen Greenblatt illustrated children's stories and that Keith Haring brought out a coloring book.

In no way must they be confused with pop art. Painters like Warhol and Lichtenstein might depict comic-book art, but for them it was contemporary culture, which they viewed with the superbly dispassionate condescension of adults. Though Warhol and Lichtenstein had grown up in the thirties, they depicted the popular art of the early sixties, an art that was in a sense foreign to them. But when artists like Ronnie Cutrone or Rodney Allen Greenblatt resurrected Woody Woodpecker or the Incredible Hulk, they knew whereof they spoke. These were no abstruse examinations of signs and flatness, as had been the case with pop. Here, writ large, were the small doodles that they, as school boys, had scribbled in their notebooks or carved into their homeroom desks.

Earlier artists and poets, from Giorgione to Fragonard and Virgil to Thomas Gray, had fully appreciated the evanescence of childhood. But the East Village artists understood, as no earlier artists could have done, that the very circumstances of one's childhood could go out of fashion, could seem no longer to fit. Whole levels of resonant loss were thus permitted to them that would have been inconceivable to previous artists. The irony was that, although their childhood went out of fashion, its visible effects were everywhere: record albums, reruns, Hula Hoops, old teeny-bopper magazines.

Their art was an impassioned tribute to everything they could no longer believe in—crew cuts and John Glenn, Felix the Cat and the Beaver. They were the last generation to experience a childhood largely free from irony, in which you said your prayers and pledged allegiance to the flag. Perhaps much was repellent in this childhood, but it was the only childhood they had had, and so they could not help but look back on it with a feeling of something having been irretrievably lost.

At least half a decade separates us from the East Village Scene, and one almost feels apologetic for writing about them at all. This book is about contemporary art, and they are not contemporary. They have been out of fashion for several years, and the pyramids of Egypt seem not as old as they. Indeed, you might sometimes wonder if they had ever been contemporary at all: Perhaps they just seemed that way. Only what is happening now can really be called contemporary: Jeff Koons, Sophie Calle, Kiki Smith. Kenny Sharf and Mark Kostabi and all the other East Village artists who certainly looked contemporary six years back, turn out to have been mere phantom artists, a trick of the light, an understandable misapprehension on the part of the art world, which, the theory goes, has now grown up. But is it possible that Koons, Calle, and Smith could also one day go out of fashion? And the answer of the art world is: Absolutely not. This is it.

Indeed, much has changed. If Max Beerbohm could call the 1890s the Age of Beardsley, perhaps we will be permitted the exaggeration of calling the 1980s the Age of Haring. For it was Keith Haring, more than anyone else, who gave to that period its most characteristic visual expression. Artists like David Salle or Anselm Kiefer might seem "weightier," but precisely for that reason, their work has never lent itself as Haring's did to the mass replication of a small number of compact and legible motifs. Obviously he neither sought nor attained Beardsley's subtlety and refinement, but his art, like Beardsley's, was born of a single formal idea, from which he forged a career almost as brief as Beardsley's. Both were artists of the line, but the thick demotic bands of Haring's cartoon-like images contrasted with the tendrilous threads of Beardsley's superfine elaborations. Beyond this difference, Haring was often as obscene as Beardsley, but oddly there seemed to be a core of wholesomeness in what he did. There was nothing effete or decadent in his art.

Haring was naive in the sense in which the Douanier Rousseau was naive. His early Art in Transit series, numerous simple images hastily painted onto the black ground of unfilled poster-spaces in the New York subway system, endeared him to the art world as a kind of Til Eulenspiegel, a merry pictorial prankster. Though he attended the School of Visual Arts, it is not clear that he learned anything there. One feels that his art would not have been substantially different if he had never entered a classroom or a museum.

Unlike Basquiat, whose populist-inspired images exuded expensive whiffs of mainstream European modernism, Haring was able, in his best work, to create a vital drawing style and occasionally even compositional flair, out of entirely populist sources. In this regard he recalls the "underground" cartoonist R. Crumb who, as a draughtsman, also has his moments. To the end of Haring's life, his art was that of a talented youth who did one thing well: drawings conceived as broad, clean lines. Earlier line drawing had consisted of thin clean lines, like John Flaxman's, or of broad messy lines like Franz Kline's. Haring arrived at a compromise, and that was his career.

What he created with that line was an entire vocabulary of postmodern archetypes, born not of the collective unconscious, but of the imaginations of suburban and inner-city youths. Throughout the nearly ten years of his career, Haring returned over and over to his Pulsing Pyramids, Barking Dogs, Flaming Hearts, and Radiant Children. They can fit into the limited confines of a T-shirt or small canvas, or they can fill every inch of every wall at the Tony Shafrazi Gallery. Once they were emblazoned across an expanse of the Berlin Wall. Haring even body-painted the singer Grace Jones and the dancer Bill T. Jones with white stripes that stood out markedly against their black skin.

It may be that the lightheartedness of Haring's style and content eventually tripped him up. Even when he later tried to express rage, in his images of entire populations being decimated by AIDS, his signature style always subverted his intentions, distorting them into something incongruously pleasant. Similarly, his bright black-on-yellow image of devils being sacrificed to a Cerberean god of the underworld, with deaths-head angels floating overhead, is compositionally perhaps the best thing he ever did, but it conveys little emotion and has little point beyond decoration.

As befitted a graffiti artist, constantly looking over his shoulder to see if the police were coming for him, Haring worked with incredible speed. I remember being introduced to him in the men's room of the Lesbian and Gay Community Services Center by Rhonda Zwilinger, whom I was about to interview in the ladies' room. He was to decorate the men's room, she the women's room, for a massive group exhibition to be held in the building. We found him sitting in one of the stalls eating pizza, beneath a large blank wall, perhaps fifty-feet square. When I passed by again after the interview, forty-five minutes later, almost the entire wall had been covered. There was an impressive vigor and energy to his design, a steamy binary equation of phallus and orifice, replicating infinitely. What most impressed me was that the paint didn't seem so much to be applied by the brush as to flow out of it, as though the myriad interlocking figures poured forth, full born and fully alive onto the complicit wall. Keith Haring was surely a severely limited artist, and even in themselves the terms of his art were not always impressive, but within those terms his mastery was absolute.

One of Haring's allies in the East Village was Kenny Sharf. His aesthetic derives from graffiti, but unlike Basquiat's raw images and words, or Haring's broad schematics, Sharf's art is rooted in a more precise kind of representation. Yet like his fellow graffiti artists, he has achieved stupendous fluency in doing the one thing he knows how to do. Once the concept of a painting is fixed in his mind, a wealth of images seem to come spiraling out of his brush with all the exuberance of an organic process. Like Haring, Sharf is a great customizer of bathrooms, and we shall not soon forget the way he took over the men's and women's rooms on the second floor of the 1985 Whitney Biennial, not to mention the adjoining corridor and telephone booths, filling every inch of every surface with Day-Glo paints that shimmered under the ultraviolet lights. There is in his art something of the virtuoso at the piano, making everything up as he goes along.

Scharf's is clearly a happy art. He is possibly the last artist to be able, without irony, to dedicate a volume of his paintings to God: "Special thanks to God who created the rainforest," he wrote in a book of his environmental images. But that was from the later eighties. His religion has not always been so mainstream. In the early eighties he invented a substitute Christianity called Jetsonism. "Jetsonism is nirvana," he explained. Jetsonism was an offshoot of a larger religion called Hanna-Barberaism.

In this unlikely faith, the Christ child and desire of all nations was none other than Elroy Jetson, whose name means much to the thirty-something crowd and, I would imagine, almost nothing to anyone else. Elroy is the ten-something son of the Jetsons, the nuclear family of a once-popular cartoon show set far in the future. He appears in various avatars in Sharf's early works. In *Elroy and Leroy*, a pair of identical twins are suckled by a she-wolf in simulation of Romulus and Remus. As Roman civilization took its legendary origin from that pair, so Elroy and

Leroy are to be the founders of a new civilization. Elsewhere Elroy is a putto floating in a nectarine-colored firmament over a rehashing of Mantegna's *Christ on Mount Olive*.

From his earlier Jetsonism, Sharf graduated to a most unorthodox pantheon of friendly ectomorphs, protoplasms, and Martians inhabiting a world of exploding supernovas, black holes, and eddying vortices of energy. Inspired by such programs as "Outer Limits," and coming to us from the time of Eisenhower, these organisms have powers far beyond those of humans. The good news is that they seem to like us and have no interest in destroying the earth. These paintings do not exist on several levels, but derive their force from the conviction with which they inhabit the one level on which they do exist. Their principal compositional trope is *horror vacui*, a dense all-over patterning that covers every inch with colors and forms.

In modernist terms, these paintings are tawdry in the extreme. The technique is slick and superficial; the colors are Pepto-Bismol pink, aquarium turquoise, and Rhodda-peep yellow. Yet the paintings are so ebullient and so clearly well-intentioned that criticism is disarmed. Like an atomic Dr. Suess, Sharf is able to touch the "child in all of us," to shed the same kind of enchantment deep within. And in the best of Scharf, as in the best of Dr. Suess, there is a quality which we might call inexhaustibleness. After a while, most paintings of high mediocrity seem to become mere paint. The energy has been depleted and there is nothing left except soulless brushstrokes on linen. But the best paintings of Kenny Sharf keep coming at you. However suspect and meretricious his artistic terms may be, I am not at all sure that this result could have been arrived at if he were not doing something right in the way of art.

Sharf's later works, it must be said, represent a partial loss of innocence. He seems no longer to be following his own impulse but rather the coaching of dealers and curators. He makes use of charged words like: *Scientists say*, *Chlorofluorocarbons*, *Corporation—oil—low cost of*. They don't quite carry conviction, and the forms don't fit together as effortlessly as before. But in an artist who is only forty, it would be foolish and unfair to write him off.

Many artists have wanted to be Andy Warhol, but no one has canvassed for the honor as aggressively as Mark Kostabi. Though this indefatigable self-promoter has not yet invested in a white wig and face powder, he exudes the same confidence as Warhol that fakery is what all art is really about. His schtick is to get others to paint his images for him at Kostabi World, his factory in Lower Manhattan. A staff of six produces between five and ten paintings a week and Kostabi sells them for $10,000 to $50,000. This in itself is not so unusual. Frank Stella, to name only the most eminent example, employs an entire phalanx of apprentices to carry out his pictorial ideas.

What distinguishes Kostabi and constitutes his lasting contribution to art is the fact that even the ideas are no longer his, since he employs others to generate these too. Far from concealing the fact, he has made it the hallmark of his success. An ad placed in the *Village Voice* read, "ARTIST'S Asst—Inventive artists wntd to provide IDEAS for Mark Kostabi paintings.... Have resume avail. $7/HR." Kostabi thus situates himself beside Mike Bidlo and Sherrie Levine in the by-now hoary tradition of artists questioning traditional notions of originality and creativity.

"I may not be a great artist," Kostabi wrote in a statement that introduced him on the game show "To Tell the Truth," "but I am a great con artist." In perhaps the most shockingly hubristic act of his career, Kostabi published a massive catalogue raisonné of his paintings when he was thirty. *Kostabi: The Early Years*, weighing as much as a side of beef and bound in sumptuous burgundy cloth, was published by a company ostentatiously named Vanity. As Sir Basil Chattington, editor of this 524-page book, wrote in the foreword, "It is as if history herself had solicited this definitive homage to Kostabi; and for a work of such noble, indeed transcendent provenance, no labor exerted or indignity suffered can possibly be considered to have been in vain."

The first chapter, by one Mavis Grace Hallowell, is modestly titled, "The Birth of a Genius" and includes an old photograph of the genius's mother in native Estonian costume, as well as high-school-yearbook shots of the genius, and pictures of the genius in buzz cut, page boy, punk, and other hair cuts suffered through the years. Like so many of the other artists of the East Village, Kostabi seems to have been the sort of bright child—every high school class has one—who might goof off, but whose flare for draughtsmanship wins him the respect of others. His earliest works, from when he was in his teens, are surely not high art, but they already display a real sense of calling.

By 1982, at the age of twenty-two, Kostabi began what Sir Basil (why have I not been able to find his name anywhere else?) calls "the Masterpieces." Here we encounter the image that has recurred over and over through the artist's career for the past ten years, a faceless mechanomorph, with jointless rubbery limbs. There is a sheer metallic glint to these images, which, in their totality, constitute as idiosyncratic and decorative a style as Haring's. Surely this is not all that we should ask of art, but it is something. Visually, most of these images are pleasant and of little essential worth. But in some, like the grisaille *I Talk to the Devil*, depicting a faceless figure gazing into a mirror, there is a true and subtle sadness. You find an honest distillation of the postmodern mood in *The Age of Anxiety*, whose two mechanomorphic forms crouch over one another, bathed in blue light. There is even something touching in *Father and Sunshine*, in which one feels a true affection between the two figures covered in a softly diffused light the color of tea roses.

Most of the art is not as ruminative as that, being boisterously smart-alecky. Kostabi's inability to resist making a joke would be irritating except that sometimes the jokes are quite funny. In one such image, he superimposes his face, giggling like an idiot, over the face of Mona Lisa. In another, irreverently titled *Baldy Paints a Masterpiece*, we see the aged Picasso from the back, putting the finishing touches on the ultra-cool sunglasses in a portrait of—who else?—Mark Kostabi. Elsewhere there are cheeky allusions to Magritte, Leonardo, and Vermeer. The standing jest is that each of these great men implicitly acknowledges that Kostabi is the greatest of them all. What often gets lost in all of this is the fact that Kostabi really does have talent, which he might some day decide to use.

Of all the artists to emerge from the East Village, Jean Michel Basquiat is the most famous and, in the opinion of many, the only true heavyweight. There are several reasons for this belief, none of them very good. Anger always impresses us more than charm, and though Basquiat had little or no charm to speak of, his art was full of a passionate conviction that many were prepared to accept on faith. Because he was black, the art world naturally assumed he must be more closely in touch with his emotions than ice people like themselves. This was the sort of casual racism they could live with, indeed live off, as long as it was never looked in the face.

Basquiat's career began back in 1978 when, in total anonymity, he started defiling public and private property with such sententious aphorisms as "If they smite you, turn the other face." He was one of the first artists to put graffiti on canvas, thus elevating what had been an urban eyesore to the ranks of high culture. He was not the only one. There were Futura 2000, Lady Pink, Fab Five, Freddy, Crash, and Daze. Why, one wonders, has Basquiat gone on to immortality, whereas they who were no less deserving will never be heard from again? Perhaps it was because Basquiat, who came from a polyglot background and had been to a private school, was not an inner-city black, but the scion of well-to-do Haitians, and thus more commendable to the snobbery of the art world. Further, he had the enterprise and shrewdness to be the kind of black the art world wanted, a noble savage whom you could dress up and take to good restaurants.

Nevertheless, for all his worldy successes, Basquiat never forsook the idiom of the street. From his triumphant entry into the art world at twenty to his heroin overdose eight years later, his art tended to be of a piece: brutally schematic images of skulls, cars, and mangled human figures competing with angry, enigmatic words against a patchwork of quite pleasant color-fields. Sometimes figures predominate and sometimes words. Usually a balance was struck, as in a painting from 1982 with the provocative title *Obnoxious Liberals.* Scribbled onto canvas are the words: ASBESTOS, SAMSON, OBNOXIOUS, LIBERAL, NOT FOR SALE. The painting is a tasteful mix of russet, off-white, pink, and bluish-grey adorned with a few humanoids and a black man raising his hands in a Picassoid gesture of, we assume, despair. And yet, aside from the words, there is nothing especially despairing about the painting, which formally is about as challenging as a Raoul Dufy depiction of a steeplechase at Longchamps.

The words themselves are what tip us off that we are to interpret this in a political context. What is extraordinary is the ease with which, as seasoned viewers of contemporary art, we can do this. After all, we are presented with a half dozen unpredicated words, removed from any context of grammar. Yet, invariably, we know how to interpret them, for the simple reason that, as seasoned gallery goers, we have seen them all before. *Asbestos* must refer to the sinister toxicity of the major corporations. *Samson*, though more ambiguous, has doubtless to do with macho role playing. The joining of *Obnoxious* and *Liberal* might have seemed like some right-wing dig at the liberal establishment, except that, this being contemporary art, we may assume that Basquiat was being ironic. *Not For Sale* is surely a comment on capitalism and the commercialization of art, of which one disapproves. The fact that this painting is and always was very much for sale is, for vague reasons, not strictly relevant. What are we left with? A black man representing oppressed humanity succumbs under the weight of illiberal corporations that jeopardize our health. Exactly!

These torturous and brutalized forms, these anguished skulls and wrecked cars and frantic scribbles are rich in sources. Unlike the other artists of the East Village, Basquiat seemed to stand for something approximating high culture. Far from concealing the sources of his inspiration, he seemed nervously eager to let everyone in on them. Seeing his works is a little like taking a quiz that everyone is guaranteed of passing: One notices the allusions to Dubuffet and Masson, Picasso and de Kooning. And this being the heyday of "appropriation," one knows better than to disparage the exiguity of the artist's visual imagination, instead praising the referentiality of his borrowings.

In a catalog essay for the Whitney Museum's recent retrospective of Basquiat, Richard Marshall showed images of these paintings side by side with the works of the European masters who inspired them. It was a tactless, terrible thing to do. On each occasion Basquiat pulled his source down a notch from brilliance into mediocrity. True, the artist has unintentionally performed the useful if somewhat pedestrian service of reinforcing for all doubters the excellence of those European masters. If Picasso had been mediocre, Basquiat seems to say, he would have painted so. Take from Twombly's scribbled images their nervous energy of line, their compulsive, feathery allusiveness, and you get this. The theory of Basquiat's career was apparently that, since Dubuffet painted like a schoolboy, every schoolboy must paint like Dubuffet.

Basquiat, however, was never so much angry as irascible. For a scalding bath of acid, we must turn instead to David Wojnarowicz, the angriest of the East Villagers. One of his earliest images is a fiery red stencil of a burning house, and one of his latest is a self-portrait photograph in which he has sewn his lips shut with ten stitches to his mouth. In between are numerous skeletons, flames encircling globes, Genêt, Rimbaud, Christ on heroin, starving dogs, buffalo falling off cliffs, and snakes devouring frogs. It is almost as though, through some hormonal imbalance, his mind found itself gravitating toward everything sickly and degraded. "I let my hands become weapons, my teeth become weapons, every bone and muscle and fiber and ounce of blood become weapons, and I feel prepared for the rest of my life," he said in one of his writings, "Being Queer in America."

Homosexuality was fundamental to Wojnarowicz's life and art. A high school dropout, he spent part of his adolescence turning tricks in Times Square. In one of his graphics from 1990, he has cut out an old photograph of himself as a ten year old and set it against a white ground. Around the image he has written: "One day this kid will get larger. . . . One day politicians will enact legislations against this kid. . . . When he begins to talk, men who develop a fear of this kid will attempt to silence him with strangling, fists, prison, suffocation, rape, intimidation. . . . All this will begin to happen in one or two years when he discovers he desires to place his naked body on the naked body of another boy."

In earlier works, you can see traces of humor, but since this humor is not especially funny, it makes a limited claim upon your attention. Unless we wish to see him as an artist like Duchamp, whose life was his art, Wojnarowicz's most impressive work is his acrylic images on wood from the mid-eighties. Like so much contemporary art, these images defeat verbal description. There is no unifying narrative core, and such is the feverish density of the imagery that a hundred things seem to be happening at once. *The Death of American Spirituality*, for example, is divided into four compartments: a space-ship zaps a Martian; a skull clenching a snake between its teeth rises amid smokestacks; a cowboy is bucking a bronco made of newspaper, with dolphins and spaceships orbiting above in a lunar landscape; Jesus Christ's head floats amid lava flows and flying rocks.

A year or two later, in *Fear of Evolution*, a neater style of collage emerges, with provocative images of monkeys and tornadoes set against an elegant background of five-, twenty-, fifty-, and hundred-dollar bills. In these he reveals a true graphic sense that qualifies him as one of the best collagists of his day. Ironically, it is hard to say what these are about, and one is left more with a sense of their elegance than of their anger. Sometimes, as in *Something From Sleep II*, amid images of hearts and a sleeping man, the dollars seem to have been torn away in parts, and heavenly blue sky is revealed behind them. Yet there is nothing hopeful about the image. It is an encomium to what is forever beyond his reach.

Wojnarowicz died of AIDS in 1992, at age thirty-eight. He was the sort of man whom Dante would have accused of willfully living in sorrow. To judge from his art, he seems always to have been unhappy, always to have found pain and outrage in the world. He did not decry injustice in order to change it, since this would have implied some leaven of ideals; rather he seemed to inhabit a hostile universe against which one could protest for the sake of protest, but without hope of change. Ultimately, Wojnarowicz's art fails to carry total conviction. He was like the Doris Day of hell. If she saw only sunshine and happiness, he, in his inverted world, saw only darkness and the pain. Both perspectives are one-sided and only a fool would suppose that Wojnarowicz's world view, because it is angrier and more passionate, must also be more informed. Nevertheless, it was this position that would come to dominate the art of the later eighties and the nineties, an art of angry intensity that had little in common with what had once taken place in the East Village.

S I X

The Reborn Figure

Much of Postmodernism is really premodernism reborn. Architecture, the site of postmodernism's first conquests, is inherently conservative, not only because it must obey the laws of gravity, but also because people who collect large buildings tend to be sobersided plutocrats who tolerate less nonsense than others. Furthermore, if, through sculpted pediments and fluted pilasters, an architect can suggest certain similarities between his patron and Pericles of Athens, the patron is unlikely to object.

This was the secret of the movement's success during the Reagan-Thatcher years. Postmodernism filled a need for grandeur and history that the suffocating uniformity of the International Style had ignored. The history that Mies Van der Rohe and Walter Gropius had tried to abolish was redeemed in the eighties, and architects were free as never before to traverse architectural time in search of what Robert Stern called "a usable past." This was part of a general mood that pervaded the eighties, inspiring everything from Nancy Reagan's revamping of the White House to the Treasure Houses of Britain exhibition in Washington, to "Masterpiece Theater" and *A Room With a View*.

Despite some frankly pseudo-intellectual doctrines that surrounded the movement, what distinguished postmodernism, at least early on, was the appeal of its pleasant colors and readily identifiable forms. Postmodernism supplied precisely those qualities that many modernists, for reasons not substantially better, had labored to exclude. No doubt the serial music of Pierre Boulez, the black-on-black canvases of Ad Reinhardt, and the voided narratives of Alain Robbe-Grillet had had their legitimate formal pretexts. But in part what inspired these men was the resolve to frustrate the bourgeois desire to be entertained. They seemed to revel in a distinctly contentious abstinence from the delights of recognizable representation, musical tonality, and compelling plots; to find grim satisfaction in having reached a terminal point, whether of elevation or abjection, to which the casually cultured could not or would not follow them. Postmodernists might find other ways to exacerbate the bourgeoisie, but tight-lipped formalism would not be one of them.

Put another way, if many modernists seemed to deliver the beef raw, without sauce or condiments, postmodernism supplied the sauces and the condiments often to the exclusion of the beef. A postmodern novelist like Paul Auster delights in narrative twists that deliberately cultivate a feeling of ornate superficiality. The pure harmonies of Philip Glass are rarely encumbered by melodic ideas to be developed and explored. And in the work of many postmodernist painters, especially from the eighties, pleasant, recognizable images return in an abundance no one had seen in a hundred years. This culture was destined to appeal to two groups, premodernists, who had never overcome their initial suspicion that a six year old could paint a Pollock, and true postmodernists, for whom modernism was an established art whose successes they envied and whose power they feared.

The grand strategy of postmodernism, especially in painting, was to bring about the redemption of meaning: meaning through recognizable images, meaning through words, meaning through philosophical doctrines, meaning through political agitation. Meaning was as totemic a concept for the art of the eighties as formal purity had been for the art of the sixties. "A poem should not mean but be," Archibald MacLeish had said long before, summing up the modernist take on culture in general. Postmodernists wanted to reverse that principle, subordinating the object's essence to its role in a larger intellectual debate.

One way to attack was to redeem representation in the face of the abstract art that had dominated for a generation. This was more easily done than might be imagined. Figure painting had never really died out in the postwar era. It was always being taught, and only in the sixties did it yield to abstraction as the reigning doctrine of the schools. Thus, by the seventies there were battalions of figure painters with some technique and nothing to which they could apply it. Postmodernism gave them the excuse they needed to create the sort of intricate compositions with complicated subject matter which, only a few years before, would have been scorned as "inartistic."

By the early eighties, figural artists were browsing around for their own usable past, and found what they were looking for it in Philip Guston and Giorgio De Chirico. Both had been pillars of modernism who eventually made peace with tradition. Their cooptation was a shrewd move on the part of the new generation, not only because both men, being dead, did not have a whole lot to say about it, but also because it seemed to prove that in the innermost closets of modernism, postmodernists were waiting to burst out.

Many conservative modernists greeted with horror the later De Chiricos that were displayed at the 1982 MoMA retrospective. How could this noble artist, whose faceless mannequins had distilled the very soul of modern alienation, so forget himself as to invent images whose untroubled clarity might, with a few adjustments, have been acceptable to any painter of the baroque? Some wondered if he had been joking or mad when he painted his self-portrait as a quattrocento artist. And what of his *Venetian*

Caprice in the Manner of Veronese, in which Arachne gazes heavenward at swans and eagles hovering in the golden Venetian air while fair women dally along classical balustrades? This reversal was worse than heresy; it was apostasy.

But the apostasy of Philip Guston appeared more shocking still, because he was a contemporary and because the style he rejected was the ruling order of the day. When he initiated the third and final phase of his career at New York's Marlborough Gallery in 1970, there was talk of betrayal. The Canadian-born Guston had been one of the more gifted members of the New York School, even though he never sought or attained a style as immediately recognizable as Pollock's or Rothko's. He specialized in pink, purple, and magenta fogs evaporating into beige along the edges, but gathering toward tangibility at their centers. He did this very well, and the artistic community saw no good reason why he should ever do anything else.

But Guston's newest art was unlike anything they had seen before. Aggressively representational, it seemed to exhume the most degraded elements of an earlier world, a world of tar and ashcans, of economic depression and heavy industry. Reaching far back into the comic-book memories of childhood, the artist pulled up crudely drawn black shoes, bare light bulbs, prickly pink legs, and what looked like a cross between an eyeball and a testicle.

Different though they were, Guston and De Chirico appealed for the same reason: they provided an authoritative legitimacy to those who had grown sick of abstraction or had never understood it in the first place. It is only a slight exaggeration to say that these two painters embody the two main sources of figuration that were of immense importance to the eighties: De Chirico representing the classicizing strain; Guston inspiring the New Imagists with his rough and slightly abstracted forms. Even where their role in the causation of the eighties was intangible they served to enunciate some of the main lines in the revival of the figure.

De Chirico became the standard bearer of a curious *passéisme*, or antiquarianism, that took hold of the art world in the early eighties. Not the least part of its appeal consisted in being the polar opposite of modernism's thirst for the new. Revivalism has been attempted often in the history of art, and twice it has been successful: in Imperial Rome, with its fertile fixation on Greek culture of several centuries earlier, and in Renaissance Europe. Subsequent revivals have been less inspiring. When eighteenth-century neoclassicists like Anton Raphael Mengs scavenged Herculaneum and Pompeii for an art that would be more legitimately classical than the art of their own time, the results were pretty paltry.

But revivalism did not reach the summit of pedantic pastiche until the mid 1800s when the members of the Académie des Beaux-Arts, having failed in the previous century to revitalize the dying, sought now to resurrect the dead. In fact, it was their dogged dedication to the corpse of the old masters, through their systematic pillaging of Titian and Veronese, that inspired the revolt of modernism in the first place, and with it the tradition of the new.

Because of the force and enduring success of this revolt, by the early 1980s it was widely believed that modernism, if it had not abolished the past, at least had no interest in it. Though this opinion wasn't true, one look at minimalists like Ad Reinhardt or Robert Morris, and you could be forgiven for thinking it was. Nevertheless, it was this opinion that gave coherence and purpose to much of the art produced under the banner of Postmodernism. And yet the classicism to which these new artists dedicated themselves was strangely compromised and impure. They could understand antiquity not in any direct way, but only through the scrim of eighteenth-century neoclassicism. This was unfortunate, for, unlike Renaissance artists, who had looked to antiquity for strength, neoclassicists like Mengs sought out all that was most weak in antiquity in order to create an art that, with few exceptions, was precious and theatrical.

This taste for neoclassicism now pervades not only the visual arts, but also novels like *Foucault's Pendulum* by Umberto Eco and Susan Sontag's *The Volcano Lover*, as well as operas like John Corigliano's *The Ghosts of Versailles* and Argento's *Casanova*. There are several reasons for its appeal. Created in the cauldron of the French Revolutionary Era, it came into being at the first moment when we can recognize our modern epoch emerging out of the feudal order of the ancien regime. It is the outer edge of the *now*, the point of crisis where present and past collide. It partakes equally of both and is equally alienated from both.

More important, it was the moment of classicism's greatest enfeeblement, the moment when it seemed most frivolous and louche. Camp, which is not a small component of this contemporary taste, is drawn to areas of weakness and excess, because true strength and seriousness cannot fit comfortably in its theatrical sense of life. But neoclassicism lends itself perfectly to this treatment, because it is the art of an age that is divided against itself and undergoing an identity crisis. At the same time, it furnishes artists with the delightful option to assume styles as they might don costumes for a masked ball, thus becoming Caravaggio for a day, or, like Alfred Leslie and Tibor Czernus, for an entire career.

The Italians seem to admire this neoclassicism more than anyone, since they, more than any other Western European nation, can claim it as part of their ethnic heritage. Carlo Maria Mariani's *The School of Rome*, with its dreamy view of marble ruins and belaureled youths in togas, is surely a central image of the postmodern movement. One of his largest paintings, it is inspired by Mengs's tawdry imitation of Raphael's *Vatican Parnassus*. All three paintings depict eminent cultural figures set into an Arcadian landscape. Whereas Apollo and Orpheus are the central figures in Raphael and Mengs respectively, in Mariani's case a self-portrait occupies that position. He is flanked by the Pyramid of Cestius, sarcophagi, a broken column, and a pair of disembodied feet. Standing amid muscular young men in

Michelangelesque poses are the artist's friends: Francesco Clemente, Mario Merz, and Cy Twombly on horseback carrying the standard of the Roman Republic.

But Mariani loves the past less than he imagines. There is little true reverence for Raphael or the other old masters, only a superficial affinity of attitude and a desultory adoption of a few formal solutions. Mariani's palette is brighter than that of his two models, causing the clashing dabs of scarlet and citron, under a blue mediterranean sky, to deflect the viewer's gaze in all directions. The chalky flesh of the sitters has none of the pulse of life of Raphael's figures; the foreground is tactlessly severed from the middle ground and the background is shut out completely; the perspective is not quite one-point and does not quite resemble anything in the old masters. Even Mengs could have done better.

Yet it was clear from Mariani's most recent exhibition at Hirschl & Adler Modern, titled Dreams, that he is a very good technician, certainly better than Mengs, whom he holds in such strange reverence. The show contained nine odd images. In one a Grecian lad sleeps provocatively amid massive marmoreal ruins. In another a youth with classical features is engulfed by a monstrous granite mouth. Generally, the painting is too slick and literal to have passed muster with the old masters, but occasionally a detail, like the face of the figure in *Third Dream—Fragments*, is so skillful that one is sorry that the rest is not nearly so good.

Whereas Mariani's classicism bastardizes Mengs who bastardized Raphael, the two Soviet emigrés Vitaly Komar and Alexander Melamid bastardize socialist realism, which in turn had bastardized David, who, it may be argued, had bastardized Caravaggio and Poussin. In all their paintings Komar and Melamid merrily assail the official art of Stalin and Brezhnev like picadors provoking a moribund bull. They once went so far as to place a wax figure of Lenin lying in state on the dance floor of the Palladium in lower Manhattan. Of course, they had good reason to be upset with their former employers. On one famous occasion back in 1977, the authorities literally bulldozed one of their open-air exhibitions out of existence, which brought home to them how much happier they would both be in America, to which they emigrated a few years later, via Israel.

Komar and Melamid are founders of something called Sots Art, whose name derives from social realism, the once dominant form of Soviet artistic expression that specialized in images of Lenin at the Finland Station or Brezhnev standing like a beribboned pouter pigeon. This is the style that Komar and Melamid themselves were taught in the Soviet academies, and formally there is little in these paintings that distinguishes them from the works of bona fide Socialist realists: They have the same compositional tawdriness, the same muddy colors and inert delineation. Essentially, what we value in these artists is their insincerity. In *Stroke*, the ashen face of the dead Stalin appears in amber chiaroscuro, his prostrate pose recalling Caravaggio's *Conversion of Paul.* Otherwise all is dark, except for an open doorway in the top right of the painting, through which a faceless apparatchik in a dark suit suddenly discovers the Great Hero's death. In *The Origin of Social Realism*, a nubile woman with flowing hair and classical drapery traces Stalin's silhouette against a column, alluding to the Corinthian girl Dibutade, who, according to legend, invented portraiture by tracing the contours of her lover's shadow against a wall.

In spite of their profound aversion to the Soviet system that persecuted them, Komar and Melamid often exhibit a peculiarly Soviet respect for high culture and Great Art, art that is difficult and impressive because of its virtuosity. In one work from the 1982 series Nostalgic Socialist Realism, titled *Lenin Lived, Lenin Lives, Lenin Will Live*, the dictator lies in state on a raised platform, his coffin covered in a scarlet pall cascading down granite steps toward a neoclassical mourner, the exemplum of Grief. There is something almost operatic about this image, with the rich dramatic chiaroscuro of flaming reds and icy blues.

Yet despite the irony in Komar and Melamid, not everything is insincere. Social realism is to them what television of the fifties and sixties is to Kenny Sharf. It is the culture of their childhood. It is not the living culture at the time they are painting, but one freighted with memories of a bygone age. Like Sharf's America in the fifties, what they depict and what they allude to may have had its horrors, but it formed part of their lives and so they must view it with some nostalgia.

Though Milet Andrejevic came from a similar Eastern European background, there is no irony in his peaceful and bucolic images. Both *An Afternoon of Acteon* and *Towards Bathesda Fountain* are set in Central Park, but the realities of contemporary urban life are transfigured and ennobled by a New Age sentiment. A woman in jogging shorts dislimbers after her run. A man walks by with his dog. A frisbee is magically suspended in air. If Virgil's Arcady exists at the dawn of history, this Arcady exists at the end. After the tempests of the modern age we are promised fair weather for the rest of time. It is easy to make fun of these paintings, since none of them is exactly good, and many of them are exactly bad. Yet despite their general weakness of conception and crudity of execution, these images have a kind of charm, born of their being so obviously and serenely well-intentioned.

Not all the artists who returned to classicism strove for the precise representation that one finds in Mariani. For some, classicism was more a matter of mood than of form. The Frenchman Gerard Garouste, for example, has pioneered a kind of expressionistic classicism. In one of his better known works, *Orion the Classic—Orion the Indian*, the mythic hunter is set in a muddy tonalist landscape, surrounded by hounds and confronted by two raging bulls. By classical standards this image is a weak piece of work, full of fumbling and inarticulate painting. Garouste expects that the viewer will be ignorant of the old masters, and thus will neither miss their telling exactitude in the hunter's formless face, nor be unduly troubled by the inept delineation of the hounds, if hounds they are, or the almost indecipherable bulls. And yet, in this age of diminished expectations, it would be churlish not to admire the energy and occasionally even the intelligence in the painter's use of the past: the daring perspectives, the elegant four-square compositions and paint textures with all the subaquatic wooziness of the late Titian.

Perhaps the terminal point in this love of classicism, its reduction to pure attitude, is Ian Hamilton Finlay, who, though enamored of the monumentality of the classical style, can't find anything worth commemorating. He says quite truly, "As public sex was embarrassing to the Victorians, public classicism is to us," yet he can discover no excuse for restoring it except that he likes the look of it. His Garden at Little Sparta in Stonypath, Southern Scotland, is a massive monument to emptiness. A cross between a Roman hortus and one of Lord Burlington's English gardens, its ten or so acres contain a house, a small lake, and some thirty monuments with names like Grotto of Dido and Aeneas, Saint-Just's Column and Monument to the First Battle of Little Sparta. "Garden centers must become the Jacobin Clubs of the new revolution," Finlays writes, though he neglects to tell us why there should be a revolution in the first place.

As gardens go, however, Little Sparta is beautiful, a fact attributable more to the fantastic lushness of the Scottish countryside than to Finlay's skill as a landscaper. It is a place full of "verdurous glooms and winding mossy ways." At every turn we encounter some new prospect of august antique gravity, but signifying nothing at all. For what meaning can we possibly assign to a grey obelisk inscribed with the words *Il Riposo di Claudio*, or the Rest of Claudius? And why is it in Italian, as opposed to Latin or English? And why does a series of fragmented stones bear the words *The Present Order Is the Disorder of the Future*, a quote from the Jacobin revolutionary Saint-Just?

Little Sparta abounds in these manufactured ruins: a head of Epicurus, a dozen sundials, the finely engraved initials of Albrecht Dürer hanging down from a tree. Occasionally, an incongruous note is struck by a birdbath shaped like an aircraft carrier or a granite sculpture of a fighter bomber. All of this leads up to the Temple to Apollo-Saint-Just, with its mansard roof and facade inscribed with the words *To Apollo, His Music, His Missiles, His Muses.* Inside the structure are lyres on pedestals, busts of Saint-Just, and other images of spurious antiquity.

In Finlay, as in Mariani, Garouste, and all the other classicizing postmodernists, the longing for "meaningfulness" is thwarted by the fact of not having much to say. The subject of their work is invariably arbitrary since it is divorced from a body of belief to which it can readily refer. An old master, even if his primary interest was figures and forms, had a context of religion or mythology in which to frame them and by which they would be immediately understandable to his viewers. But contemporary artists are denied this body of belief, and so, when they invoke Christian or classical symbols, they have to settle for a kind of ornamental pointlessness. Mariani's title, *Dreams,* is thus shrewd because it relieves the artist of any obligation to preserve logic or coherence. Like many postmodernists, he is content to go through the motions of meaning, but the meaning itself is mysteriously left out.

David Hockney is a bridge between these spiritual children of De Chirico and those who, following Guston's example, strain toward an aggressively contemporary style. His paintings, drawings, and photomontages are usually set in the here and now, yet a sense of serene timelessness lifts them out of their contemporary context. If Guston and De Chirico presaged the formal terms of postmodernism, Hockney, more than anyone, registered its mood as early as 1966 in *The Splash,* depicting a swimming pool whose crystalline waters are momentarily disrupted by a submerged and unseen diver.

Hockney was the first to discover in art an oasis of postmodern peace in the calamitous world of late modernity, a Californian dreamscape of sun decks, track lighting, and lithe male bodies. Here is art under sedation, with all the noise of modernism phased out. It is a sustained surge of nitrous oxide, which, though it leaves one vaguely conscious, causes all the problems of the world to seem infinitely remote. Among the artists of our century it is rare indeed to find anyone as unabashedly content as David Hockney seems to be.

He anticipated the art of the eighties in another important sense, namely in the fickleness of his formal terms, his insistence on being able to pick and chose from a clashing diversity of styles and periods. Though he ranges restlessly between realism, abstraction, and photomontage, his best work, surely, is his portraiture from the sixties and early seventies. In *Looking at Pictures on a Screen*, we find Henry Geldzahler examining reproductions of Vermeer, Piero, Van Gogh, and Degas. With his hand held judiciously behind his back, the bearded and bespectacled critic looks dashing in a beige suit that underscores the blond tonality of the work as a whole, from the greenish-white background to the amber-colored floors. A similarly static pose inspires the portrait of Fred and Marcia Weisman, surrounded by their sumptuous collection of modern art. Fred, in profile, wears a suit while Marcia, several feet away, stands full-frontal in a billowing pink dress, before their mod, angular house framed against a pale blue sky.

Most impressive and rare in these portraits is Hockney's masterful ability to compose a picture through very subtle but effective mashaling of the lines in a visual field. In his portrait of Christopher Isherwood and Don Bachardy, the implicit orthagonal of a rug or wall, the way the blue shutters behind them intersect the head of Bachardy and the profile of Isherwood, are subtle in the extreme. Hockney has found inspiration in such works as Rembrandt's *Syndics of the Cloth Draper's Guild*, where the sitters are elegantly framed by wainscoting. But unlike most postmodernists, he has looked to older painting not to spoof it, but to enhance his own contemporary practice.

Hockney surely anticipated the mood of the eighties, but what he actually created during that decade was something of a falling-off. One rather unfortunate detour was his photographic collages, in which a hundred microphotographs of a face, for example, were pasted together into a screwy composite. In *Pearblossom Hwy*, from 1986, this technique managed to work a memorable change on a desert scene of tumbleweed and turquoise sky. But most of his other Polaroid composites are vaguely unpleasant to look at, if not downright ugly. Despite its allusions to analytic cubism, Hockney has yet to produce anything in this mode that proves why it is necessary in the first place.

He was also greatly influenced by the passionate, lecherous, multiform works of the late Picasso, which many critics had disparaged as lacking the integrity and refinement of the Spaniard's early works. Hockney loved the opulence of jazzed forms and lubricious colors, the bold lava-like outpouring of visual creativity that was all the more remarkable for being the fruit of Picasso's extreme old age.

Under the influence of these later works, Hockney painted *Nichols Canyon*, a maplike, aerial image of a snaking country-road set amid hilly fields of strikingly illogical pink, blue, and orange. This style seems to suit Hockney in that he, like Picasso, is an artist of stunningly fecund facility. Unfortunately, most of the images he has created in this style, like many late Picassos, come too easily to the artist and cost him too little, which is why, despite their appeal, they rarely strike deep.

Hockney is usually placed, with Francis Bacon, Lucian Freud, and Frank Auerbach, in what has been called the School of London. He certainly seems to embody what is often called the Englishness of English art. He has exhibited throughout his long career a pastel-like lightness of color and a daintiness of touch which, even in paint, tend toward the insubstantiality of drawing rather than toward the hard materiality of paint and felt form. Thus he can easily be assimilated into that long tradition of English art that embraces everyone from Nicolas Hilliard and Turner to Ben Nicholson.

Nationalist considerations such as this, which had been largely abolished under late modernism, were largely restored under postmodernism. Thus, when it came to the redemption of meaning, especially meaning of a grave and pregnant sort, one looked instinctively to the Germans, who, true to their grim

Teutonic stereotype, brought us Sigmar Polke and Anselm Kiefer. These two artists were part of what, by the early eighties, was known as Neoexpressionism. They favored violent forms of expression, crude, brutalized images whose scale and energy derived in large part from the gestural abstraction of the New York School.

The best of these artists is Gerhard Richter who, because his finest work is abstract rather than figurative, will be considered in another chapter. Some of this work can be effectively energetic, like Rainer Fetting's *Self-Portrait in a Yellow Hat* and K.H. Hodicke's tawny scene of *Summer*, glimpsed through an open window. But most of it is sound and fury, signifying little. Why, for example, are the figures in Georg Baselitz's crude paintings shown upside down? To express cosmic disarray, a topsy-turvy world, comes the answer of the ductile art world. In all fairness to the critical record, however, it should be said that when his canvases are themselves turned upside down, which I believe to be the way he painted them, they look a little better.

How people sound when they talk about contemporary German painting, with its full freightage of meaning, can be gleaned from a discussion of Sigmar Polke's *Paganini* of 1982. The painting depicts the famous violin virtuoso as he lies dying, with the devil fiddling at the foot of the bed. Tiny swastikas, at first unnoticed, become increasingly numerous the longer you look. They mingle with the background, hang from the devil's tail, get caught in the eyes of the dying man.

In the 1989 catalog to *Refigured Painting* at the Guggenheim, Thomas Krens wrote of this work, "There are three primary constellations of imagery in the painting: first, the mythology of the Faustian pact; second, the legend of virtuosity embodied in the hand of the maestro; and third, the burden of historical consciousness, reflected in the painting's ironic and obsessive engagement with the swastika. . . ." Krens then discusses the history of the swastika, which meant "good luck" in Sanskrit. "In using the symbol, and thus invoking a dire set of associations, Polke may be suggesting that which seems benign and restorative in one period has the capacity to change, even to the point of malfeasance, in another. . . . Creation involves the knowledge of destruction, of death itself."

And yet, when we look at the work itself, we are underwhelmed. Despite the overall left-to-right flow of the composition, it does not really cohere. The whitewash effect of the left half causes it to seem empty, while a dark brown mass on the right destroys the balance. A background of blue and grey lozenges, though not unsuccessful as wallpaper, clashes unpleasantly with a pastel of pale blue circles, a coil of canary yellow, and a tasteful dab of tangerine. As for the figures, Paganini appears to be more stuffed than dying, and while the devil is portrayed with a certain verve, the figure of death juggles skulls that look like a cross between floppy disks and regulation soccer balls.

In other words, there is nothing terribly Mephistophelean or even Faustian about this overly large work. Furthermore, although Paganini may indeed have made a pact with the devil, he was Italian rather than German, and therefore of questionable use in any parable about National Socialism, the soul of the German *Volk*, or such other things as preoccupy certain German artists. It is hard, therefore, to see how a work of such entrenched mediocrity can be said to carry "the burden of historical consciousness," whatever that is.

Anselm Kiefer is surely the most highly regarded of the German neoexpressionists and perhaps the most highly acclaimed living artist. Robert Hughes, not prone to hyperbolic praise, suggested in 1987 that Kiefer may be "the best painter of his generation on either side of the Atlantic. Kiefer's ambitions for painting range across myth and history, they cover an immense terrain of cultural reference and pictorial techniques. . . . He has tried to shoulder the content of historical tragedy."

It must be said that Kiefer plays the Sturm und Drang role to perfection, separating himself from the rest of the world through walls of impenetrable taciturnity. Of the forty Germans featured in the Guggenheim's exhibition, he alone refused to be photographed for the catalog. (True, C.O. Paeffgen sent in a self-portrait with a finger up his nose, but at least he didn't leave the space blank.) Furthermore, Kiefer, whom Hughes finds refreshingly free of "the pompous narcissism that fatally undermines the work of other artists to whom he is sometimes compared," has the irritating habit of being photographed making the Nazi salute. Now to some of us this tends to mean only one thing, but his supporters are quick to point out that what Kiefer is really doing is forcing the Germans to confront their past.

Kiefer's paintings are never beautiful, at least not in any pretty sense. They are massive hulking surfaces, so theatrical that they could serve as the backdrops for stage settings of Wagner or Strindberg, grimly modulating between muddy earth tones and ashen greys. In *Shulamith*, one of his best-known images, we seem to enter a deep dungeon at the end of whose steep perspective is a small hearth, burning eternally, it may be supposed, in memory of the Holocaust. The place is dark and eerily uninhabited, and we are not noticed as we trespass over the cold stone floor. *Hoffman von Fallersleben on Helgoland*, a later work, offers the same perspective of wasted, war-torn landscape, voided once again of any human habitation.

In *The Ways of Worldly Wisdom: Arminius Battle*, we look on a massive black and white prospect of woods, presumably the Teutoberg Forest where Arminius routed the Roman legions. Around the woods are crude penny-portraits of German worthies like Karl Marx, Carl Maria von Weber, Lessing, and Bismarck. If we subtract from this image, as from most of Kiefer's art, the appearance of intellectual weightiness and impacted historical association for which he has been so celebrated, what are we really left with if not some very weak paintings, frail in conception, listless in execution, unlovely to look at, and impressive only because of their size.

Furthermore, the terms in which this meaning is conveyed are so vague that they could mean almost anything at all. More often than not it is the well-wishing indulgence of the viewer that turns Kiefer's inarticulateness into ambiguity and his affectlessness into dispassion. We may assume, for example, that the artist was against Germany's role in the Second World War rather than for it: but if instead he were really ruing Germany's defeat, the form of his art would not need to be much different from what we see now.

Another artist who rose, like Kiefer, on the expressionistic tide of the early eighties was the Italian Francesco Clemente. He is a humbler, less bullying artist than Kiefer, with the same weakness in drawing, but with a better color sense. His paintings, like Julian Schnabel's, consist of roughly drawn, multilayered images taken from high and low art, competing with words and decked out in clashing colors. In larger works like *Hunger*, depicting a man biting a snake, or *Rain*, representing a naked figure with an umbrella, the painting is clearly crude. Clemente's nonrepresentational art, however, can be surprisingly subtle, especially his small watercolor abstractions on pondicherry paper: fiery irradiations of red, orange, and green coalescing into mandalas.

His best work is found in his watercolor self-portraits, showing considerable skill in a difficult medium, and reveling in that passionate color sense that is his greatest strength. His disembodied face is seen everywhere amid exploding scarlets and lavenders, free-floating in a sea of amniotic fluids, grasping at naked forms, touching itself. From these moody images he can pass on to a much less intense, far more frivolous kind of figuration. Twenty-four gouaches on antique handmade Indian rag paper, titled *Francesco Clemente Pinxit*, are elegant parodies of Mughal miniatures, depicting naked men in what I take to be homoerotic poses. There is a brittle minuteness to the details, mimicking the fineness of their Islamic sources. But things start to go awry as one set of abstract patterns is invaded by another clashing set; men carry around banners with Latin inscriptions; a massive telephone is hooked up to a man's penis and another man tries to insert an egg in his anus. Occasionally, there is a real and fabulistic resonance, as in a scene of four men on a lawn gazing up into a starry night with three moons. It is in images like these that Clemente reveals the connection to other Italian painters like Enzo Cucchi and Sandro Chia, who, like him, are members of the movement known as *transavanguardia*.

Though Italians like Clemente and Germans like Kiefer played a major role in reinvigorating the art world in the early eighties, it was the Americans who were, though surely not the best, at least the most prominent younger artists on the postmodern scene.

The paintings of David Salle, who is foremost among these artists, have much to do with *appropriation*, a term that has been buzzing around Lower Manhattan for close on ten years. As buzzwords go, however, *appropriation* seems to lose a little more of its buzz with each passing day. Salle was one of the first to exploit the concept and he has been one of the last to let it go. For him, appropriation is the act of removing an image bodily from its intended context to give it new meaning by placing it in the context of another work.

Of course, there is nothing very new in all of this. Modern art has been nourished on the flotsam of world culture ever since Parisian prostitutes donned African masks in *Les Demoiselles D'Avignon* and the Rhine maidens met Cleopatra in the pages of "The Wasteland." But nothing in modernism prepares us for the impacted density of allusion in Salle's most recent paintings at Gagosian, in which ancient sculpture and Renaissance painting, advertising and pornography, clash and interact with all the illogic of an image bank suffering a seizure.

Typical of Salle's appropriations is *Pressed-in Sturges*, whose title contains the sort of dopey pun that only SoHo could find clever. Evidently an allusion to film director Preston Sturges, the title prompts us to look for cinematic allusions in the painting, although, if there are any, I have not been able to spot them. Divided horizontally into halves, the top is a festive Mediterranean scene of goat masks, garlic charms, and peasant women in kerchiefs. The lower half, by contrast, contains three black-and-white images of a naked woman. Illuminated from the front by the phosphorescent gleam of a T.V. playing into the night, she holds a musical instrument to her pudenda, then another object so ineptly painted as to be anything from a coke bottle to a vacuum cleaner.

The problem with these images, as with all of Salle's depictions, is that he does not know, and has no inclination to learn, how to paint the figure. His brush is plodding and amateurish in a way that cannot be excused by his having other ambitions than to paint well. When he tries to copy a Gericault, this lack of formal sophistication becomes an embarrassment. It is only the cynical certainty that no one whom he wishes to impress could possibly see the difference, or could care less about it if he did, that induces Salle to persist in painting this way.

In the central section of the lower half of the same work, the naked woman exposes her buttocks for the viewer's prurient inspection. This is an image that recurs often in Salle's work. In *The Burning Bush*, from 1982, a woman presses her fanny against the picture plane. In *King Kong*, a year later, and in *Tennyson*, a year after that, three more women repeat the pose. That the painter has a taste for this body part is clearly too simple an explanation. Surely he must be questioning our voyeurism, or commenting on the degraded status of women in society, or such other things as contemporary painters like to do.

The critic Kevin Power helps us out: "[Salle's] concentration on the female posterior recalls Norman O. Brown's assertion that the excremental vision constitutes the symbolic essence of modern civilization. Indeed, American civilization remains in a youthful stage and its attention may well be focused on eroticism."

Such readings as these, however lacking in method, confirm Salle as one of the heavies of contemporary art. His work is rife with allusions to high culture, though one suspects that they are intended to impress precisely those who will understand them least. Given that SoHo's sense of the past does not extend much beyond two seasons ago, it may be asked how many in the art world will get Salle's allusion, in one painting, to the eighteenth-century Northern Italian painter Fra Galgario? But then, the point was never that they should identify the image, especially since it has no real relevance to anything in the painting itself. Its unique purpose is to inspire a vague feeling of portentousness, which, to judge from the critical response, Salle has succeeded in doing admirably.

In this regard Salle is yet one more of many fetishizers of "meaning." To fetishize meaning is to adore significance for its own sake, which is very different from actually having something to say and then saying it. Like Finlay and Mariani who adore monumentality without having anything worth commemorating, Salle's paintings do not give off meaning, but the pure form and appearance of meaning, which is reduced in the process to an empty act. For surely no one who urgently wished to communicate something would have chosen terms as staggeringly inarticulate as these.

Much the same could be said for Julian Schnabel. Perhaps the foremost achievement of this irascible mignon of the market consisted in coming up with snappy titles for his bloated paintings. Indeed, Schnabel is to titles what Homer is to epic verse, Wagner to music, and Michelangelo to two-dimensional representation. What is a good title? It is one that lends a painting the semblance of depth, while also directing the viewer to see in it what isn't there and thus to attribute to its author some spark of passion or intelligence which to all appearances he lacks.

Circumnavigating the Sea of Shit is an early painting and one of Schnabel's very finest titles. In it he has used shattered plates glued onto Masonite. The overall pattern seems to strain toward representation without ever quite reaching it, and the only thing corresponding to the title is a pervasive earth tone. Nevertheless, the smashed plates on Masonite are supposed to signify passion, since people who break quantities of plates are usually worked up about something. It is for this and other reasons that are not substantially better that Schnabel has gained a reputation as a "passionate" painter. After the coolness of minimalism, Schnabel is credited with putting the passion back into painting. But here again, what is most remarkable in Schnabel is not the quality or nature of this passion, but the fact that passion is being expressed at all.

Exile, from a year later, is set against a gold ground on which we see one of Caravaggio's homoerotic young men offering himself to the viewer along with a basket of fruit, but copied with such maladroitness that it is almost unrecognizable. Above his head and at his side are moose antlers, which a doll-like figure on the right uses to angle one of the young man's fruits. Above the doll, in the right-hand corner, the Ayatollah Khomeini looks out beyond the picture plane. Does this allude to the Shah of Iran in exile, lamenting his lost wealth, symbolized by the gold, or is it Khomeini himself, exiled in Paris for most of the seventies, longing to change Iranian society? Or is it a searing indictment of the Alaskan pipeline and the displacement of whole herds of caribou? We can only guess.

In abstractions like the Maria Callas Series, the arcane references have been removed. These works are oil on velvet and have the facile appeal of pure colors not obviously missapplied. But they have been done too quickly, without enough thought given either to the structure of a painting or to the forms that fill it. This shift from representation to abstraction underscores the central fact of Schnabel's art, its relentless mutability. He is able at any point to swerve from gestural abstraction to finical representation to simple words scribbled across a canvas. Ever fickle in his choice of forms, he is finally faithful only to his image of himself.

Erich Fischl's paintings have more coherence than Salle's and Schnabel's, and thus are easier to enjoy and even to admire. They are, to coin a term, hyperrealist expressionism, and his nude figures, at their best, seem to be somewhere between Willem de Kooning and Philip Pearlstein. Fischl's work often has a mercurial quickness of touch that recalls de Kooning, but he applies it to a far more dry-eyed conception of the world, which, like Pearlstein's conception of it, seems intent upon savoring every blemish. But if Philip Perlstein's nudes were the first in art history with body odor, Fischl's exude clouds of Aquavelva and cheap perfume. Whereas the sexuality of Pearlstein's nudes is severely neutralized, when they are not downright ugly, Erich Fischl manages to endow his figures with a certain sexual charge. They are never so much nude as naked. Their tan lines indicate that they have just now removed their clothes and are not yet entirely comfortable in their exposure. It is in this form, however, that they live out their lives of forced leisure, watering lawns, lounging around Club Meds, resting up in hotel rooms, or lusting after one another. They are not of the upper class that buys art and is redeemed in the transaction. Nor do they wear black, read French thinkers, befriend minorities, or enter into daring forms of sexuality. They are just average. The art world can forgive any excess of wealth or of penury, as long as it is picturesque, but the ordinariness of the middle class is beyond the pale of redemption, and it is this fact that sets a certain disagreeable snideness over Fischl's earlier works.

We understand that the lives these people lead are fatally compromised and false. Everyone is supposed to be having fun, yet no one really is. One feels a dangerous undercurrent of insecurity and nervousness just below the surface of these provocatively enigmatic scenes. In *A Visit To/ A Visit From/ The Island*, Fischl crudely contrasts, in adjoining panels of the painting, the sunbathing white tourists and the storm-tossed black natives. *Daddy's Girl* represents a naked man in a deck chair caressing a little girl in a scene heavily fraught with overtones of molestation.

Here is the point at which the adolescent boy enters as the hero of the piece. In *Bad Boy*, he is engaged in an act of voyeurism. In *Birthday Boy*, he lies on a motel bed with an older woman to whom he has just lost his virginity. He alone among Fischl's recurring cast of characters has the semblance of a face, an expression, an identity. The very nervousness and indeterminacy of his state afford him, for a year or two, an insight into the absurdity of the adult world to which he desperately wants to belong. In a larger sense, adolescence, with its lankiness and riotous complexion, is an emblem of humanity in general, beleaguered, compromised, and confused.

At their worst, Fischl's images are little more than over-priced versions of LeRoy Neiman's. Neiman is best known for his Super Bowl scenes and sex kittens in *Sports Illustrated* and *Playboy*. But Fischl does have his moments. There is an impressive purity to early works like *Rowboat*, with its scarlet hull against blue water. Real drama emerges from the tawny color and steep tilt of the floor in *The Sewer*, in which a seductress in lingerie sits in an office chair beside an old sewing machine. Likewise, some of Fischl's oil-on-paper beach scenes have a delicious fluidity to them, and there is even some fairly good figure drawing in one 1983 charcoal on paper of a girl in the shower. His more recent works have left suburbia and white America in search of more exotic formal and mythological truths, which he has not yet found, but which he one day might.

Alice Neel's role in contemporary art is problematic. Since she was born with the century and died an old woman in 1984, can she be considered a contemporary artist, let alone a postmodernist? Though there were always perceptive people who could appreciate her, for most of her long life she did not quite fit into any of the acknowledged patterns of the art world, and thus was left to her own devices. Only in the seventies did the fact of her being a woman and of her having been so long ignored finally endear her first to feminists and then to everyone else. And at that point, Neel, who had always been good, promptly became even better. She merits inclusion in any consideration of contemporary art for three reasons: because she became relevant only recently, because she was in harmony with the works of far younger artists, and because the images she was making in the seventies and early eighties were among the most vibrant of her time.

It is ironic that Neel, one of the finest American portraitists of the century, should be best known for her worst work, a depiction of Andy Warhol in a brassiere. Sloppily painted and weakly conceived, it lacks those virtues that her other works so conspicuously abound in: an integration of the whole, an energizing of the parts through painterly tours de force, and above all, a profound psychological penetration. Though Neel made stunning cityscapes and still lifes at various points in her career, portraits were just about all she ever really wanted to do. In the thirties, when Marx was taken very seriously, Philip Rahv of the *Partisan Review* used to chide her for her bourgeois fixation on the individual rather than the collectivity. Ms. Neel kept painting her portraits.

The style in which she painted them, seemingly by the hundreds, remained remarkably constant without ever locking into a formula. Because no two sitters were alike, and because Neel connected with every one of them on a personal basis, each portrait was fundamentally different from any of the others. Her sitters were by turns sullen and boisterous, and she was sullen and boisterous with them. The texture of her paint is always generous and fat, the compositions and perspective always slightly skewed and improvised. In thus transforming her sitters into art, Neel had a mind of almost Mozartean fertility: Formal patterns on which a lesser artist might have based a career spilled from her palette once and were never seen again.

She arrived at her distinctive style around 1930, and waited patiently for half a century until the art world saw her point. This style is one of extreme directness, often full frontal, yet allied to a certain abstractness of touch, as though probing the sitters and finally prodding them into life. Already in her early portrait of the naked, voluminous Ethel Ashton, Neel has perfected her signature sturdy black outline, which describes large, sagging breasts and a corpulent midsection. One shudders to think what Philip Pearlstein would have made of these wallets of fat, but Alice Neel is all sympathy.

As in certain images of the photographers Kertesz and Atget, the soul appears with such immediacy in these portraits that we feel a kind of interest or responsibility for the sitter. We should like to know more about the labor organizer Patty Whalen, with his eyes fiercely alive, his aquiline nose, his massive hands balled into fists. We are saddened to learn that Max White, the intense young man in the black suit and open-necked shirt, would one day develop arthritis in those large hands of his. We are likewise consoled to know that the sallow young man in a hospital bed in *T.B., Harlem*, from 1939, who looks to be at death's door, was destined to live another forty-three years.

Neel, who became estranged from her affluent family when she decided to become an artist, was temperamentally a liberal in the Eleanor Rosevelt mold. She seemed open to everything and everyone, from Ed Koch and Bella Abzug to babies and downtown aesthetes. Though this spirit remains constant, its expression changes with the times. The postwar Ben Shahn gloominess of *Two Black Girls* and *Two Puerto Rican Boys*, both from the fifties, gives way in the next decade to something much lighter and more mod in the portrait of Red Grooms in striped pants and tweedy jacket, looking directly at us in his scarlet shirt and orange tie, while Mimi Gross, in slacks and white plastic boots, looks off to the side. In the next decade, Robbie Tillotson, wearing bell-bottoms and an afro, is depicted with no more or less sympathy than the Fuller Brush man in his zoot suit and narrow bowtie, who seems to lunge toward you to sell you some of the brushes stuffed into his lapel pocket. In an entirely different mood, *Mother and Child* (a portrait of Neel's daughter Nancy and her granddaughter Olivia) shows a black-haired young woman, wearing a green dress, pressing the child to her face in one of the sweetest images of maternity since Raphael or Correggio.

Alice Neel's life, it is said, was not easy. In addition to difficulties with her parents, she had a child who died of diphtheria, and, as a young woman, she tried to commit suicide when her husband abandoned her. Yet her art is among the most profoundly joyous of our depressive age, and its joy is the more important and persuasive for having been wrested from grief.

SEVEN

The Remains of Abstraction

When Ad Reinhardt painted the last of his black-on-black canvases in 1966, he felt confident that painting was dead and that he had just killed it. One year later, Reinhardt was dead and painting was still very much alive. Though it has since then become a rite of passage for the residual avant-garde to sound the death knell of painting, the medium continues to outlast all of its would-be coroners. Which is why, even in a climate as inhospitable as the present one, there are plenty of artists who try with varying success to uphold the tradition of abstract art.

It takes courage to attempt abstraction today, whether in painting or sculpture. Abstraction requires a kind of honesty. It will not allow the artist, by hiding behind his figures or his politics, to conceal his weaknesses. He stands naked before an art world that is often hostile to his apparent conservatism and to the apparent presumption of placing oneself in contention with the greatest artists of the past century. Granted some abstract painters, like Peter Halley and Phillip Taafe, have tried to palm off their paintings as subversions of abstraction, with the calculated result of deflecting attention from the formal failings in their work. But, abstraction usually inspires a kind of honesty in those who use it, and artists like Ross Bleckner and Terry Winters, whatever their strengths or weaknesses, seem genuinely committed to the life of forms.

If there is one thing that distinguishes abstraction today from what it was a generation ago, it is the general relaxation that has settled over its devotees. They all seem implicitly to recognize that they exist at the end of art history, that painting no longer has a manifest destiny and that providence has not appointed them to help it get there. Theological disputes about gesture or hard edge, about flatness or painterliness, do not concern these artists overmuch.

Early abstract art coalesced around certain formal core convictions: In the twenties and thirties, geometric abstraction predominated in the works of Kandinsky, Mondrian, and Albers. After the war, American artists of the New York School, influenced by surrealist automatism, were overwhelmingly gestural, passionately entering into the very spirit of the paint like calves lolling about in clover. The sixties, by contrast, were divided between the postpainterly abstractions of Helen Frankenthaler and Larry Poons and the pared-down minimalism of Ad Reinhardt and Frank Stella.

But today, instead of these neatly divided schools, we have a truly postmodern omelette that mixes together all of the above without rhyme or reason. At any one moment, Ross Bleckner is painting images that recall the mood and sometimes the forms of such Orphicists as Kupka and Robert Delaunay; Cary Smith's paintings are very respectful and respectable variations on the neoplasticism of Mondrian; Therese Oulton's impasted canvases revel in the dense, layered painterliness of Richard Pousette-Dart. A good many artists, foremost among them Elizabeth Murray, Susan Rothenberg, and Donald Sultan, have sought a compromise between abstraction and figuration, though almost invariably leaning toward the former.

And yet, for all that, there is a palpable nervousness among contemporary abstract artists. Something unimaginable forty years ago seems to be coming to pass. Abstract art, despite its apparently chaotic liberty, turns out to be more limited than representational art ever was. It suddenly starts to look as though we may reach a point, especially in painting, where very few variations on abstraction will have remained unexplored or unclaimed.

For this reason there is something almost in the nature of a miracle whenever a contemporary artist is able to pull off one more truly original abstraction, to invent a formal vocabulary that has never been seen before, but that looks inevitable after the fact. In exploring our contemporaries' attempts to do just that, to mine one last great abstraction from the nearly bankrupt quarry of visual art, we will pass over many fine artists like Agnes Martin and Esteban Vicente who were part of earlier movements and who have continued to make memorable paintings in those older styles. What concerns us is how the latest generation of artists has responded, in postmodern terms, to the summons of pure form.

Gerhard Richter, one of the finest painters alive, has done so in a way that presents us with a seemingly irresoluble paradox. At any moment, he can turn from the chromatic carousal of his abstract paintings to nit-picking representations that seem, depending on your perspective, either polemical or pointless. Many artists have attempted to work in more than one style at a time, and most were decidedly better at one than at another. But I can think of no artist in whom the disparity is greater, or the drop in quality steeper, than Gerhardt Richter. From the outset, he seemed incapable of having a weak formal idea or a good representational one. Such is the descent from his noble abstract images to his inert figural works, that one feels like imploring the artist not to waste another second of his valuable life on anything other than abstract painting.

Richter's early representations are in a vaguely pop key, studiously sanitized and banal, yet possessing the tough immediacy of photography, on which they are often based. One work comprises forty-eight grisaille portraits taken directly from photographs of eminent twentieth-century intellectuals: Einstein, Thomas Mann, Mahler, Heidegger, H.G. Wells, and so forth. In an age less cynical than our own, we might suppose that Richter were honoring these indisputably worthy men. Instead, we now wonder to what ironic purpose he means to turn them. In either case, they don't provide much of anything beyond the intellectual sport of seeing how many sitters you can name, which I believe not to have been the point.

A later series depicts the joint suicide of the leaders of the Baader-Meinhof gang, the seventies terrorist organization. Images of prostrate corpses seem covered over in tracing paper or frosted glass, as though the traumatic horror of death could be bearable only through such alienating mist. These works are oddly cool and unmoving. One imagines that if Richter had been entirely bored by his subject, they would not look very different from what we see now. It is thus hard to imagine what his purpose could have been in painting them.

As this art reveals, Richter seems no more given to levity than Anselm Kiefer and Sigmar Polke, his equally hard-blowing compatriots. Something in the German character renders its artists incapable of taking up a brush without supposing that the fate of the nations hangs in the balance. Perhaps this is why, when he painted his first abstractions, Richter chose a sullen grey monotone. Across the length and breadth of the canvas he spins a superfine tracery of grayish webwork whose stippling effect sometimes acquires the matness of sharkskin, sometimes the pachadermatous roughness of a rhino. Grey was the obvious color. White would have been too life affirming; black might have suggested a passion he couldn't feel. But grey is the color of absence and alienation, of the impossibility of true, unmediated feeling in the modern world. It is, or was, the color of postwar Germany, the color of its drizzly, numbing rain, of an economic miracle that was smothering the fields and meadows of the old world in a grim concrete epidermis.

Then quite suddenly, around 1980, these gloomy evocations lurch into life. With crystalline clarity, screaming yellows streak across ice sheets of arctic blue and fiery field's of ox-blood red. At their best, Richter's later abstractions have the prismatic sheen of crushed opals or sheered off mica. They are not conspicuous for their heart or soul, any more than Richter's figural art has been. Though he gives abundant pleasure through his art, he does not seem to take pleasure in doing so. The only thing these astonishing paintings have going for them is their excellence, and that, it turns out, is quite enough.

It would be hard to conceive of any abstractions more different from Richter's than Sean Scully's vigorously geometric exercises. Yet they are ultimately allied in their committment to the great cause of painting. If the seventies and eighties had never happened, Sean Scully's art would not be much different from what it is today. Born in Dublin in 1945, raised in London, and living in America since 1975, Scully hearkens back to an older style of abstraction, free of gimmick or irony. Compared with the paintings of Stella and Reinhardt, two forebears in the geometric abstraction he practices, Scully's art is relaxed, as befits postmodernism. Painting's destiny does not interest him greatly, and if it has any further to go in its march, Scully is content to be left behind. His art is undemonstrative and humble, profoundly soft-spoken and entirely sincere.

Unlike Richter, whose formal ambitions go in several directions, Scully always knew exactly what kind of art he wanted to make: geometric painting with heart. But if his career can be seen as an incremental progress toward this goal, *By Night and By Day*, from 1983, is a hesitant early step. In an irregularly shaped tryptych, stringy black lines ascend vertically across a yellow field, with coal and rust-colored striations to one side and squat beige horizontals on the other. But the colors are weak and ill-assorted, the composition shaky. Only around 1987, in *A Happy Land and Empty Heart*, does Scully enter his more classical and less experimental mode, an idiom of gentle harmonies and precise balances.

In his most recent show at the Mary Boone Gallery in May 1993 Scully has largely outgrown the earlier affectation of joining canvases into polyptychs, and has found happiness in straight squares and rectangles. Aside from a lingering bad habit of placing a smaller canvas within a larger one, which is no different visually from painting the contents of both onto a single canvas, there are no tricks to this art. What you see, in the immortal words of Frank Stella, is what you see.

If Richter is interested in gestural abstraction and Scully in geometric abstraction, Terry Winters is scarcely less devoted to the biomorphic abstraction pioneered by, among others, Arshile Gorky and William Baziotes. Superficially, there is something undeniably pleasant about Winters's best work. In *Fertile Region*, amoeboid brachypods, ciliated spores, and nameless fungi float in a rich amber broth. Elsewhere, thickly impasted polyhedra are deployed across the canvas like an alignment of planets.

But after you have seen several of Winters's abstractions, a variety of compositional and textural problems seem to arise. In *Lumen* for example, from 1984, forms fill the canvas in an orderly way, but without energy or movement. In *Good Government*, from the same year, one senses a lack of organic connectedness of form to ground, as one plane is inertly superimposed on another. And then there is the problem of touch. You can always judge a good abstraction by its refusal to remain mere paint. The excellence of Pollock and de Kooning derived largely from the way the very texture of the paint suggested something more than mere paint, the way it was able to awaken whole sequences of extra-artistic association. But in Winters, this doesn't happen: Paint stays paint, a glutinous material as yet unenlivened by any Promethean fire.

Given these weaknesses, one wonders what inspired the Whitney's decision to grant a retrospective to an artist whose work consists of straightforward and undistinguished abstractions on canvas, especially when the present Whitney curatoriate is no friend of abstraction, and when they could easily have found a dozen other artists more deserving of the honor. My conspiracy-minded suspicion is that Winters was chosen precisely for being lackluster, thus proving that abstraction, and with it formalism in general, is indeed as dead as the curators like to think it is. If we had only Winters's abstractions to go on, we should have to concede the point. These tame, unironic, garden-variety abstractions have that tony, expensive look that makes them ideal for banks and hotel lobbies. But Winters is still a young artist who very possibly could develop a more interesting, original and satisfying style than he has found to date.

Richter, Scully, and Winters, different though they are, create abstract art with a directness closer to modernism than to the work of more recent painters. Though they have no exact precedents in earlier art, they would be immediately legible to most painters of the New York School forty years ago. To find truly postmodern abstraction, we have to turn to painters like Peter Halley and Pat Steir. Abstract art like theirs, created in the spirit of postmodernity, tends to be either coyly ironic or incandescently sincere, reflecting an almost New Age sensibility.

Though Pat Steir's Waterfall paintings at the Robert Miller Gallery were among the finest things exhibited in New York during the past season, the artist took her time before arriving at so perfect a formal resolution. For much of the earlier part of her career, there had been something hesitant and irresolute about her art. A series like *Night Chant Series*, consisting of crudely slapdash O'Keefian orchids painted in white against a black ground couldn't decide whether it was coming in the direction of figuration or going in the direction of abstraction. There wasn't much more promise in her *Brueghel Series (A Vanitas of Styles)* whose composite forms recalled Jennifer Bartlett's tile-like accumulations of images. Occasionally there were tremors of painterly bravura, but Steir could not sustain them for more than a few square inches at a time.

Nothing therefore could have prepared us for her Waterfall paintings. The masterpieces of abstract expressionism, with which these surely deserve to be compared, were noble, powerful, and serious. But they were never charming, let alone enchanting. Steir's latest paintings, by contrast, give off a thrilling New Age assurance that all is well with the world. Even the titles have the beauty of poetry: *Waterfall of the Asian Night*, *Waterfall of Reverie*, *Waterfall of Ancient Ghosts*. These paintings are deeply spiritual without being meditative or withdrawn, without losing touch with the world. Like a two-toned Pollock, Steir is able to energize every inch of the composition. Her mastery of touch charges every particle of paint with some of the more interesting tactile textures found in an abstract painting. From the height of these tall, emphatically abstract paintings, rivulets of golden light gush out of hidden veins, deliriously cascading down the blackened lengths of canvas like falling stars to create some of the most joyous art of the past generation.

The mystical element in Steir's work, the shrill luminosity of painted light against nocturnal ground is paralleled in the latest abstractions of Ross Bleckner. His grandly maximalist images, like hers, revel in a bigness that recalls Pollock. Bleckner was always interested in abstraction, but his forms were once very different from what they are today. Typical of his earlier work is *Wreath*, from 1986, in which blue, black, and orange stripes pulse from high to low, qualified by a single bend sinister of red pigment toward the top. From painters like Larry Poons in the early sixties Bleckner has derived a love of overall patterning, as well as a general unwillingness to endow his unusually happy paintings with drama. Instead, *Wreath* is all of a piece and remarkably free of internal tension. There is no sense of one part being subordinated to another. Though obviously appealing, this and other of his works rarely rise above what, paraphrasing Harold Rosenberg, we might call apocalyptic wrapping paper.

It is therefore surprising that of late a religious sensibility no less intense than Steir's has found its way into Bleckner's art, replacing decorative patterning with real spiritual and emotional power. His grounds become dark like the midnight sky. Before this almost theatrical setting, something is happening, an event or an act that we cannot quite describe, but that seems charged with overwhelming importance.

Architecture of the Sky I, one of his most profoundly satisfying images, is nothing more than a dark greenish-grey field stippled with white lights converging, as in a Mercator projection, upon a point just above where the canvas ends. This charming, preindustrialized view of heaven recalls the concentric metal orbits inside an armillary sphere, the sort once used to chart the Ptolemaic cosmos. In *Telescopic Life*, from 1989, arrows irradiate from a center of light as a bevy of doves rise up around it. Here is the supernoval radiance of the daylight into which the newborn struggles out of the night of the womb, the flash of light rumored to be on the other side of death. Its supersaturated brilliance recalls the symbolist hysterics of Strauss's Zarathustra.

Despite their theatricality, the abstractions of Bleckner and Steir are compelling because there is something about them that is obviously sincere. But if there is something postmodern in the directness of these paintings, there is something entirely different, but no less postmodern, in the irascible irony of Phillip Taafe and Peter Halley. Now irony is not an easy thing to achieve in an abstract painting, for pure forms tend toward pure feelings. But the ability of these two artists to find irony in such sere soil proves that they are among the more intriguing abstract painters of recent seasons, if not the best.

As regards his paintings Taafe has great expectations that seem less ironic than touchingly naive: "I am actually trying to lay the groundwork for some kind of paradisical situation on earth. . . . I guess I have a hope that when they are in the hands of powerful individuals, people who make profound decisions with respect to the direction of the world, my paintings could enable a more humanistic perspective to emerge and evolve." (Powerful people, of course, being those with enough money to pay for anything as costly as a Phillip Taafe.)

The art by which Taafe intends to erect his New Jerusalem grows out of two earlier traditions: the op art of the late sixties and the pattern and design painting of the late seventies. In a fit of retro madness, he essentially reproduces the "mod" art of the sixties, but places a screwball postmodern spin on it. These images hold out to us the prospect of a known pleasure, such as we have found in earlier abstract artists. But at the last moment, as we grasp for it, Taafe retracts it with a sardonic smirk.

Thus *Four Quad Cinema* is a sequence of spiraling fanwheels with black dots filling the spaces in between. Clearly the painting is inspired by Bridget Riley's art of two decades earlier. But whereas Riley's optics tricked and pleased the viewer at the same time, there is something angry and aggressive in Taafe, something that wants to hurt the eye by exaggerating Riley's innocuous style to the point of absurdity.

Trinity, a parabolic checkerboard in brown, yellow, purple, and pink, sends up Victor Vasarely just as *Four Quad Cinema* sent up Riley. Possibly the most discredited artist in existence, in the sixties Vasarely painted pleasant geometric abstractions that cannibalized and made palatable the revolutionary advances of an earlier vanguardism. This, naturally, was long before the vogue for cultural cannibalism, the kind Taafe himself practices.

As cannibalism goes, however, Taafe is most successful in a work that is meaninglessly titled *We Are Not Afraid:* Two yellow bands and one blue band of simulated rope are set against a sheer field of scarlet. The postmodern cheekiness consists in reducing the macho modernism of Barnett Newman, with all its high seriousness and neosublimity, to pleasant wallpaper patterns.

If Taafe parodies such things as op art, Peter Halley goes after the hard-edge abstraction of Ad Reinhardt. When he undertakes to explain his reasons for doing what he does, he sounds like this: "The elements of modernism are hyper-realized. They are reduced to their pure formal state and are denuded of any last vestiges of life or meaning. The are redeployed in a system of self-referentiality which is itself a hyper-realization of modernist self-referentiality."

Translated into deeds, this vaporous palaver inspired Halley, in his imitations of Reinhardt, to subvert the tradition he seems to honor, to raise our hopes with the expressed intention of disappointing them. Treading the hair's breadth between vanguard and old guard, Halley constantly runs the risk of having uninitiated viewers think he is being sincere in his imitation. To defend himself, therefore, against even the appearance of sincerity he draws out of hard-edge abstraction layers of nauseous banality that one wouldn't have imagined it to possess.

One of his favorite tricks is to present the viewer with what looks like a straightforward abstraction, and then, through its title, to insist that in fact some goofy form of representation in going on after all. The cubic masses in *Prison*, for example, attest to his love of violent chromatic contrast, stark black along the edges and shrieking yellow in the center. Yet in the center of that center are four vertical strips of black, the reason, and the only reason, that the painting is called *Prison.* Thus what looked like straight abstraction turns out to have been crude figuration all along. You have the setup and then the punch line and before you know it Greenberg's formalism has received an unceremonious slap in the face.

Later paintings recall the circuitry of transistor radios, an association the painter welcomes. In *Glowing Cell with Conduits*, from 1985, dull orange is placed cheek-by-jowl with a stomach-churning Pepto-Bismol pink, which itself clashes with another layer of fleshtone pink. This pink on pink is clearly a snotty allusion to Malevich's high modernist white on white and to Reinhardt's late modernist black on black. A further subversion consists in using Day-Glo paint, that goofy fad of the sixties counterculture. Halley is playing an elaborate game. His is a kind of scavenger culture that nourishes itself on the chewed up, spat out remains of one's predecessors. Yet his final comeuppance will occur, one suspects, when he takes his place with Taafe in the history of taste, rather than with Bleckner and Steir in the history of art.

Why is it that no one talks of the death of sculpture? Perhaps because sculpture was never paramount the way painting was, which made its demise a little beside the point. Sculpture never had to carry the burden of art's destiny. If it was heading inexorably in any special direction, no one seemed to be watching, and as long as the work was good, no one was complaining. But if the first years of postmodernism, from about 1978 to 1986, saw a marked resurgence of painting, in the past half dozen years sculpture has replaced painting as the medium of choice for younger artists.

Perhaps this is because sculpture offers a wealth of extra-artistic associations that particularly endear it to an art world increasingly bored by art itself. Since sculpture exists in three dimensions rather than two, it can give what painting can only suggest. This fact has been fully exploited by contemporaries, especially installations artists, in their determination to break down the boundaries between life and art. Everything from the slick neo-geo consumerism of Ashley Bickerton to the scatter art of Cady Noland's thousands of cans of Bud Lite and Janine Antoni's cubes of lard and chocolate, has been made in the name of sculpture.

But the sculpture that concerns us here is abstract. There is no greater uniformity to contemporary abstract sculpture than to contemporary abstract painting. Each artist, left to his or her own devices, strains to find a distinctive style. Beyond the fact that their works are all abstract there is little plausible connection between Christopher Wilmarth's cool parabolas of etched glass and David Hammons's darkly menacing and suggestive forms; between the semiabstract stickmen of Joel Schapiro and the tubular candy-cane striations of the French artist Daniel Buren.

One broad generalization we can make is that contemporary abstract sculpture favors experiential suggestiveness over formal purity. One of the forebears of contemporary practice was Eva Hesse, whose multiform objects of string, steel, or polyester anticipated present-day sculpture by stressing emotional intensity over form. This fact, combined with the circumstances of her life and with her being a woman artist in the male-dominated sixties, has made Hesse a kind of cultural lodestar for younger artists.

Hesse, whose parents had fled Hitler and came to America when she was a very young girl, had a hard and unenviable life.

As she once explained in a letter, "One cannot be cool when one constantly feels fear." Everything she did filled her with anxiety. Her relentless fretting over her gifts prompted Sol Lewitt to offer the following curious counsel: "Try to do some BAD work. The worst you can think of and see what happens, but mainly relax and let everything go to hell."

But Hesse never heeded his advice, preferring to give herself over to the twin gods of whining and work. "Maybe because my life has been so traumatic and so absurd—there hasn't been even one normal, happy, even happy [thing]—and I am the most easiest [sic] person to make happy and the easiest person to make sad too, because I think I have gone through so much. I mean it never stops."

Even her impressive successes were never unalloyed by sadness. When she appeared, for example, in a group show at the Owens-Corning Fiberglas Center in 1970, her biggest and most widely reviewed exhibit to date, one critic went so far as to call her "one of the most accomplished and promising artists of her generation," who was now at the "outset of a brilliant career." A few days later, after a brief coma, she was dead.

In her brief lifespan, however, Hesse had covered a lot of ground. She began as a painter, making gestural abstractions in the style of de Kooning. But soon she turned to sculpture, creating forms that reacted against the dominance of minimalism and that reached back, through artists like Beuys and Gunther Uecker, to Surrealism, with its instinctive feel for the associative richness of materials. In Hesse's case, these materials were high-tech lengths of galvanized steel or fiberglass that were "mod" by the standards of the time. Though she shared with the Minimalists a taste for industrial material, she did not use it to deflect feeling, as they did, but to harness feeling and inspire it in the viewer. Thus she rejected Minimalism's hard edge for organic shapes like *Repetition Nineteen III* whose irregularly shaped chalices of light, formed from fiberglass and polyester resin, look like a cluster of pallid plants from the ocean floor.

Sometimes Hesse's work, by seeming to scoff at Minimalism,

anticipates the irreverence of later postmodernists like Peter Halley and Philip Taafe. One of her best-known works, *Sans Two*, consists of two rows of fiberglass boxes one on top of the other, looking very much like melted down Donald Judds gone partly to seed. Likewise, her *Accessions* consists of massive cubes of galvinized steels with rubber tubing knitted into their sides. Though the cube was a stock form in the minimalism of Tony Smith and George Sugarman, Hesse endowed it with all the repulsive and treacherous suggestiveness of Meret Oppenheim's fur cups.

Hesse's art also anticipates contemporary practice in its ceaseless changefulness. In the five years separating *Ringaround Arosie*, with its lengths of electrical wire coiled into mouths, eyes, and nipples, and one of her last pieces, *Untitled (Rope Piece)*, a convoluted tangle of interlocking ropes, Hesse seems to have adopted and discarded no fewer than a dozen distinct styles.

Whereas Hesse was thus constantly shifting allegiances from biomorphic polyester to tangles of cord and temperamental squares, Jackie Winsor discovered the cube early on and she has remained faithful to it. Before the cube, however, she tried out a number of other options. Her earliest works were uneventful Masonite blocks, with rubber and painted metal strips added to relieve the pared-down tedium. Treading the fine line between minimalist objecthood and pure theatricality, Winsor next twined together huge stumps of cord, the sort that could hold an ocean liner to its moorings, before she moved on to her charming fence pieces, elegant wooden wattles whose multitude of nails formed incongruously delicate patterns for the eye.

Her first cubes, from the mid-seventies, seem to be a response to the same minimalist art Hesse had responded to in her *Accessions*. Winsor's *1 × 1* and *55 × 55* are based upon Sol Lewitt, but, for all their discipline, they have a handmade, down-to-earth feel. Since the eighties, Winsor's works have hovered around forty inches cubed, and within the limited terms of her art, she has been astonishingly inventive. One cube is an immaculate white block with a small hole perforating its center on all six sides. Another is fashioned from industrial concrete and then burned or exploded. At other times a cube is decked out in vibrant green and scarlet and mirrored glass. Some of her later works have admitted an element of jauntily postmodern impurity. *Gold Piece*, a large mongrelized cube bedizened in pink and deep purple and goldleaf, aspires to be a sphere. Within the context of Winsor's career, the sheered off corners are big news, and they prove that, just when you think Winsor has squeezed all the possible transformations out of the cube, she can come up with something entirely original and lovely.

As I am probably not the first to remark, the best of these cube sculptures look like Agnes Martin's paintings conjured into three dimensions. Like that great lady, Winsor is Canadian, which leads one to speculate about the Canadianness of Canadian art. If such a thing does exist, and it probably does not, it consists mainly in a purity of soul and line, such as we Yankees imagine to exist in abundance in the far north: the clarity of uncontaminated streams and steel blue skies, of bull moose prancing in paradaisal satiety across miles of permafrost. Both women tend to avoid strong colors and to project the frailty of drawing onto the sturdier mediums of painting and sculpture. Though they are as committed to geometry as their fellow minimalists Ad Reinhardt and Tony Smith, Martin and Winsor endow their lines and angles with the fragility of cobwebs, invariably revealing their personal mood and touch.

Jean-Pierre Raynaud, by contrast, scrupulously avoids all suggestion of human touch in his flawlessly geometric art. Though he is one of the most original living sculptors, Raynaud is not widely known outside France, even though the French esteemed him enough to make him their representative at the 1993 Venice Biennale. There seems to be something typically French in Raynaud's passionate rationality and rationalized passion. The pristinely white tiled gridwork from which he constructs his sculptural environments incarnates that rage for order that the French call *l'esprit geometrique*.

Raynaud's love of clarity was expressed early on in the

controversial windows he made for the Abbey of Noirlac. They could be called stained-glass windows, except that they weren't stained, being as pure and pellucid as a swig of Perrier water. What raised eyebrows was the fact that their only reference to religion was the pointed ogival arches into which they were formed. For a man like Raynaud, however, their surfeit of purity and liquid clarity was all the religion one really needed.

It was in this spirit that he created *Maison*, an inhabitable sculpture and reified mathematical concept in which the orthagonals of quattrocento perspective are projected into the third dimension. To enter such a structure is to pass from this world into one of pure geometric peace where everything is knowable once its constituent axioms have been disclosed.

Though the grid has been a constant in modernism since Mondrian, and though sixties artists like Lewitt and Martin had quite a run with it, Reynaud's obsessive use of it far surpasses anything else of the kind. Every inch of wall, floor, and ceiling in *Maison* is covered over in a fantastic expanse of sparkling porcelaneous tile, exuberant and chaste at the same time. Yet, into this grid irregular elements of the real world are occasionally admitted, although they too are transformed into mathematical terms: windows, electrical outlets, ashtrays, and a Mozarabic doorway are all translated into geometry, as though through a mad parody of Plato's supersensible world. Then, in defiance of all logic, an actual Romanesque baptismal font appears out of nowhere, together with real palm trees and a real bed. This mania is pursued with such tough integrity that the slightest modulation, a shift in floor level, or a slight change in the size or density of a tile, takes on the quality of high drama. This is the astonishing environment into which, like some saturnine prince of the Renaissance, Raynaud has chosen to retreat from the clamorous complexity of an imperfect world.

Of all the sculptors working today, Anish Kapoor strikes me as the best that postmodernism can offer as a credible alternative to the art of the immediate past. In his finest work Kapoor achieves what modernism and premodernism achieved at their best, namely beauty and perhaps even a little truth. Before modernism this was usually evoked through a telling correspondence between the truth of an object and the formal skill of its depiction: the peerless silhouettes of Velasquez, the dimpled draperies of Fra Angelico, the fanning impastos of a Rembrandt sleeve. Modernism increasingly achieved this more through energy than through fidelity to retinal reality: the abstracted balance of a Mondrian grid, the careering lines of Arshile Gorky. But how will postmodernism create this effect? Indeed, can postmodernism achieve this energy at all? Therein lies one of the great questions in contemporary art.

The beauty of Kapoor's sculptures is different from the beauty of modernism. He officiates over a purely visual experience that expresses nothing of himself. His *Adam* is a mansized monolith of distressed limestone, hewn into an upright cubic rectangle. At first it is easily legible in modernist terms. The hulking, shattered mass of stone recalls, perhaps too closely, the later works of Isamu Noguchi. By this reading, it is not much to look at: derivative, unexpressive, and obvious—at best mediocre. And then you see, a little above the center, what looks like a black patch whose flawless contours are obvious and banal in their geometric purity. Only on drawing closer do you see that it is not a patch after all, but a void, a black hole, quarried out of the living rock. It is thus a precise and mannered artifice lying at the heart of the virile modernist pose. There is beauty here, but it isn't the beauty of the eye or the mind. Rather it can be called the beauty of the spirit, the pleasant incongruity of this rich and absolute blackness, unnatural in its perfection, lodged in the rough-hewn naturalism of the stone.

This optical illusion obviously appeals to Kapoor, because he has used it often. *At the Hub of Things* is a perfectly described hemisphere painted a bright Kleinian blue. Once again, the form itself is not created by the sculptor, but presented to him unchanged by geometry itself. But as we peer into that deep convexity, we seem to stand at an abyss, looking into a precinct of infinite darkness in the very midst of a well-lighted gallery.

In this and other strangely evocative sculptures, Anish Kapoor has arrived at what may be the first postmodern art which, in its very postmodernity, can vie with the formal integrity of earlier art. If postmodernism does indeed turn out to be something more than a fad, if it is indeed the way of the future, it will be so not because of the inanities of Jeff Koons, or the false dramatics of Julian Schnabel, or the political radicalism of Group Material, but because of the sober, probing beauty of Anish Kapoor's sculptures and the handful of other contemporary works that stand comparison with them.

EIGHT

The Radical in the Studio

Early in the sixteenth century, Cardinal Ippolito de' Medici created a human zoo. As Jakob Burckhardt tells it, he "kept at his strange court a troop of barbarians who talked no fewer than twenty different languages, and who were all of them perfect specimens of their races. Among them were North African Moors, Tartar bowmen, Negro wrestlers, Indian divers, and Turks." It was a veritable banquet of human diversity.

Now the cardinal, being a humane man, did not keep his possessions in cages. Rather, he brought them along on embassies to impress dignitaries with their native dances and songs. This was long before anyone had heard of the inalienable rights of man or considered that what united humans might be more interesting than what kept them apart. At a time when many regions of Europe had not altered their ethnic makeup in a thousand years, when Ligurians felt an ancient hatred for Venetians, and Burgundians still looked on Normans as semi-pagan upstarts, one was more apt to be intrigued by the differentness of people than by their similarities.

The idea of a human zoo scandalizes us. It challenges everything we claim to believe and much we do believe. Yet if the members of the menagerie assemble of their own volition for purposes of self-promotion, we are apparently prepared to applaud them. Welcome to the Whitney Biennial of 1993. This was the occasion on which eighty-two artists, in 142 works, merrily collapsed their common humanity in a withering sequence of self-imposed stereotypes about racial, physical, and sexual identity.

The generalized human being and the radicalized individual, those noble stock heroes of the modernist project, were personae non gratae at the latest Biennial. Each artist came as a self-appointed spokesperson for a special-interest group, one might almost say a political action committee. Yet the perverse result of this sustained treble of anger was that all of the artists, whether lesbian or gay or bulimic or black or Native American or Hispanic, started sounding like the same actor taking on and casting off a succession of masks, until all that fabled multicultural diversity presently gave way to its opposite: a single nameless, voiceless, raceless, desexed cypher, the type and emblem of statistical oppression.

The emergence of political art in the late eighties and nineties is part of the larger shift in interest from the work of art in itself to the meaning it articulates and the cause it propounds. Surely all art is a compromise between form and content, and until modern times the two tended to exist in fairly even condominium. But compromise is nothing that this generation wants, any more than the last generation wanted it. In yet one more instance of the continuity between modernism and postmodernism, the desire to remain radically faithful to an artistic ideal is preserved in more recent art, except that the ideal has changed. For just as the painters of the sixties sought art's enduring essence, the zero degree of pure form, so many artists today aspire to an equally absolute rejection of formal purity in favor of pure communication, in the very act of which form itself often vanishes.

For my part I square with what Pascal said in respect to literature: "Meaning receives its dignity from words rather than bestowing it on them." (*Ce sont les sens qui recoivent leur dignité des paroles, au lieu de la leur donner.*) As regards the visual arts, Pascal was implicitly rebutting the sort of critic who believed that any crucifix, because it had been carved by a Christian and because it communicated the revealed word, must be superior to the Apollo Belvedere, because that had been sculpted by a pagan who believed in obscene fables. That Pascal's injunction has been disregarded is clear whenever the art of de Kooning and Picasso is censured because its authors are thought to have been disrespectful to women; whenever the inert work of Judith Leyster and Angelica Kauffman, two middling talents of the seventeenth and eighteenth centuries, is exuberantly praised because they are imagined, erroneously, to have been feminists *avant la lettre*.

The absolute degree of meaning's ascendency over form was reached in *AIDS Timeline*, an installation at the 1991 Whitney Biennial by Group Material, the artists' collective. Using charts, graphics, and television monitors with doctors chattering learnedly in white coats, not to mention a few appropriated and pretty forgettable paintings on the walls, the piece communicated to us that AIDS is bad and not good. But suppose that precisely the same setup had been mounted to advocate, not AIDS awareness, but safety on the highways (Buckle up, America!) or heaven forbid, an anti-abortion screed. Though its aesthetics would be identical to *AIDS Timeline* we can rest assured that the installation would never even have been considered by the curators, and that its very status as art would have been vigorously contested.

Perhaps the main difference between this Biennial and its predecessors, and the best that can be said for it in the way of intellectual honesty, is that it has not pretended, as its predecessors pretended, to represent the mass of American artistic activity over the previous two years. For several years it had been clear to perceptive people that art no longer interested the curators of the Whitney. Now, for the first time, the curators conceded the point. "The 1993 Biennial Exhibition presents new directions in American art over the past two years," the official statement of purpose declared. "The works of 82 artists confront critical crises that are altering the fabric of American life. In particular, the artists raise important questions about the changing role of the artist in society. The politics of representing racial and sexual difference, the boundaries between art and pornography, the function of art as a socio-political critique, the interrelationships of self, family and community, and the influence of new technologies."

Given this detailed laundry list of buzz-themes, it is difficult not to believe that the artists were chosen less for their art than for what, to put it as crassly as possible, they could bring to the table in the way of marketable marginality. Not just anyone could get into Ippolito's zoo and not just anyone could get to exhibit at the Whitney. That standards have been replaced by quotas is proved by how easy it was to label each artist according to his or her political identity: Janini Antoni—Feminist; Sadie Benning—Lesbian; Robert Gober—Gay; Christine Chang—Asian American; Jimmy Durham—Native American; Miguel Gandert—Latino; Glenn Ligon—Black.

The Whitney Biennial was a country club from which only straight white males were excluded. Doubtless, the curators felt that some rough justice was being carried out, given that there were many clubs where straight white males excluded everyone else. It was difficult to find many artists in the show who were just white males. There were some, but fewer than the demographics of the United States or the art world justified. What we were seeing in the latest Whitney Biennial was, to coin an ugly word, the donutization of the art world—all margins and no center. This must have seemed strange to many straight white male artists, who felt every bit as disaffected as their more exotic colleagues and every bit as scornful of established authority.

But, to invoke Robert Hughes's phrase, they were "the pale, patriarchal, penis people" and there was not a great deal they could do about it.

Though the straight white male artist is often absent from these exhibitions, the straight while male is present in the art to a compulsive degree. One of the key concepts buzzing around the art world today is "the Other." Deriving from the writings of such fashionable French thinkers as Simone de Beauvoir and Jacques Lacan, the term usually refers to minorities who have been marginalized by the center of society. In contemporary art, however, the straight white male has become the Other, an inscrutably dangerous stranger, an Ishmael. But worst of all, he can never be acknowledged as such, for that would require those minorities that now stand squarely in the center of contemporary art to yield their foremost claim to relevance, the fact of being marginalized.

The white man's offensiveness derives from his terminally unglamorous centrality. He is beset by homosexuality because he is straight, by ethnic groups because he is white, by the educated because he does not understand them and is not interested in them. The white man comes, not from Manhattan or San Francisco, but from Ohio, or Long Island, or Baltimore; that is, from mediated, inauthentic places. You just know that his life, which of course is led in quiet desperation, must be unexamined, and thus not worth living. Why does he go on living? No one in the art world seems to know.

He has appeared in many forms over the last generation. In separate performances pieces, Robert Morris and Chris Burden both dressed up as square white males, with buzz cuts, neckties and all. To themselves, these artists must have seemed rather like the dashing duke in *Rigoletto* and the elegant count in *The Barber of Seville* disguising themselves as bumpkins. And the cream of the jest was that most of the onlookers did not see that these were really happening artists just pretending to be squares! Jeff Koons has based his career on incarnating the pleasant-looking whiteboy. He is a high-tech, Baudrillardian simulacrum of the clean-cut all-American boy, bright-eyed and bemused at the attention he is being paid.

The whiteboy does not make art, except for the occasional still life of a bowl of fruits. The whiteboy does not look at art, except to visit the Norman Rockwell Museum, or to marvel at Andrew Wyeth's Helga portraits. He is the toothy, pimply young man holding the American flag in Diane Arbus's famous photograph. He is the middle-aged American tourist in Duane Hanson's stunningly precise waxwork figure, khaki shorts and all. In Alex Webb's *St. Augustine Florida*, a pleasant looking middle-aged whiteboy and his wife are photographed on a bench, looking out at a traffic light that epitomizes the dreary pointlessness of their lives. When Ida Appelbroog depicts him as Santa Claus with children crawling all over him, he becomes a child molester. In a hundred canvases by Erich Fischl, he can be seen sunning himself beside the pools of Club Med. How is it possible to be this unglamorous and not explode?

In the new quota system, as in the old, not all races are created equal. In general, one's aesthetic relevance is a function of one's distance from the center, defined by this purely notional straight white male. Blacks can always be relied on to give good value, but, with the successes of Glenn Ligon, Adrian Piper, and Carrie Mae Weems they can hardly be considered novelties at this point. Women and homosexual men are always desirable as well, provided their art is about feminism or gay rights. If not, they become traitors to their marginality. Latinos, Asian-Americans, and Native Americans do not have the resonance of blacks or homosexuals, the great richness of historical hurt that the art world wants, but at this point they are new, a factor by no means to be discounted.

It may at first seem strange that there was no specifically Jewish art in this Biennial, aside from Nancy Spero's verbosely mediocre work. This reflects a general feeling in the art world that Jews have been so fully assimilated to the white world that they are of no more consequence than white people in general.

Their identity has instead shifted to gayness or femaleness, the new preconditions for their relevance.

The reader must excuse the suffocating vulgarity of the foregoing. Yet the point needs to be made that many an art-world player is prepared to act upon these and similarly racist or sexist impulses, so long as they are not obviously racist or sexist, and so long as he or she can appear, in the process, to be attacking racism and sexism.

Only one truly radical work appeared at the latest Biennial: the grainy video of the Rodney King beating made by George Holliday on March 3, 1991. Its unique importance in this discussion consists in the fact that Mr. Holliday is not an artist and has never aspired to be one. Although Marcel Duchamp once set a snow shovel in a gallery and claimed it as his work of art, at least he stopped short of attributing artistry to the manufacturer as well. Yet that has not deterred the Whitney curators from nominating this video clip as a work of art, for no other reason than that it fitted some political agenda that they had, or liked to think they had.

Unlike Mr. Holliday, Janine Antoni at least thinks she is an artist. She achieved considerable success with a two-foot-by-two-foot chocolate cube that showed teeth marks where she had gnawed the surface. Another work began as mass of lard that the artist had chewed up and spat out and then collected into a cube. How this was accomplished, or how long it took, I am not eager to learn. Yet the authority of this work, at least for those who attribute any authority to it at all, derived from the almost obsessive, martyr-like compulsiveness implied in it. What Ms. Antoni objected to was the way the patriarchy demanded that she be slim. The idea that she might be imposing this obsession on herself, that most men really don't care one way or the other what she looks like, is the sort of thing that, in the etiquette of nineties, you simply do not say to a radical feminist artist.

Sue Williams, another feminist artist, scored points for her imperishable puddle of plastic vomit. Presumably the unnaturally abundant outpouring of a bulimic binge, it lay on the floor before a large yellowish painting, covered with skilless depictions of fat thighs, liposuction, and other acts of bodily alteration. Among the welter of words, we read: "One thing I've gotten with age is free to choose. I chose fat thighs." The artist, of course, is not speaking in her own voice but is imitating the sort of person who talks this way. She knows, and we know, that the speaker is deceiving herself, that the dictatorship of the phallocratic patriarchy has in fact left her without a choice.

Fairly typical of the ethnic art at the Biennial was a piece by Pepon Osorio, who speaks for the Latino community. In the present exhibition, he is represented by an installation that simulates a movie set of a typical Hispanic living room, as indicated by a number of klieg lights. A murder has taken place and the shrouded corpse lies in a puddle of blood on the floor. The room itself is full of gaudy gewgaws and Mariological images, thus stereotyping the typical Hispanic home.

On the outer walls that flank the installation are rows of videos, as in a rental store. The point of the piece, according to the artist's commentary, is to expose the way Hispanics are regularly stereotyped in movies and to see what can be done about that. Is this then what art, the tradition of Phidias and Michelangelo, of Apelles and Raphael, has come to. Advocacy that Latinos deserve meatier roles in Hollywood films? Let us accept that they do; let us accept that Mr. Osorio is free to transpose such banalities into his art. Is there any reason why any of the rest of us should be interested in seeing it?

But there is a higher level of falsehood at work in this and similar pieces in the Whitney show. In pleading for us to break down the stereotypes about Hispanics, what it seems Osorio really means, what he truly agitates for, is not an end to stereotypes, but rather the right of Latinos, and every other ethnic group, to appoint their own stereotype. To object that people are more than these stereotypes, that they can and usually do transcend them, is the sort of humanist drivel associated with the white establishment.

Naturally, Osorio's work is condescending in the extreme. It is insulting first of all in supposing that we need to be told that Latinos are human. Furthermore, there is a tacit compact between the artist and those who are in a position to view his work, that is, well-to-do museum-going white folk. The mere fact of their being in this position exempts them from the work's anger. The putative target of this work, as of most political art today, is the whiteboy whom we met before, that dimly descried, ever-receding and entirely notional Other.

In most of this art, the voice or identity of the artist is far more important than it ever was in modern art. In retrospect, there seems to have been remarkably little direct communication in modernism: rather, we were constantly overhearing it. A painting by Rothko has tremendous meaning without having a message. It is the distillation of an experience that the painter had and that we also have when we encounter his art. Even in the provocative works of dada or surrealism, the object is a distillation of the artist's mind or mood, but not a surrogate for the artist himself.

By contrast, most of the art of the latest Whitney Biennial derived whatever authority or interest it had from the identity of the artist. It is ironic, then, that the curator Lisa Phillips could write in her catalog essay: "One of the most powerful developments among artists in this emerging generation is a deliberate rejection of... an authorial voice." What she is saying is in one sense true: Most of these artists no longer use materials to express themselves the way one of Pollock's drips or one of de Koonings lunges could be said to express the artist's inner state. But in a much larger sense Phillips's statement is false. Osorio's stage set is about Hispanic stereotypes. Sue Williams's puddle of plastic vomit is about being a woman in a patriarchal society. But suppose it came out that Osorio had really been the author of Williams' piece and Williams had been the author of Osorio's piece. Immediately all authenticity would vanish from both works, as it became clear that each artist was assuming an identity to which he or she had no right. The object would not have been altered by so much as a molecule, yet its authenticity would have evaporated, and so we should have no further use for it.

Political art, which, in its extreme form, was enshrined in the latest Whitney Biennial, is a strikingly recent development. All art has a political dimension to it, just as it has a psychological, anthropological, and religious dimension. But until the end of the eighteenth century, the very circumstances upon which explicitly political art depended didn't exist. Such art requires a political sphere in which a large portion of the population has a say in its own affairs. Propaganda, of course, is as old as human artifice. But the Assyrian friezes of Nishapur, the Prima Porta statue of Augustus, and Rubens's Marie de Medici Cycle did not acknowledge a political realm. Rather, they were the means by which those in power sought, through magnificence or intimidation, to remain in power. The premise of these works was stasis: The premise of true political art is change.

Surely there was protest art as early as the sixteenth-century Reformation, when protestants and papists calumniated one another in such mass-produced engravings as Sebald Beham's *The Roman Clergy's Procession into Hell* in which the mounted pope leads a stately carriage of cardinals and bishops toward a flaming palace of perdition. Yet such works as these neither sought nor attained the status of high art. They merely bastardized the traditions of high-art engravings to make some passing point.

High art first met politics on the streets of Paris in 1793, when a jubilant mob carried Jean-Louis David's *Dying Marat* from the artist's studio to the galleries of the Louvre. Two generations later, Delacroix's *Liberty Leading the People* showed the unnecessarily bare-breasted Marianne leading the Parisian workers, students, and bourgeoisie on to victory against the forces of reaction and revolution. Though this was propaganda paid for by those in power to justify the status quo, it acknowledged the new realities of a citizenry which, either as an enlightened electorate or as an enraged mob, was determined to have a say in its leadership. As such it was political art, even if it had none of the acerbity that Daumier, Delacroix's contemporary, was purveying in his mass-consumption lithographs.

Modern political art came about, in a sense, when the vine of Daumier was engrafted onto the oak of Delacroix, and the person who did it was Gustave Courbet. Courbet, that fiery communard and befriender of anarchists, was indeed a pivotal figure, at once the first modernist and the first to turn high art against the established order, in this case the bourgeois state of the Second Empire. In doing so, he set the pattern for most of the political agitation in the art of own own day. Since then, to the extent that art is explicitly political, it has leaned overwhelmingly to the left. With the possible exception of the futurists, it is hard to think of a single right-wing artist of any importance who, even if he were royalist like Degas, chose to agitate for his position in his art.

To say that art is more politicized today than ever before is imprecise. More accurately, political art seems to be more highly valued than other forms of art, and more highly valued than it used to be only a few years ago. After all, a great deal of political art was made during the sixties, often by prominent artists, but neither they nor anyone else considered such work to be of any real artistic consequence. It was an adjunct to their real work, rather like what pro bono work is for lawyers.

According to art historian Irving Sandler: "The political awareness of vanguard painters and sculptors did not lead them to put their art in the service of their politics.... Political radicalism and artistic radicalism were kept separate. What the artists did in the streets, so to speak, had no influence on what they made in their studios." In many respects, the rough and ready posters and slogans that plastered the sixties have recurred in much the same form in the nineties. But what had been the adjunct to the career has become the career itself. It has usurped the career.

One artist who has been making political art steadily for more than a generation is Leon Golub. Just as the figural painters of the eighties looked to Philip Guston as a forebear of their art, so many recent political artists have been inspired by Golub's example. Surely he was not the only one making political art back in the sixties, but he was one of very few who made it the bulk and substance of their careers, and one of even fewer who, through the truculence of his tone and style, presaged the enragé art of recent years.

Born in 1922 in Chicago, Golub was weaned on the WPA style of the Great Depression. Though the same could be said for many artists of Golub's generation, he never doubted, as many of them did, that art can and must answer to a social, rather than a merely formal, summons. For a time, during the postwar period, his work took on a dour, Ben Shahnian character, with overtones of Picassoid existentialism. It was only when he was in his forties that Golub arrived at the style he has made his own.

At ten feet by twenty-eight feet his *Gigantomachy* is bigger than Picasso's *Guernica* or Pollock's *Blue Poles*. The fact of its being painted onto banner-like lengths of unmounted canvas gives to the work a rough and ready urgency. Nude male figures appear against a blank background whose nondescriptness only heightens the riotous violence of the action. They fling themselves into a doomed conflict which, before their predestined defeat, will threaten the throne of Zeus. They are the primordial proletariat, the outcast and oppressed, hereby inaugurating that conflict which, according to Marxist mythography, will recur through all the sanguinary annals of human history.

In time, however, Golub grew dissatisfied with this existentialist universality. He began looking for something more rooted in the specifics of the here and now. The result was a series of headshots of famous politicos, ranging from a vaguely disobliging image of Nelson Rockefeller, smiling a toothy, smarmy, crocodilian smile, to a marginally more idealized image of Ho Chi Minh.

Golub neither seeks nor attains subtlety. His most famous images, scenes from the lives of mercenaries, manage to be simultaneously ambiguous and one dimensional. If there is any symbolic resonance to the soldiers carrying a prisoner upside down on a pole, it is that they incarnate arbitrary and disinterested aggression. Since it is not, however, in the banality of their evil to be sullen all of the time, the mercenaries are sometimes seen horsing around and acting macho, as one jovially kicks another in the pants, while a third looks on laughing. But invariably their sport turns treacherous. In one interrogation scene, two men in fatigues belabor a man hanging down from a pole. Another painting shows these same figures, in different clothes and of different nationalities, assailing a prostitute. But the most damning indictment of all is reserved for *White Squad*, in which they lounge around laughing, entirely oblivious of the corpses that lie everywhere about them.

Despite their violence, the tone of these paintings is strangely affectless. Even Golub's earlier existential works, inspired by passionate men like Pollock and emotional men like Ben Shahn, betray this inability to feel much of anything. Whatever his private convictions, as an artist Golub is an amoralist. This is not to say that he advocates amorality. Rather, he sees it as the acting principle in the world. Conscious of his essential powerlessness against something so big, the artist can only utter these grim and ineffectual protests. His native element is that chilly moral void that remains after all sanitizing illusions have been stripped away from the world. It is cognate with the despairing cry of the man with his arms raised in the *Fifth of May*, Goya's famous firing-squad scene, except that it is incapable of the tragic sense of life. What defines the world for Golub, what makes it so awful, is its blind and baleful neutrality.

Golub's execution is invariably listless and unappealing, as though it would be an obscenity for anyone to paint well in such a rotten universe as this. Many people seem to have been far more moved by Golub's work than I am and have been more forgiving of his unconcern for composition and paint textures. But even as political art, Golub's paintings are one-sided tributes to the banality of evil, qualified by a directionless anger that presumes to present the problem but has no clue to the solution.

Unlike Golub, who came to political art only in his forties,

Hans Haacke began his career in art as an angry young man. And though he is no longer young, he remains as angry as ever. Haacke has as much claim as anyone to originating the political factoid installation, of which the *AIDS Timeline* mentioned above is only one eminent example.

He accomplished this in the long ago days of the Greenbergian sixties, in an installation-performance piece called *MoMA Poll Question*. The museum's visitors were asked the following: "Would the fact that Governor Rockefeller has not denounced President Nixon's Indochina policy be a reason for you not to vote for him in November?" Twelve percent of the visitors responded, and of them, 25,566 or 68.7 percent said yes, whereas 11,563 or 31.3 percent said no.

Essentially, Haacke's art was inspired by the thinking of the New Left that came to prominence in the sixties. Though a sympathy with the downtrodden is implicit in his work, it is nowhere evident. Instead, Haacke's virulent hatred of big government, capitalism, and the military induces him to go after politicians and rich capitalists.

Sol Goldman and Alex Dilorenzo Manhattan Real Estate Holdings, A Real Time Social System and *Shapolsky et al Real Estate Holdings*, both from 1971, attacked slum lords, itemizing their various holdings in Manhattan and explaining through words and pictures how, among other forms of provocation, they had allegedly used pimps and the Mafia to attack residents.

Subsequent installations went after the trustees of the Guggenheim, listing what companies they owned or were chairmen of, as well as the misdeeds of which these companies were purportedly guilty. A similar work devoted to the Metropolitan Museum's corporate sponsors, informs us that: "Mobil's management in New York believes that its South African subsidiaries' sales to the police and military are but a small part of its total sales. . . ." The effect of both these works is to suggest that culture is overwhelmingly saturated with and contaminated by money; that there is an evil world just below the surface far uglier than the pretty colors in which it is usually painted.

If there are heroes in the world, they are not in Haacke's art. Like Golub, he wouldn't know what to do with the heroism of the little man struggling against great powers, something that interested earlier political artists like Ben Shahn. Haacke is uniquely interested in the wealthy, in their aggressions and, as he sees it, their hypocrisy.

He goes after no one as aggressively as he goes after Peter Ludwig, owner of the Trumpf chocolate manufacturers and creator of the Ludwig Museum in Aachen, Germany. With a grim display of disinterest, he lists one after another the malfeasances of Herr Ludwig: he is wealthy; he has sold some manuscripts in Switzerland to the Getty Museum in Malibu; he has employed workers in Eastern Germany; he has commissioned portrait busts of himself and his wife by Arno Breker, who had been a prominent artist during the Third Reich. Now Herr Ludwig is by universal consent an unusually generous philanthropist. But for Haacke that makes no difference. In the name of the revolution, all of the man's philanthropy must be reduced to nothing, and the weapon of choice is to be a sequence of vague and unpersuasive innuendos.

If Haacke is an artist of the barricades, Barbara Kruger learned her strategies of subversion in the belly of the beast. Having spent several years on Madison Avenue, she now devotes herself to turning advertising against the corporate interests that fuel the industry. For Kruger, everything is about power and those who have it and those who do not. Her spiritual and political essence can be summed up in an us-them equation pitting white people with penises against everyone else. The former are big business, governments, and scientists with their arrogant claims to knowledge. They have the power, but We have morality, and if We could only organize We could take over. We, of course, also includes the art world showing strength with the presumably grateful underclass.

At the heart of Kruger's images is a conflict between their strident directness and their inscrutably enigmatic message. Against a shattered mirror we see a close-up of a woman in pain and the phrase "You Are not Yourself." There is the flash of a mushroom cloud and then the words, "Your Manias Become Science." United States foreign policy is implicitly attacked in an image of two blond children, Dick and Jane, in crew cut and braids, the quintessential scions of the fifties middle-American nuclear family. He shows her his biceps, above the caption, "We don't need another hero."

Several strains of postmodernism meet in these aggressively ironic photomontages. Like Mariani imitating the mythologies of Raphael, Kruger is an antiquarian, whose predilected style is the Russian avant-garde. Most of her photomontages are black and white, enlivened with violent reds, as in the banners of the Bolshevik Revolution. Now as then, the enemy is still capital, but it is also male aggression, with overtones of psychosexuality that would not have sat well with bolshevism.

And yet one suspects that the real motivation for Ms. Kruger's revolution turns out to be nothing more than style. She likes the look of red against black; she admires the virulent conviction of Rodchenko and Tatlin. Like Ian Hamilton Finlay contemplating the overthrow of governments in his pleasant Scottish garden, Kruger is not so much interested in the radicalism of the Soviet revolution as in its really snazzy graphics.

Like Kruger, Krzysztof Wodiczko creates images that have the punch and directness of advertising rather than the nuance of fine art. He is not a subtle man, and such areas of grey as exist between black and white don't interest him at all. Instead, he wants to make his point as provocatively as possible and he succeeds. If anarchists or nihilists ever sought the services of a first-rate Madison Avenue firm they would be lucky to get something on the order of Wodiczko's art: a product of often exhilarating cleverness, with all the intellectual stamina of a car commercial. Whatever you think of his politics, you will find that these unfailingly provocative images linger in the mind long after most other political art has faded away into over-funded irrelevance.

Wodiczko's material is light itself, the particles of a beam zapped onto some particularly august and cherished public monument. In the process, the monument is totally subverted from its original purpose by collages of light and masonry that make the same kind of psychotic sense as John Heartfeld's incomparable antifascist images from the thirties. There is the further pleasure of knowing that the owners and inhabitants of these public buildings have no legal recourse. The structures are totally transformed, and yet, since the offensive medium is mere light, they have not really been altered in any way. The ultimate subversion!

"The attack must be unexpected, frontal, and must come with the night," Wodiczko has written, "when the building, undisturbed by its daily functions, is asleep and when its body dreams of itself, when the architecture has its nightmares. This will be a symbol attack, a public psychoanalytical seance, unmasking and revealing the unconscious of the building's body, the 'medium' of power."

Night is a necessity, of course, since light projected onto a surface would be invisible during the day. But the night has other attractions that Wodiczko may have been the first visual artist to discover. Night is a parody of day, a quiet zone, a context of elegance and leisure. It was for this reason especially that night, that most elegant and ceremonious of stage settings, had to be invaded and defiled by Mr. Wodiczko.

Since the early eighties, the artist has been circling the globe, hoping to foment the revolution with his provocative displays of son et lumière. The Scotia Tower in Halifax, Canada, an angular monolith of glass and grey concrete, was too tempting to resist. Wodiczko's subversion was accordingly deft and simple. He projected a gold-braided uniformed arm onto the side of the building, thus transforming the entire structure into a soldier standing at ramrod attention. Those fascist Canadians!, the work cries out, even though the exact nature of his grievance against them is unclear.

The Art Gallery of New South Wales, in Sydney, Australia, is a long, flat, austerely classical building with a portico in the center and a colonnaded pavilion at either side. Its imperialist monumentality was simply too much for Wodiczko. On the opening night of the Biennale of Sydney, with the blessings of the gallery's directors, he projected onto the center of the building the headless torso of a man, whose arms stretch all the way to the pavilions in an emphatic gesture of grasping, colonialist power-lust. Those fascist Aussies!

Not long afterward, the Nelson Column in London's Trafalgar Square was turned into a nuclear warhead. Onto its large plinth were projected the treadings of a panzer, and the top of the neighboring South Africa House was adorned with a discreet swastika. Wodiczko has, or thinks he has, something on everyone. In 1984 he projected chains onto the New Museum of Contemporary Art in SoHo to protest the fact that "at the time of this projection the space above the museum was slated to be converted into a group of luxury loft condominiums."

These chains would later reappear in an Italian context. Though the Venetian republic was surely belligerent five hundred years or so ago, in recent memory it has been behaving itself quite well. That doesn't stop the ever-angry Wodiczko from projecting his chains onto that city's Arsenal. Why Venice, for God's sake? Because "they have turned [the city] into a tourist playground and imaginary 'refuge' from the politically and economically troubled world of today." The idea that anyone would want to take refuge from such things makes Wodiczko angry. He knew what to do. Tanks and missiles needed to be projected onto the base of Verrochio's great equestrian statue of Colleoni, the famous fifteenth-century general and, we may imagine, protofascist. The world-famous Campanile was transformed into a tourist, with a camera around its neck and a row of bullets at its hypothetical waist.

Whatever you think of the artist's harebrained division of the world into noble underclass and fascist oppressor, it is impossible not to admire the sheer visual ingenuity with which Wodiczko has gone about his business. The art he practices is in its cradle, but it is hard to imagine anyone ever doing it better than he has done.

What projected light is to Wodiczko, the light-emitting diode is to Jenny Holzer. Upon it she has woven her theoretically provocative words, many of them from a series called Truisms, into postmodern samplers. In these enigmatic works, what you see is what you are. How you respond to such dark utterances as MURDER HAS ITS SEXUAL SIDE or ABUSE OF POWER COMES AS NO SURPRISE or MONEY CREATES TASTE, whether with boredom or with an expansive sense that your life has new meaning, says more about you than about the artist.

It must also say something about our culture that Holzer has achieved as great a success as she has. That she had arrived in a big way was proved, not by her Guggenheim retrospective in 1989, but by her reception a year later at the Venice Biennale where she won first prize as the American entry. But it was not the prize that indicated her success so much as the fact that her Truisms were printed onto T-shirts and baseball caps and briskly marketed inside the American Pavilion. Before long, in almost any major city you visited, here or abroad, you could find people wearing Jenny Holzer's aphorisms. Soon they were in contention with Warhol's sententious vacuities as the heavy utterances for our time.

The turning point in Holzer's career came in 1982, when she was thirty-two. That was when she took over the famous electronic board above Times Square to flash the words "Private Property Created Crime" and "Torture is Barbaric" to a mass of confused motorists and pedestrians. Until that time, her Truisms had been printed on posters and pasted around urban centers on bus shelters and parking meters. Thereafter, they could be found on bleeping matrices of light-emitting diodes, the medium with which Ms. Holzer has become identified. Though she has subsequently diversified into metal and marble, the burping diodes remain her signature.

At their best, her installations can have a hard-edged, glinty elegance that amounts to beauty. It was impressive, at her Guggenheim retrospective, to see those ribbons of lights winding majestically round the spiraling rotundity of the white interior. In Venice, she orchestrated into being a tranquil zone of gently buzzing lights and cool marble floors into which her Truisms were incised in several languages.

But what seems to appeal to her most is the subtle subversiveness her words acquire when placed in circumstances of especially abject banality, the farthest one can get from the glamorous parochialism of the art world. Thus MONEY CREATES TASTE was beeped along the length of the luggage carousel at the Las Vegas Airport. On the Caesar's Palace flash board she wrote: LACK OF CHARISMA CAN BE FATAL. High above London's Picadilly Circus, an electric signpost flashed the words: SAVOR KINDNESS BECAUSE CRUELTY IS ALWAYS POSSIBLE LATER. Even baseball hasn't been safe from her predations: YOU MUST HAVE ONE GRAND PASSION appeared on the scoreboard over Candlestick Park in San Francisco.

There are two audiences for this art, the actual audience and the real audience. The latter watches the former, though the former doesn't realize that it is being watched. The words on the scoreboard at Candlestick Park are seen by the fans, who have no idea what is going on. But the fans themselves are being watched, in a sense, by the art world, which learns about Holzer's piece through magazines, books, documentation, and word of mouth. Thus, whenever Holzer flashes her words at Candlestick Park, or Picadilly Circus, or Times Square, the art world senses a frisson of excitement at the thought of all those people who have not the remotest idea of what is going on; all those people who do not go to art galleries, who do not read *Artforum*, who are not in on the joke. Life is good.

How can you interpret these works? Who is speaking in the works of Jenny Holzer? Or more precisely, how many voices are there here, and do any of them belong to her? We assume that when she says, "Abuse of power comes as no surprise" or "Murder has a sexual side" she is speaking, not in her own voice, but in imitation of the sort of people who say such things or think such things. But how is it that we can know this?

There is an unspoken and yet crucial act of faith involved in one's experience of Holzer and of most other political artists at work today. When Chris Burden scribbles the word *nigger* onto one of his works on paper, we naturally assume that he is imitating and calling to account the sort of people who would use such words in earnest. Surely no one who sees Burden's work supposes him to be calling anyone a nigger. He is vaguely imagined to be bravely embattling racism, and he is praised for this. But if a real Klansman were ever to stand before this work, he might suppose that Burden was a racist, and would perhaps praise the work just as exuberantly.

Herein lies one of the paradoxes of contemporary political art. In order to communicate in even the simplest way, all art presupposes a shared vocabulary and a shared set of habits and expectations. How else could it be that despite the elliptical obliqueness of much contemporary art, it is so easily understood by those who go to see it? Without that bedrock of shared attitudes, this understanding would be impossible. The logical consequence of this fact, in most cases, is that contemporary political art can be understood only by those who already accept its premises and its conclusions. Yet *ex hypothesi*, they are the last people whom this art needs to reach, if we accept that it has anything to say in the first place. And *ex hypothesi*, those who would seem to need it most, unenlightened bigots and chauvinists, are least apt to encounter it, or even to identify it as art when they do.

At this point, an inevitable question presents itself: What do Holzer and most of the other political artists of the moment hope to accomplish by their art? For political art must have a political purpose. Almost by definition, it must strive toward some practical result. It may well be that in her own mind Holzer was raising peoples' consciousness, using her various "deconstructionist strategies" to call into question the most basic premises of contemporary Western society. But such a goal, even if it reflected her sincere wish, would be so ill-defined and so essentially impractical, as to be almost a retreat from politics into the comfortable complacency of doing nothing at all. Is there not then a palpable tremor of despair underlying her calculated subversions, a radical rejection of the sort of genuine, if less glamorous, political activism of social realists from the thirties like Ben Shahn and Reginald Marsh?

Ultimately, the art of Jenny Holzer, Pepon Osorio, Hans Haacke, and so many of their contemporaries, for all its talk of mobilizing and organizing and empowering and overthrowing, is to real politics what pure mathematics is to arithmetic. In other words, at the very root and wellsprings of this art, far below the point where most of these artists cease to know themselves, there is really a complete rejection of politics, or, dare we say it, a more or less total apathy.

In part this mood results from the chastening effects of experience. The revolutionary temperament can withstand anything except its own success. Today's artists know, even if they will not admit it to themselves, that the lessons of revolutionary France and Russia, perhaps of America in the sixties, have been this: that the implementation of radical politics has been empirically shown to engender monsters. Any descent into the real world is necessarily fatal to the purity of one's ideals. Furthermore, someone will have to take responsibility when things start going wrong.

And yet, radicalism is somehow so intoxicating to these artists that they are loath to abandon it just yet. Instead, a new kind of radicalism had to be devised, one so purely theoretical that there could never be any risk of its being put into practice. Thus, by adamantly withdrawing from the real world, by rescuing politics from the sordidness of any application, art has become the medium by which radicalism is redeemed. Just as you can have Marlboros without the tar and Big Macs without the fat, so you can now have the rush of radical politics, the virulent, expansive, corybantic joy that only bracing jolts of self-righteousness can confer, without every having to descend (for it is a descent) into the arenas of action.

This is what art has done for politics. But what has politics done for art? It has given contemporary art something to do, something to talk about. In the process, it has become a kind of ornament in contemporary art very comparable to a patch of newsprint in a cubist collage: the point of which was less what the print said than the visual effect of so many inches of pure pattern. Politics has become nothing less than a new aesthetic, neatly filling the vacuum caused by postmodernism's retreat from the older formal ambitions. In other words, it has replaced modernism's art for art's sake with something equally valued in itself and for itself, pure politics instead of pure form. Yet the "valid" critical response is as aesthetic as it ever was: By approving the message and the authenticity of the attitude it conveys, one admires, one likes, one enjoys the art.

Despite the fervid hopes of many people, contemporary political art has not succeeded in indissolubly merging art and politics. Rather, they have merely traded places: Art has become political so that politics could become aesthetic, with each one travestying and finally betraying the other.

NINE

The Art of the Body

Postmodernism, like modernism before it, wants to see just how much it can get away with. It strains to test all limits and to call all things into question. Where it will end up remains a mystery. For the time being, however, the French performance artist Orlan seems to have gone about as far in the way of art as anyone ever should. And even those people who feel they can no longer be shocked by anything may yet be shocked by her.

Orlan belongs to the tradition of artists who use their own bodies as the locus of their art. In the seventies, the German *aktionismus* artist Rudolf Schwarzkogler seemed to go as far as possible when he systematically amputated his penis inch by inch. But since it later transpired that he had faked the whole event, it was widely recognized that there was still work to be done. Though many have used tattoos to transform themselves into human canvases, Orlan, I believe, was the first to turn herself into malleable sculpture, by staging performance pieces in which actual plastic surgery was performed on her body and face. In a photograph published in Barbara Rose's recent article about Orlan in *Art in America*, the artist's face emerges amid baroque chiaroscuro out of the theatrical shadow of an operating table. Because of the camera angle, we see Orlan as from below. Her face is covered over in a thin membrane of latex, with openings at her nostrils, at her tearing eyes, and at her mouth, whose scarred and bloodied lips are tugged at by two surgical implements and tweezed by a third.

Even before her present mania for self-revision took hold, Orlan could do some outrageous things. In one performance, Rose writes, "Orlan stationed herself outside the Grand Palais, site of FIAC, the French art fair, next to a life-size photo of her torso transformed into a slot machine that she identified as an automatic kiss-vending object. Customers who inserted five francs in the slot between the breasts could watch the coin descend to the crotch, at which point the live artist jumped off her pedestal to reward the purchaser with a real kiss."

In a tableau vivant from 1983, *Saint Orlan as a Baroque White Virgin Armed with a Bouquet*, the pale, moon-faced lady is wrapped in billowing, alabastrine drapery recalling the robes of Bernini's swooning *St. Teresa in Ecstasy*, an historical figure with whom, apparently, she identifies. Orlan is borne aloft, against a background of fanciful clouds. Underfoot, a crown, flowers, and a basin are overturned through the presumed violence of her sudden ascent. Bright light floods her face, and one breast is illogically bared. More posture art than body art, this tableau recalls Cindy Sherman and Tseng Kwong Chi, who also photograph themselves in highly artificial and contrived circumstances.

But unlike these American-based counterparts, Orlan upholds the culture of Europe, of the Renaissance and the Baroque. At the same time, she resembles architects like Ricardo Bofill and painters like David Ligare and Carlo Maria Mariani, in being either unwilling or unable to see beyond the surface of that tradition to its force and substance.

Orlan can also be seen in terms of the French obsession with refinement and feminine beauty. All cultures, of course, value these things, but none has pursued them with the same intellectual precision as the French, who lead the world in haute couture and luxury cosmetics. It is no coincidence that the French critic and poet Theophile Gautier can lay as fair claim as anyone to having coined the phrase "art for art's sake," or that the French novelist Barbey D'Aurevilly remains the foremost legislator of the laws of Dandyism. Their goal was to transform life into art, to quarry from existence itself, from the most personal object of all, the human body, the stuff and matter of artifice.

But if these men laid the theoretical groundwork, Orlan is the logical consequence. On her forty-third birthday, in 1990, she had the first of seven operatory performances, which, according to Ms. Rose, eventually "will totally transform her face and body." The reason for the operations has little to do with vanity, according to Rose. They are rather an attempt to conquer the last frontier of art, which was also the first frontier, the body itself. In her operations Orlan is inspired by the ancient painter Zeuxis, who, according to legend, depicted Venus by combining the traits of all the most beautiful women of Croton, basing the nose on one of them, the hand on another, the breasts on a third, and so on.

Orlan stands the Zeuxis parable on its head. By insisting that life imitate art, she has sought and found in several classical paintings and statues the features she wants to engraft on her own face: the nose of the Diana of Fontainebleau, the mouth of Boucher's Europa, the chin of Botticelli's Venus, the eyes of Gerome's Psyche, and the forehead of the Mona Lisa.

Each of the hospital rooms in which the operation takes place has a reproduction of the work of art from which the body part is to be taken, presumably to guide the surgeon's hand. The room itself is transformed beyond recognition: In one performance, *The Mouth of Europa and the Figure of Venus*, Orlan, her surgeon, and his female assistant appear in shimmering silver lamé gowns designed by Paco Rabane. While Orlan lies across the operating table with a mike to her face, reading from a romantic novel, the surgeon goes about his business removing or inserting something (it's hard to say) into her bared fanny.

In what I believe is a later moment in the same piece, after the surgeon has started operating on her mouth, Orlan gazes, ever conscious, into the camera's eye, a stream of blood dribbling down the side of her face. All around her are sumptuous clusters of grapes and apples, as in a Neapolitan still life. In *Cloak and Harlequin*, her fifth and latest operation/performance, Orlan, covered in saffron and plum-colored robes, lies flat on the operating table, holding in her left hand a pole with a death's head and horns, in her right a candy-colored pitchfork.

The interpenetration of flesh and artifice of which Orlan is an extreme example has occupied the artistic imagination through the ages. It is the force behind the myth of Pygmalion, who sculpted Galatea out of marble and then fell in love with her, and it inspired the ancient Greeks to chain down their statues lest they walk away. The self-scarifying Masai and the tattoo-covered Maori have wrought similar transformations on their bodies through the centuries. But the modern founder of body art was Marcel Duchamp, who not only dressed in drag in the twenties, but even had words shaved into his hair.

His example, however, was not widely followed until the seventies, when it was picked up by artists hoping to squeeze one last shock out of modernism. In addition to such *aktionismus* artists as Hermann Nitsch, Rudolf Schwarzkogler, and Arnulf Rainer, the American Vito Acconci achieved something of immortality with his infamous *Seedbed* of 1971. In this performance at the Sonnabend Gallery in New York, the Bronx-born artist built a low ramp under which he hid twice a week for two weeks, each time for six hours. When visitors entered, he would masturbate and shout out sexual fantasies involving them.

In a refinement on the same theme at the Marian Goodman Gallery only a few months ago, Anselm Kiefer's *20 Jahre Einsamkeit* (20 Years of Solitude) featured a table with several dozen codices and ledgers, on each page of which was the trace of one or, as I believe, more than one ejaculation, the register of how the artist consoled himself in his solitude.

Astonishingly, in the context of the art world there is nothing very astonishing about Kiefer's ledgers or Orlan's performances. Body art, which became big in the seventies, has given way to what we might call Art of the Body, an artistic obsession with body fragments, body fluids, clothing, and sexual apparatus that now occupies the center of the art world to the same degree as political art. Obviously, art has always had a fundamental interest in the human form, from prehistory down to the present. But that form of body art must not be confused with these more recent developments. The body, which earlier artists viewed as a vessel of the soul, now stands objectified as a fascinating, treacherous, infinitely complicated contraption in a state of alienation from its owner.

In the catalog to Corporal Politics, a recent exhibition at MIT, Helaine Posner refers to "a startling phenomenon in late-twentieth-century art, the striking preponderance of the body fragment as a highly charged metaphor for the psychological, social, political, and physical assaults on the individual. The disturbing isolation of body parts and limbs, internal organs, and bodily fluids, emphasizes the vulnerability of our bodies and implies physical violence, sexual oppression, and ultimate loss. . . . The dismembered body is the site for the investigation of some of our most urgent contemporary concerns, including sexism, sexual identity, reproductive rights, homophobia, social inequality, brutality, disease, and death." She goes on to say, "This war on the body and the experience of disconnection it engenders is most often revealed in the work of female and gay male artists. From perspectives outside the white male power structure they are in a painfully privileged position to comment on and critique the politics of division, exclusion, and loss." Or, as Barbara Kruger said less turgidly in one of her photomontages, "Your body is a battleground."

A natural consequence of this attitude is the camp fascination with plastic surgery and other forms of corporeal revision. Now that these surgical emendations are so widespread, now when one hears increasingly of cloning, transsexualism, virtual reality, and sperm banks, have we reached the end of humanity as we know it? No, we have not.

That is the sensible if boring answer to the hare-brained question posed by Post-Human, an exhibit that toured Europe in 1992. According to Jeffrey Deitch's catalog, the show explored "the implications of genetic engineering, plastic surgery, mind expansion, and other forms of body alteration to ask whether our society is developing a new model of the human being. It poses the question of whether our society is creating a new kind of posthuman person that replaces previous constructions of the self."

Now common sense is compelled to admit that just because Michael Jackson had a nose job, or Zsa Zsa Gabor had a face lift, this does not spell the end, or even the radical transformation, of the human condition. But, naturally, this fact doesn't deter the author from answering his own question in a paranoid affirmative: "Within the next thirty years the fear that we may not be able to distinguish real humans from replicants will no longer be just science fiction.... Art may have to fuse with science, computerization, and biotechnology to create further 'improvements' on the human form."

The catalog, which favors a somewhat spastic form of free association, provides numerous images of transformation: Jane Fonda, Ivana Trump, Pat Sajak, three plasticine icons of the mass media who, through aerobics or cosmetic surgery, have reinvented themselves. Much is also made of the polymorphous villain of *Terminator II*, that indestructible machine with no sense of humor, who, threatened by the wrath of Schwarzenegger, dissolves into a puddle of mercury. This figure, we are to believe, is the Apollo Belvedere of the future, digitalized perfection that looks without pity on human frailty.

That the old certainties have been disrupted does not seem unduly to disturb the author or the artists he includes in his exhibition. One doubts they were ever that big on humanism anyway. Despite their tone of dark foreboding, they seem to look forward to the day when virtual reality and genetic engineering will rid us of all unhappiness, ugliness, and imperfection, and plastic surgery, as a last resort, will airbrush away any lingering unpleasantness.

Modernism's alienation is preserved in Deitch's view of things, but translated into the language of today. "The decentered television reality that we experience, with its fragmentation, multiplicity, and simultaneity, is helping to deepen the sense that there is no absolutely 'correct' or 'true' model of the self," he writes, blowing hard. But where modernism trembled at what seemed to be the very real threat of nuclear war and possible enslavement, this art has a shrill, manic glee to it: The world is going to hell, and we have the best seats in the house! In place of the old alienation, you have repressive tolerance in a sunlit, Californian dystopia whose hollowness only artists can understand, because they are more sensitive than the rest of us.

When the historians of the future look back (if they look back) at the sort of art enshrined in the Post-Human exhibition, they will wonder at its abundance of prostheses. Legs, arms, breasts, and buttocks in wax, rubber, or plastic are to these artists what right angles and grids were to the artists of the sixties. Everyone's doing it. The appeal of prostheses is vague yet manifold: Though mimetic like high art, they have a popular, extra-artistic source which jives nicely with the high-low debate. At the same time, their apparent realness and ultimate falseness, combined with their being mass-produced, can be linked, if you want, with Baudrillard's theory of simulacra, not to mention Benjamin's *The Work of Art in the Age of Mechanical Reproduction*. Finally, their relevance to the sexually adventurous sounds a note of gay liberation, not to mention intimations of physical infirmity that take on a special resonance in the age of AIDS.

Typical of this trend is Kiki Smith, daughter of the late esteemed minimalist Tony Smith. Though she has changed her formal terms often in her brief career, her orientation in the body remains constant. One untitled work from 1986, before she became directly interested in body parts, consisted of twelve empty glass jars, elegant in their crystalline clarity, the sort you might find in an alchemist's laboratory. Engraved into their surface, in Gothic type, were the words: *Sweat*, *Urine*, *Semen*, *Diarrhea*, *Vomit*, *Pus* etc. The power of the piece was supposed to consist in the contrast between the pale purity of its forms and the revolting quality of their contents. Similarly two sculptures from the same year were bronze casts of the male and female urogenital system. Another work consisted of hundreds of shimmering glass spermata colliding in primordial strife, a postmodern, safe-sex analogue to Michelangelo's *Battle of the Centaurs.*

But Smith is best known for her human figures in plaster and beeswax. These faceless entities lie huddled on the ground, bend over on all fours, or hang from meathooks as haggard, lifeless skinnings. An interesting comparison suggests itself between Smith and George Segal, who also made life-size plaster and papier-maché figures. Though separated by a single generation, they seem worlds apart. For Segal, the body is a coherent whole that had a soul once, but has lost it under the weight of that existential anguish which, if culture is any guide, ceased to exist sometime after 1975. Segal's figures carry the burden of a postwar world, where Auschwitz is a fresh memory and nuclear annihilation a present threat.

Smith, by contrast, raises the banality of her figures a few notches. They are full-grown abortions that have never lived and never will live. They have not lost their souls since they had no souls to lose, and they had no souls to lose since, for Smith, as for everyone like her, the body is the ultimate fact of human existence, the one eternal truth (eternity in the art world being anything from six months to a year). What is their problem, these voided, aborted human possibilities? We shall never know for certain, since art of this sort, battening upon the roomy credulity of its viewers, can be sustained only through portentous vagueness.

One of Smith's most recent works is *Bloodpool*, which has had a certain international success. It looks like an aborted fetus in an early stage of development, a few months old perhaps, its spinal column still externalized as a spiky white concatenation. It is hard to fathom what this work could possibly mean. As a successful member of the art world, Ms. Smith surely cannot be anti-abortion, yet such a work could profitably be enlisted by pro-lifers to point up the sordidness of the process. Doubtless the meaning of the work consists in a generally cynical take on the human condition. It is not a tragic vision, as is Segal's, but a coldly dispassionate one: This aborted infant is neither more nor less dead than Smith's earlier desquamations, or than any of us.

Robert Gober, who shares many of Smith's concerns, seems to have taken his time before arriving at his present fascination with body parts. True, in the early eighties *Crouching Man* looked like the first gay George Segal sculpture, but Gober then moved away from explicit reference to the body. His sinks, from the mid-eighties, are his best work, in fact the only work that makes any credible claim on one's attention. Their faucets and drains removed, they resemble radically schematic faces like Arp's.

After that work came his cribs, which, tilted at severe angles, suggest imprisonment and childhood anxiety, two recurring themes in contemporary art. *Three Urinals*, from 1988, is Gober's homage to Duchamp, that other great urinal-appropriator. But over the last eighty years, what had started out as a shocking gesture now carries with it intimations of the gay lifestyle and "bodily fluids in the age of AIDS."

Whereas the body parts in Kiki Smith's art are somewhat schematic, the legs and torsos Gober has used over the past few years are scrupulously accurate, down to the hair on the legs and buttocks, and to the single trouser leg, sock, and shoe that adorn a single limb in isolation. They can be seen either as amputations or prostheses or, because they are often jutting out of the wall, as synecdoches of some missing person.

Why is the rest of the body missing? Doubtless to signify "absence, loss, memory and/or desire," or something like that. To whom does the leg belong? Given its simple felt shoe, grey sock, and black pants, one readily supplies the missing rest: You have seen this man a million times, buying materials at Pearl Paints on Canal Street, visiting the galleries on Greene Street, or sipping expresso at Elephant & Castle. He is your basic artist type. But there is something almost balletic about his dismemberments, the way they lie on the floor or protrude illogically from a wall. In other works of this sort, a wax torso resembles a depressed pillow, one side male and hairy, the other female and breasted; a man's buttocks are bared and covered with musical notation; a similar figure in underpants, sneakers, and socks has hideous chunks hewn from it.

If Smith and Gober have used sculpture to express their interest in the body and its parts, many others have chosen photography, often using themselves and their bodies as subject matter. Cindy Sherman is one of the most protean of these self-portraitists. Like most contemporary art, her images are not much to look at formally, at least not in the way that the images of Steichen or Weston were. Their interest consists almost entirely in the message or attitude communicated.

It will be some time perhaps before people realize just how narcissistic Ms. Sherman really is. She is surely a pretty woman, with small ruddy features and a slender body, which, at an earlier moment in her career, she found ample occasion to expose to the camera (though she has had the rare forbearance never to reveal herself totally naked). Perhaps some will find this physical assessment of Ms. Sherman to be politically incorrect. I defend it on the grounds that no one could have exposed herself as often as Sherman has without feeling a strong measure of exhibitionism. Surely there is some part of her, and nothing very subconscious either, that can live with the thought that men are admiring her body.

While we're on the subject, am I the first to observe that few artists strip naked before the art world unless they feel confident that they have, as it were, something to show? With the exception of John Coplands, whose septuagenarian self-portraits reveal an ungainly, overweight walrus of a human, most of this art is undertaken by women like Karen Finley, Hannah Wilke, and Carolee Schneeman, all of whom, at the time of self-exposure, are young and by no means unpleasing to look at. Men seem to feel this naturalist summons less than women, but when they do, as Robert Morris did in the late sixties, you can rest assured that there will be an impressive physique in the offing. Naturally one appreciates that it is the imperatives of art, of self-expression and the truth, that compel these artists to remove what they're wearing. Yet for some of us it remains a nagging puzzle why those less certain of their desirability seem content to remain within the more traditional avenues of artistic communication.

To return to Ms. Sherman, her earliest works from the late seventies, when she had just graduated from SUNY Buffalo, were artfully shot in black and white. At the time, these images were genuinely original, because they were entirely constructed and because they disowned both the straight, undoctored formalism of traditional photography and the snapshot journalism that Gary Winogrand and Lee Friedlander pioneered in the sixties. Generically titled Film Stills, they exude the brooding, treacherous suggestiveness of every Hollywood B-film you ever refused to watch, though there are also hints of kitchen sink and nouvelle vague directors. In one shot, Sherman appears as a Bardotesque sex kitten gazing into a mirror. In another she is aproned and in the kitchen, glancing coyly over her shoulder. Sometimes she appropriates Hollywood's "epic shot," from below, to become the ingenue in the big city, resplendent in print dress and flower bonnet. Around each of these cleverly conceived and constructed stills, the mind readily constructs an entire fifties film.

Since 1981, however, Sherman has been coming at us in living color. No longer imitating B-films, she seemed by the mid-decade to be undergoing a profound multiple personality disorder and to be recording for the camera each stage of her psychosis. Occasionally she is a femme fatale or society matron, but usually she is the quintessentially bubbleheaded white girl.

Her surroundings are suffocatingly suburban, and the colors that saturate these images are about as natural as a closet full of double-knit polyester. Often she appears cinematically illumined in T-shirt or tank-top and shorts. Someone is pursuing her. She is wet and scared. She hears something that causes her to look up suddenly. If this were any other artist, such an image would be a deadly serious comment on male aggression against women. For Sherman, it seems to have little purpose beyond dressing up and acting for the camera. There is nothing very serious in these pictures: Sherman is rare in contemporary art in wanting first to amuse herself and then to please her public.

Sherman's third and latest phase is fabulistic, with storybook warlocks, genies, and demons. Colors and images have now become more stagey and artificial and prostheses abound. In one image she is a checkered pirate with an eye-patch, standing before a raging fire. She goes from being an angry fertility god rising out of a wheat field, to being a drowning victim, a snouted subhuman brute, and an evil genie in a turban. As a genie she reveals a most impressive pair of breasts—which turn out to be plastic prostheses. In another work, she is a murder victim, with her buttocks exposed. But these also turn out to be false. Surely their falseness is a tease, rather than the result of any demureness, since Sherman's most recent works at the Whitney Biennial were extremely crude images of a fake penis and vagina. It was amusing, by the way, to hear one of the Whitney guides explain these images to a flock of suburban housewives by saying in all sincerity that the artist, having grown tired of the way collectors bought everything she made, decided to create something emphatically unsalable. But then, to Ms. Sherman's astonishment, the collectors went for these works too! Surprise, surprise.

Cindy Sherman, mistress of disguises, never appears twice in the same shape or form. The British team of Gilbert and George, by contrast, are ever and always the same. Beginning with a performance piece called *The Singing Sculpture* from 1971, several years after they met and fell in love at London's St. Martin's School of Art, the two men appear in all of their several hundred self-portraits in grey suits, pressed, antiseptic, and anonymous. Not only do they refuse to change, but each so resembles the other that they seem interchangeable. It is as if J. Alfred Prufrock had looked into a mirror and fallen in love with his own reflection.

Who these two men are we may never know, but who they appear to be is clear to anyone versed in the taxonomy of British stereotypes. For they are above all typically English (even if Gilbert was born in Treviso). They come from a four-square middle-class family of shopkeepers or functionaries and they know their place. They are what is sometimes called the backbone of England. They keep the Tories in power and worry that the Pakistanis are taking over their sceptered isle. Furthermore, they have unlimited affection for the Royal family, especially the Queen Mum, though they never took to Fergie or Princess Di. In this sense, they are oppressively conformist.

Even their homosexuality is of a typically English sort. In the aviary of homoeroticism, they are the pallid pigeons, with no beautiful plumage or charm of song. They are the only gays who are not especially interesting, and they would choke before bringing up the subject, as that would not be proper. The poignancy in this art, if there is any, is that we seem to know them better than they know themselves. They appear to be trapped in their little lives without perceiving their imprisonment and thus with no hope of discovering a way out. Only we can see the disquieting undertones, which threaten at any moment to break through the edgy civility of their pose.

This diffident self-depreciation, however, is a ploy to make more emphatic the raunchy homoeroticism that is the recurring theme, if not the only theme, of their art. However shocking Robert Mapplethorpe's gay images might seem, at least he could do other things too: flowers, portraits, statuary. Gilbert and George have only one thing on their mind, and that is young men, generally between the ages of fifteen and twenty, though one senses a willingness to compromise on either end. Translated into the terms of heterosexualism, they would be a pair of foxy grampas (since both are now in their fifties) leering at every young filly who comes their way. But because they are homosexuals we are required, I suppose, to see everything they do as daring and intelligent.

On the other hand, fascinated though they are by gay sex, Gilbert and George do not seem, like Mapplethorpe, to have seen too much of it, at least not in their public personas. On the principle of "No sex, please—we're British," the genesis of their art is in a severe repression and frustration that finds its outlet in exuberantly patterned and colored images of doctored photography, silk-screened onto glass.

Like so much contemporary art, these images are murderous to describe in any other than the vaguest terms: The all-over riot of clashing colors and forms is physically perplexing and occasionally inconceivable. The team kicked off the 1980s with *Ass*, whose title is quite apt, since it surely does depict a pair of male buttocks, parted and ready for anything. *Dog Boy* evokes a lad of about ten standing with his best friend near a storefront, framed by yellow roses. In two immortal masterpieces, *Shit Faith* and *Buggery Faith*, crudely drawn excrement emerges from four abutting anuses in one work, while the other represents four penises touching at the tips.

Ultimately, despite Gilbert and George's astonishing productiveness and the dizzy diversity of their exploding pinks, greens, and oranges, there is a tedious sameness, even a uniformity, to their works, which takes you by surprise. What better proof than the pair of images, *Life* and *Death*, in which there is nothing especially vital about the one nor mortuary about the other. Like everything else by Gilbert and George, both works are cheerful, garrulous, and slightly hysterical. Perhaps this is why the two men are a little more interesting in themselves than in their art, which succeeds only in cloying the viewer before it ever gets the chance to satisfy.

With relief, then, we turn to the far tamer art of Robert Mapplethorpe. If any one person incarnates the art of the body, Mapplethorpe is surely it. So much humbug attaches to him, whether in the form of uncritical adulation or philistine condemnation, that he more than anyone would gain from having his mystique systematically dismantled. Ultimately, Mapplethorpe was a better-than-mediocre photographer who, but for the posthumous furor, would probably be seen as one of the brighter lights of one of art history's dimmer ages.

His early works from about 1970 have aged remarkably well and do not look nearly as frumpy as a lot of the other art of the period. He was, in fact, ahead of his time in the sense that what he was doing in the early seventies would come to dominate the mainstream about a decade later. If it took any courage to depict black male nudes in 1980, it probably took far more to make *Leatherman Two* in 1970, a pop photo of a scowling biker in a black chain cap, surrounded by a bright red frame, with images of an Adam's apple and a man's legs set in between. Already this and similar images feel remarkably postmodern, given their appropriation of earlier images, their archness, and their insistent lack of formal purity.

Contrary to the progress of almost every other postmodern photographer, Mapplethorpe graduated from doctored prints to straight photography: compared with someone like Richard Prince, Mapplethorpe is formally one of the most conservative photographers of his age, arriving at his scrupulously honest images the old fashioned way, by focusing the camera. With the possible exception of the excellent Nicholas Nixon, he is perhaps the only photographer to make a name for himself in the eighties through straight photography. His two favored subjects were portraiture and erotica.

As regards the former, one is struck by how consistently he makes all his subjects seem rich and famous, until one realizes that in fact they are all rich and famous: the singer Patti Smith; a yawning David Hockney; Brice Marden seated sideways in an armchair; Arnold Schwarzenegger in 1976, flexing his pecs beside a tasteful curtain. Like all good fashion photographers, Mapplethorpe created more glamour than he recorded. Each of his images is carefully crafted, leaving the sitter dazzled by a style he probably never realized he possessed. Notwithstanding the raunchiness of Mapplethorpe's homoerotic images and the conservatism of his photographic technique, honesty was not one of the man's virtues.

Very rarely did he seek to penetrate beneath the shimmering surface, and only twice did he memorably succeed. In one self-portrait, a full-frontal shoulder view from 1980, he appears naked and heavily made up, with a flounce of blown-out hair. I find this image oddly moving and sad. His famous wolverine features seem belabored and vulgar beneath the layers of cosmetics, yet through them transpires the soul of the man, confused, out of breath and a little disoriented—the very type of human frailty.

In his splendid dual portrait of Philip Glass and Robert Wilson, from 1976, the sitters look directly into the camera, facing us cross-legged in simple chairs with two boards joining behind them to divide the composition neatly down the middle. This was the first Mapplethorpe image I saw, reproduced in Roland Barthes' *Chambre Claire*. It was Glass who especially impressed me. I found and still find in that face a seriousness and generosity that impart to the image, as a work of art, an inexhaustible interest and life.

Mapplethorpe's later portraits are very competent, yet they impress me less. They are all glamour and sheen. He truckles to his subjects with a servility that a more honest man would not have allowed, as in his image of Richard Gere, coiffed and bare breasted, or the prunefaced Louise Bourgeois grinning stupidly as she holds her "daring" phallus sculpture under her arm. Sometimes, it must be said, these portraits succeed in being very glamorous indeed. Francesca Thyssen is seen in profile like one of those daughters of wealthy Florentine banking families painted by Fillipo Lippi. Mapplethorpe accentuates her languorous eyelids and her beautiful profile amid a swirl of arabesque drapery clustered with diamonds and pearls.

Flowers are the link between the polished glamour of these portraits and the hard-core pornography of his homoerotic art. Thanks to his evocative tonalism, grapes become testicles, and orchids and calla lilies are emphatically suggestive orifices. This is taken furthest in *Poppy*, from 1988, in which the flower is held luminously aloft against a pea-green background, its stem twined by the hairy, testicular bud of an unopened flower. It is possible that Mapplethorpe thought he was being subtle.

At least in his outright pornographic images, he frees the air of such perfumed pretension. A recurring image in his work, a fixation almost, is the black male nude. In *Man in Polyester Suit*, from 1980, he crops the image at the figure's neck, so that it becomes all body and no head. What we notice first are the large black hands and then, through the open zipper of his pants, what must be, unless the man is a midget, a very large penis. A year later we see the magnificent physical specimen of Ajitto. Yet I feel bad for Mr. Ajitto. He sits naked on a pedestal, his face buried in his knees, needing money and submitting to this strangely driven photographer. He resembles the sort of black man Leni Riefenstahl photographed in Africa, whom she admired and Mapplethorpe admired, because, as they both knew, the black man was closer to nature than their civilized selves.

In the catalog to Black Males, an exhibit in Amsterdam back in 1980, the novelist and essayist Edmund White gushes, "Mapplethrope turns his subjects into antique bronzes. When he photographs the wonderfully articulated back of a man sitting on a pedestal, or when he shows us a white-haired young man in *profil perdu* staring off into a stylized distance, or when he anatomizes the abstract shapes of body parts—a head from which the face has been cropped, or an open, rising hand beside a leg, or the great lyre of muscled legs and buttocks—in these pictures Mapplethorpe looks at the black male body as a thing of beauty."

That there was any sympathy between the photographer and his specimens is not obvious from the images Mapplethorpe left us with. Artful though the images are, the exploitation seems palpable, only a cut or two above the soft-focus female centerfolds of *Penthouse* magazine. One has the strong impression that these images were designed to appeal to well-off white men whose tastes tended toward the exotic, or to well-off white women who felt they weren't getting enough attention from their banker husbands.

Naturally Mapplethorpe was a racist, except that, unlike most racists, he befriended blacks instead of wanting to persecute them. But at least in his art, his entire position toward these subjects is to deny their general humanness and to concentrate entirely on their race. In part this has to do with the dusky sheen of their skin, a legitimate interest of photography. But more than that, it involves a sense among many gay white men that the Negro is kinkiness incarnate. The black man, as an object of their sexual attention, is the polar opposite of the white woman society had intended for them.

The dewy-eyed soft-core feel of the Black Males series gives way to something far more explicit in Mapplethorpe's depictions of white men. *Mark Stevens (Mr. 10½)* is a headless torso in leather pants extending his impressive manhood, as it were, over what is supposed to suggest a meatblock. An image from two years later is titled *Joe.* There is something amusing in the personal touch of a first name, since every inch of the man's body is trapped in a suit of studded black leatherette, qualified only by a breathing tube that loops from his mouth in a spry parabola. *Joe and Tom, Sausalito* is the innocuous title of a triple image of one man urinating into the other's mouth. Here, as in all the other images of white male homosexuals, deadpan dispassion is of the essence. Any tremor in Mapplethorpe of involvement or interest or astonishment at what they're doing and the whole structure of his artifice comes crashing down.

Is this art obscene? Of course it is. Should it be censored? Of course not. Obscenity is crudely understood by many who express an opinion on it. Cultural critics have made life too easy for themselves by surrendering the entire issue to the courts, thus carelessly identifying obscenity in the legal sense with obscenity in itself. Judges have to observe due process, but critics do not. They can and must rely on their better judgment. So what if that won't stand up in court? They are not in court.

In theory, there is an easy way to determine which art is obscene and which is not, if, as is unlikely, you do not already know. Just ask the artist, since he knows very well what his intentions were. The problem, of course, is that, in circumstances in which the work really is obscene, the artist will almost surely lie. He will record every outrage he can think of, and yet, the moment he is queried on it, you can be quite certain that in no time at all he will be talking like a Greenbergian formalist. Thus, Robert Mapplethorpe's many defenders will insist that he was merely exploring tonal values, curves and rectangulations, solids as opposed to voids. Or he is seen as weaving a poignant, elegiac chronicle of love between men.

In fact, these images were explicitly intended to scandalize and shock. Can you prove it? they demand, donning for the nonce the mantle of the Philadephia lawyer. Well no, because such things are not susceptible of proof in any legal sense, as we all know. But it is peculiar that the very people most eager to extol and defend Mapplethorpe have, apparently, not the slightest misgivings in misrepresenting everything he stood for.

But if we could reach Robert Mapplethorpe in whatever region he now inhabits, and ask him what he was really up to in all those images of men urinating into one another's mouths, or in his self-portrait with a bullwhip up his rectum, he would no doubt reply, with the honesty of death, that it was his intention first to have a good time and second to shock a whole lot of people. And who were these people? The sort he grew up with: the nuns and priests he met in parochial school, the repressed librarian with the pinched expression; the school disciplinarian with black rubber-soled shoes; not to mention all the bull-necked squares in middle America. This is what he set out to do, at least in the obscene part of his work, and this is what he succeeded in doing.

Now, if this was his aim, as I believe it was, then the government was not only justified, but even obliged, not to fund his art. By upholding modernism's hoary aim of shocking the middle class, Mapplethorpe implicitly declared himself the enemy of certain basic values that the American government and most of its citizens hold dear, for example, the conviction that it is not polite to photograph yourself with a bullwhip up your ass. As such, he should not have been censored by the federal government, and of course he was not, but neither should he have sought or received the enthusiastic blessing of those whom he meant to scandalize.

In the case of the Mapplethorpe controversy specifically, there were extenuating, complicating circumstances: Money was given not to an exhibition of his works, let alone to him personally, but to an institution that used that money for many different things, only one of which was a Robert Mapplethorpe show. Nevertheless, intellectually the principle of the thing remains the same.

Obscenity in the sense in which I conceive it requires intentionality of provocation. The reason Mapplethorpe's homosexual images are obscene, while the sculpted nudes on the Hindu temples of Madya Pradesh are not, is that Mapplethorpe intended to shock, whereas the medieval sculptors of Northern India had no intention of doing so. True obscenity requires two players: the scandalous and the scandalized. If Jesse Helms and Robert Mapplethorpe had not shared the same moral scale, the same register of sensibilities, it would have been impossible for Mapplethorpe to know how to shock Helms or for Helms to know when to be shocked.

Now, it is nowhere written that what is obscene cannot also be great art, nor that what was once an obscenity must remain obscene forever. Opponents of the idea of obscenity point to Manet's *Olympia*, which outraged Paris in 1863, but is now a universally recognized masterpiece. The implication is: The Philistines thought it was obscene, but now we know better. More exactly, it was indeed obscene once and it isn't anymore. And the reason it was obscene is that Manet created it with the intention of shocking *Le Bon Bourgeois* of his time and he succeeded in doing so. That we are no longer able to see its obscenity today means that we are not fully living up to Manet's expectations of his viewers. It has required all the industry of scholars like T. J. Clark to restore to the work the punch it once packed. In exactly the same way, anyone who cannot be shocked by Robert Mapplethorpe's imagery, as many in the art world seem unable to be, cannot experience it as Mapplethorpe intended.

And the unshockable viewer might as well also give up on Andres Serrano, that other "victim" of the NEA. Born of a Cuban mother of African descent and a Honduran father, Serrano made his fortune with *Piss Christ*, a genuinely obscene image of a crucifix in a yellow substance that turned out to be the artist's urine. One's views on this image are necessarily ambivalent. There seems to be a distilled quietness to this and similar images, representing a profoundly internal and ruminative religion. If it were not for one ingredient, the work would be hardly objectionable, and perhaps even moving.

The same could be said for *Black Mary*, a subaqueous figurine beaded with hundreds of tiny pearl-like bubbles, and *Black Jesus*, a typically Victorian tombstone image, inexplicably darkened. I would guess that only a person of some kind of devoutness could have made these images. Serrano claims that they assail the commercializing of religion in America. And perhaps he was telling the truth when he wrote that, "Religion depends largely on symbols, and as an artist, my job is to explore the possibilities in deliberate manipulation of that symbolism."

If Serrano sincerely believes that he was merely examining symbols, he has some very serious problems in communicating, which in fact is what his real job is—"as an artist." *Piss Christ* certainly looked like an attack on Christianity itself. In matters of such consequence, it is important not to mumble.

No such loftly purpose, however, could possibly have been imputed to his lastest show at Paula Cooper, with its large Cibachrome images shot in an unspecified morgue, of the victims of suicide, drowning, rat poison, and other forms of violent death. These stridently colored photos are in such extreme closeup that one never has a sense of the whole body, only the horror of the circumstantial details: the goose-flesh of rigor mortis, the caked blood at the throat, the knife wound to the foot. The melodramatic mood is essentially that of erotic photography, and it takes a moment to adjust to the actual subject matter.

Serrano, interrogator of American values, is playing yet again the gruesome game of Test the Taboos! In terms of sheer daring and outrage, the art world has not seen the like in, what, two weeks? An entire culture stands accused of having fostered and then tolerated such an idiotic show as this. What was worst about these fuzzily focused images was not their competence, which was workmanly, but the fact that Serrano was incapable of raising so tremendous a subject out of feeble, fumbling mediocrity, and that most of the art world was so far gone in the way of the discernment that there was no possibility of their ever finding out.

Serrano may sensationalize death and exploit his subjects, but he does at least manage not to poke fun at the corpses. That was left to Joel-Peter Witkin, who recently won a fourth National Endowment of the Arts grant, which, one is sorry to note, he deserved as one of the more gifted artists of his generation. As Witkin recently told a *Vanity Fair* reporter, "The first thing I should say is, I'm not a monster." The reader will have to decide that for himself.

Witkin follows in a long line of shocking imagists that includes Bosch, Arcimboldo, the younger Teniers, Fuseli, Doré, and John Heartfeld. He surpasses them all, however, for the simple reason that his images are real: neither paintings nor photomontages, they are actual registrations of the objects in the camera's lens. His predecessors furnished us with an escape clause, the soothing knowledge that their images, however revolting, were mere inventions, mere paint. Witkin does not allow this escape. He scrupulously fulfills photography's promise to tell the truth. What we see in the picture really exists. The event depicted, however grotesque, is really happening. The fact that he shoots his images in black and white and plays with the negatives to give them a nineteenth-century feel, in no way detracts from their veracity, but if anything, gives point to it.

Witkin places a special burden on all who write about him, since his elaborately composed pictures beggar all description. It was with only slight exaggeration that, in the afterword to one of his photography books, he added this extensive solicitation of new models: "A partial list of my interests: physical prodigies of all kinds, pinheads, dwarfs, giants, hunchbacks, pre-op transexuals, bearded women, active or retired side-show performers, contortionists (erotic), people who live as comic-book heroes, satyrs, twins joined at the forehead..." That was the first fifth. In a later book another solicitation ended thus: "Hermaphrodites and taratoids (alive or dead). Beings from other planets. Anyone bearing the wounds of Christ. Anyone claiming to be God. God." In the event, Witkin got only about half of what he asked for.

In all of Witkin's works the aesthetic is that of Victorian photography, steadfastly black and white, with infinite attention to those details of objects and materials that once fascinated the pioneers of the new medium. The tone and first impression of these photographs is invariably one of Victorian high seriousness, with all its moral and scientific pretensions and preoccupations. Everything depends on Witkin's being able to maintain this unflappable deadpan. Thus it takes a moment for the eye to adjust itself to the astonishing perversity of the art, which is its real point.

Mexican Pin-up, one of his tamer images, features an ordinary, well-set woman with a quantity of needles riddling the nipples of her large, bared breasts. In *Eunuch* a man is mounted from behind by a dog. In *Man Without Legs 1984*, a masked man's torso is fully developed, but his body, except for its prominent penis, ends at the waist and rests on a skateboard. The mask itself is typical of the artist. It is the first thing we see, but what we take to be the point is in fact a distraction from the real point, that the man has no lower body. Meanwhile *Savior of the Primates* features a crucified monkey, and *Madame X* is a blindfolded man with large breasts and no arms covered in drapery like the Venus de Milo. Wearing lingerie and masks, an adult pair of black Siamese twins are joined at the top of their heads and thus must gaze into the camera sideways.

Only recently has death entered Witkin's work in *John Herring, Person with AIDS, Posed as Flora with Lover and Mother*. Part of its punch consists in trying to determine how he got all these people, especially the frumpy-looking mother, to humor the mustachioed subject in his fanning, garlanded, Little Bo Peep hoopskirt. The image is "tastefully" composed in the manner of a baroque painting, with neatly balancing repoussoirs. As nineteenth-century clouds break in the background, Mr. Herring stands on a damask rug, and a naked child dressed as an winged putto holds a pinwheel near the subject's head. One is not sure what to make of the image, especially on learning that the subject, who once helped out around the photographer's New Mexico home, subsequently died of AIDS. Since he cooperated willingly, the exploitation is somewhat intangible. Yet one has the disagreeable sense that Witkin is mocking his subject even as he immortalizes him.

Where Witkin goes beyond the pale is in *Still Life, Marseilles, 1992*, depicting an "aesthetically" composed table decked out in watered silk, upon which is set a pewter platter of endives, seashells, crustaceans, and fruit; in the center you see the severed head of a deceased man, his boneless desquamated face so composed that his eyes and mouth are wrenched shut in an expression of what, in life, would have been emphatic disgust. Yet the top part of his head sports a melon (I believe) serving as a prosthetic cranium filled with lilies and baby's breath.

In a still more disgusting image, the flabby, corpulent figure of a man sits casually back in a chair, facing the camera almost frontally. He is naked, but that's not the important thing. He fingers himself, but that isn't important either. What is important is that he has no head, that his neck terminates in a collapse of neatly folded flesh. This is not trick photography.

With this image, it would seem, Witkin has gone as far in the way of the art of the body as one can ever go, surely as far as I, for one, am willing to follow. It is hard to imagine where else the perverted ingenuity of idle minds will take us next. Suicide as performance? Murder as performance? In the case of the headless man, it is scarcely consoling to learn that his corpse, like all the others in Witkin's photographs, was donated to a hospital in Marseilles for scientific purposes, and that that institution gave Witkin permission to compose them as he wished. The fact remains that the owner of that body did not donate it for so frivolous a purpose. Without becoming too moralistic, we may legitimately ask whether it is right that a man's entire existence should be thus reduced to the provocative punchline of a pointless joke.

TEN

Art Art

Once there was a movement called NO! Art. Few people now remember it and fewer still speak of it, which seems about right. According to Simon Taylor, writing in *Abject Art*, a volume of essays accompanying the Whitney Museum's recent exhibit of the same name, "Committed to a radical leftist ideological position, these artists [Sam Goodman and Boris Lurie] were outraged by the complicity of their fellow artists with the moneyed elite." Their short-lived movement seems to have started (and ended) in 1964, when the two artists filled the Gertrude Stein Gallery in New York with huge mounds of papier-maché excrement doused with brown paint, to which traces of red were added to indicate hemorrhoids. Goodman said of these works, aptly titled Shit Sculptures, "I'd like it understood this is my final gesture after thirty years in the art world. This is what I think of it."

But if Goodman and Lurie thought they were on to something original, there were mistaken. Beginning with Duchamp's inverted urinal in 1913, the coprophiliac tradition in the twentieth century has by now become almost venerable. Piero Manzoni, an otherwise accomplished artist, canned his excrement in neatly labeled, weighed, and numbered tins that he displayed in galleries. Andy Warhol made his discreetly titled *Oxidation Painting* of 1978 by urinating onto a canvas covered in metallic paint. Lest women should be left out of the discussion, Hannah Wilke's Phallic/Excremental Sculptures simulated feces in terracotta, while Shigeko Kubota's infamous Vagina Paintings resulted from placing a brush in her pudenda and squatting over a canvas on the floor.

The point of these gestures, of course, was to show contempt for art and all it stood for. "No more Art! Demolish serious culture!" cried Henry Flynt, one of the leaders of Fluxus, that Dada-inspired death-of-art movement that flashed in the overheated pan of the sixties. Like Dada itself, Fluxus was to all appearances resolutely anti-art. Its members began by hating the reverential pomposity with which art was celebrated and ended up despising art itself.

But the joke was ultimately on them, and the punch line was delivered in a recent Fluxus retrospective at the Walker Art Center in Minneapolis, which afterward went to the Whitney. Not that the show was bad. To the contrary, it was a model of thorough and respectful curatorship and it taught a great deal about a difficult and unusual movement. Indeed, it was the curators' scrupulous labeling of each turd, their punctilious dating of each tuft of mottled junk, that finally and irreversibly betrayed everything Fluxus stood for.

At times, in the act of honoring this art, the curators explicitly contravened its intentions. On top of Ben Vautier's *Total Art Match-Box*, containing about thirty blue-tipped matches, one read in the Belgian's shaky English: "Use these matchs [sic] to destroy all art—Museums, Art Library's—Ready-mades, Pop—Burn Anything—Keep Last Match for this Match[box]." The final injunction was especially directed against those who had ideas of keeping the object as a work of art. But of course that didn't stop the catalog from dating the piece; describing its materials as one might a sculpture ("Commercial Matchbox with

Matches, Offset one Card Stock Label"); and then measuring it: $1\frac{1}{2}'' \times 2'' \times \frac{1}{2}''$. It is now a prized possession of The Gilbert and Lila Silverman Fluxus Collection.

But there is a far deeper irony at work. The curators' reverence for anything as irreverent as Fluxus points to a paradox at the very core of recent art, a paradox that qualifies the success not only of Fluxus itself, but also of Dada, the grandsire of all the anti-art movements in our century. The truth is that in rejecting art, these artists proved that they were unable to keep away from it. By profaning it, they paid it unconscious and unwilling homage.

Consider *Ben's Window*, an installation piece created by Vautier in London in 1962. This piece required a storefront with a large window in which the artist lived for fifteen days without once leaving. Now, as martyrial exercises go, this act of self-sacrifice in the name of art couldn't compete with Chris Burden's being stuffed into a locker for five days or his lying for three weeks in a bed placed in a gallery. By comparison, Vautier's performance was one of exemplary domesticity: He had a bed, a wash basin, a television, and a stove. Vautier's point was to prove, as though proof were needed, that this performance, like everything else, could be seen as art. "I sign everything as art, the universe, the Pope, hens, kicks, etc.," said a chalkboard hanging from one of the walls.

A later work, *Ben's Museum*, displayed among other things a shell, some wood, and a bit of dirt. Beside them was a sign: IF SINCE DUCHAMP EVERYTHING IS ART DOES THAT MEAN THAT THIS TOO IS ART? IF THE ANSWER IS YES WHY GO TO MUSEUMS AND NOT JUST DOWN TO YOUR CELLAR? A still more dramatic statement of this sentiment was his Kick in the Pants Certificate, which read, "The present attestation is to certify that I Benjamin Vautier have effectively kicked M.____ in the posterior and that this kick must by [sic] considered a work of art." Other certificates authenticated bites, slaps, and kisses.

What does all of this prove? There is a point in the history of every artistic medium, whether visual art or music or literature, just as there is a point in the life of every user of that medium, when an earlier devotion turns to contempt, when the appetite momentarily sickens and the votary turns away in disgust. It was probably this that inspired Marianne Moore to begin a poem called "Poetry" with the words, "I, too, dislike it." Surely this feeling was not invented by modernism, but it was modernism that first expressed it and placed it squarely at the center of our cultural habits.

Indeed, this attitude, which once reduced the poet to silence and stilled the painter's hand, has now become the foremost material of their art. The fact of having nothing to say is often what one has to say. It was this attitude that inspired Hugo von Hoffmansthal's Lord Chandos to forsake literature in an elegant, if fictional, letter to Sir Francis Bacon. It was this attitude that induced John Cage to create music that was nothing other than silence; that guided Ad Reinhardt's hand as he painted the last of his black-on-black paintings; and that moved Ludwig Wittgenstein to found a school of philosophy on the idea that philosophy was utterly impossible.

Yet the real paradox of this contempt is its proximity to a kind of love. No earlier centuries could have mounted an anti-art movement because, among other reasons, culture for them was a means to an end. Music, poetry, and painting were to delight and to teach. One would never have assigned to art the importance that Fluxus did, since, after all, it was just art. As long as culture remained this means to an end, it was impervious to anti-art. Only when it was revered in itself, as much modernist art seemed to be, could it encounter this contempt. But just as only profoundly religious people can be satanists, just as profanation and blasphemy require as much spiritual enterprise as orthodox devotion (if not more), so the anti-artist shares with the aesthete and the culture vulture an unshakable conviction about the importance of art, and consequently about the importance of its overthrow. Without this confidence he could not function at all.

At some point in our century, each province of culture—whether music, literature, or painting—experienced this contempt. But music and literature managed to move on. They became reintegrated with their material to the point of being able to create freely in it. This is why composers and novelists no longer feel an overwhelming impulse to interrogate their own traditions. They just write their novels and tone-poems as best they can.

Not so with art. It is the artness of art that continues to fascinate the art world, the need constantly to examine and reexamine the process of art itself. Nothing exists outside of this art: It is self-referentiality incarnate. Thus Sherrie Levine challenges ideas of originality by painting exact copies of Malevich or by photographing a Walker Evans photograph. In a similar spirit, Mike Bidlo copies Pollocks and Matisses. Meanwhile Sophie Calle fills empty frames with words recollecting paintings stolen from the Isabella Stuart Gardner Museum in Boston. Andrea Fraser, in one of her performance pieces, pretends to be a tour guide leading visitors through the Whitney Museum. No fewer than four artists at the most recent Whitney Biennial, Glenn Ligon, Jimmie Durham, Denise Green, and Fred Wilson were represented by installations that were really mini-exhibitions, thus defining a new subgenre: the curated-show-as-artifact.

As yet, no suitable label exists for this art. It is not really anti-art since most of it does not explicitly attack art. Rather, it is "Art Art." Art Art is what occurs when artists see their medium as an end in itself. It must not be confused with art for art's sake, which conceives of something outside of itself, for example beauty and refinement, to which end art is the means. Art Art is entirely different. It is fascinated by, morbidly involved in, everything concerning contemporary art: frames, paintings within paintings, art world politics, semiotical explorations of meaning, exploitation of concepts like kitsch, abstract enquiries into the interplay of high and low culture. From California to

New York and from England to Japan, artists are taking art as the subject of their art.

One of the more memorable examples of Art Art could be seen in autumn 1992 at the Ronald Feldman Gallery in SoHo. It was a show of sixteen paintings by the justly neglected Soviet artist S.Y. Kochelev. It was difficult to see what had prompted the gallery to devote an exhibition to this man, since he was clearly a dull, if pleasant, official Soviet artist, whose work was full of sunny semi-impressionistic scenes of boys pulling tractors and girls dancing in native costumes. There were also pleasant images of geese and village elders and gossiping townswomen in kerchiefs. Perhaps the most banal image of all was one called *The New Teacher*, in which two young women gaze admiringly at a taller, older woman, the embodiment of authority.

But the viewer was distracted from these works by the extraordinary circumstances of their display. They were shown in a dimly lit sequence of rooms, whose gilt doorways and wainscoted walls were so dreary as to remind one of nothing so much as some regional museum in Minsk, Magnetogorsk, or Smolensk. The benches in the center were huge, ugly things. Worst of all, in full entropic Soviet style, the ceiling was leaking something awful, and a rattling tintinnabulation of drips and drops was detonated into metal and plastic pales, creating a noise that resounded through the gallery. Many people at this point got fed up with the artist and the gallery and left. Some, however, were enchanted by the fluency of the artist's technique. Among them, rumor has it, were major curators and collectors, who enquired eagerly into the price of the works.

It was at this point that they were let into a secret. S. Y. Kochelev didn't exist. He was a figment of the imagination of another man, the prominent Russian installation artist Ilya Kabakov, who had invented him out of thin air and had painted sixteen pictures in a protracted parody of the socialist realist art he was brought up on. When they learned of the hoax, collectors really fell in love with the work, and the four paintings that were for sale promptly sold, in all their tawdry glory, for $50,000 each.

Another installation artist who has successfully exploited the curated-show-as-artifact is Christian Boltanski. The propriety of his inclusion in this chapter on Art Art is, to be honest, moot. Though his work has a strong sense of emotional, if not formal, beauty, Boltanski is rare among contemporary artists in being able to see beyond art and politics to those human realities that underpin both. "For me," he once said, "painting isn't provocative or moving, only life is moving." Forty years ago, anyone could have said that. But no artist talks like that today without being sincere.

Boltanski creates installations whose vitrines, or glass cases, recall such Fluxus artists as Joseph Beuys and Marcel Broodthaers. He lovingly fills them with children's toys, old photographs, and personal effects of people whom he doesn't know. One such work was *Inventory of Objects That Belonged to a Woman of Bois-Colombes*, in which the vitrines were filled with glasses, teacups, saucers, and elegant cake knives, all belonging to a nameless woman who otherwise would have slipped forever between the cracks of history. Unlike Beuys's posthumous vitrines, which merely stuffed a lot of his belongings into cases, in Boltanski's works a mysterious presence begins to rise like a conjured spirit from out of the inert matter.

The same curatorial impulse inspired *Reserve—Detective*, from 1987, consisting of hundreds and hundreds of photographs hung on the walls of the Stedelijk Museum in Amsterdam. These included rough and ready snapshots of babies, adolescents preparing for first communion, and women in bikinis. "The photographs originally appeared in the magazine *Detective*. A weekly specializing in news items, it presents an indiscriminate blend of assassins and victims, the unintentional heroes of forgotten dramas." Other installations featured sixty-two members of the Mickey Mouse Club in Albi, black-and-white images of Dijonais children with lights behind them and electric wires trailing from the back, one of the artist's signatures. Here, as in much of Boltanski's work, there is a discreet, delicate humor, a humaneness so rare in today's art that it distracts one from what, it must be said, is the artist's general lack of formal ambition.

One of the principal concerns of Art artists, in accordance with such fashionable French theorists as Barthes and Derrida, is to examine whether visual and verbal meaning is possible, and if so, what the mechanics are of its communication. Foremost among those whom such questions interest is the American Joseph Kosuth, like Boltanski, primarily an installation artist.

It may be that Kosuth does not see his art as being about art at all. He seems to see it as a radicalized questioning of meaning itself, with distinct implications for the well-being of the world. His art is rife with references to Barthes, Wittgenstein, and de Man. Yet, to the extent that his installations work aesthetically, Kosuth practices a form of art far older than perhaps he realizes. His material is words themselves, arranged not calligraphically as in Islamic manuscripts, but in clean, elegant lines that recall Roman epigraphy and the Aldine tradition of book printing. Naturally, Kosuth would make more inflated claims for his art, but this in fact is what is happening in his installations.

His first important work, part of the emerging conceptual art movement, was *One and Three Chairs*, from 1965, now in London's Tate Gallery. This installation consisted of a photo of a classroom chair, the chair itself, and beside it, on a placard, the definition of chair. At the time he created it Kosuth was twenty years old, which was remarkably young—or remarkably old, depending on how you looked at it. At the same time, the work certainly seemed, and continues to seem, terminally cool and perhaps a little dull in its surly avoidance of any trace of human touch. Ironically, the wooden chair itself, the sort that can be found in a million homerooms across America, strikes an oddly schoolmarmish note, which accords well with the annoyingly teacherly tone that one often encounters in Kosuth's art.

Text/Context, from 1979, consisted of two billboards placed in what I take to be New York's garment district, bearing the following legend: "This text/sign wants to see itself as part of the 'real world,' but it is blinded by those same conventions that link you to it, and blinds you to that which, when read, is no longer seen." Another sign from two years later informed the passerby that, "That which presents itself, here, as a whole can only be recognized as a part of something larger (a 'picture' out of view), yet too inaccessible for you to find the location (a 'construction' which has just included you.)" It is hard to imagine any pedestrian in the throes of enlightenment hastening home to tell the good news to his family. But then, wasn't the real point of the piece to confuse him all along?

Kosuth's work becomes aesthetically interesting only during the later eighties. His finest achievement is *Zero & Not*, which has been installed in several venues, most spectacularly the Leo Castelli Gallery. All along the walls of the large, columned white space ran rows of immaculate typography, each one obliterated with a canceling black line, but in such a way that you could still read the words beneath. This was a reference to what the French semiotician Derrida calls "relevance," the process by which a word is obliterated from a text, but also preserved, thus affecting our reading through indirection. But the text itself, as well as the references to Derrida and other Frenchmen, had nothing to do with the appeal of the work, which resided exclusively in the sheer graphic snazziness of the words.

The obsessiveness suggested in covering an entire gallery with words, and then canceling every last one of them, is very much in keeping with the manic nature of a good deal of Art Art. Like the paintings of Jean Dubuffet, this art finds its inspiration in the mood of madness, if not in the forms. Starting with the conviction that genius and madness are closely allied, this art seems to go through the motions of madness in the hopes of inducing that genius. So far, however, the results have not been promising. There is little empirical basis for the guiding assumption of this art, that what is insignificant once becomes great after ten thousand times.

Yet it is this notion, this premise, that seems to have moved Hanne Darboven, in her 1993 show at Castelli, to fill hundreds of pages of foolscap with meaningless lines of illegible script.

And it was this notion that inspired Chris Burden's *Other Vietnam Memorial* at the Museum of Modern Art in 1991. Its eight massive copper leaves formed a book that reached from the floor to the ceiling and listed, or seemed to list, each of the three million Vietnamese who died in the war.

One of the progenitors of this "obsessive art" is the Japanese On Kawara. There is, I believe, a measure of autoracism in his work: a playing up to the art world's preconceptions of the Oriental, specifically the Japanese. This stereotype of the Oriental as dehumanized, unfeeling machine has been with us since the days when Godzilla wrought havoc on Tokyo Bay back in the fifties. Whereas we work to support our leisure and raise our families, the Oriental does so because he has been programmed to do so and because he has no imagination that might induce him to act at variance with his conditioning. It was in this spirit that, when asked his age on a certain day in 1986, On Kawara answered that he was 19,821 [days old].

Kawara began in the sixties as a conceptualist, and he can be seen as the reduction to absurdity of the documentational urge that characterized that movement from its inception. He often documents his projects on crisp regulation typing paper, bound in sober black books that ceremoniously underscore the utter frivolity of what he is doing. In *One Million Years*, he has registered every single year from 998,012 B.C. all the way to 1988, when the work was made. It should be said, in fairness to Mr. Kawara's madness, that there is something impressive about actually visualizing a million numbers, and seeing how tiny human history is compared with the immensity of what went before.

In 1966, Kawara began making his Date Paintings, small black placards with the date they were painted etched in precise white paint, often accompanied by a box containing newspaper clippings from that day. A similar mood inspired *I Got Up*, in which Kawara recorded the time at which he awoke each morning (usually around 9:30 A.M.) in neatly sans serif inkpad letters, on the back of a postcard from wherever he happened to be. On the front were kitschy images of Berlin, of the Economic Miracle, bland scenes of highways and glinty, airborne planes sailing into the heavily retouched blue yonder.

It is one of the paradoxes of this art that it provides an abundance of information about the artist and yet tells us nothing about him. We know something so private as the minute he awakened every morning for years on end, but one brushstroke of de Kooning tells us more about its author than all the volumes of fatuous documentation by and about Mr. Kawara. He has transformed himself into a statistic, a cypher. Just as Orlan transformed her body, through plastic surgery, into the material of her art, so Kawara forges, or quarries, his art out of the very materiality of his life, the hours that grow into days and the days that grow into years.

This obsessive impulse has captivated Allan McCollum as well. He is the creator of surrogates, useless, unnamable objects, which, we may suppose, parody the fetishized comsumer commodity. McCollum's earliest memories are of the assembly line. "When I was a child, both of my parents worked on the assembly line of a large aircraft factory in Southern California. On Christmas, the company invited all the employees of this huge industrial complex to bring their children to an enormous party in one of their larger warehouses, and all of us were given exactly identical Christmas gifts. There were stacks upon stacks of these gifts, all in identical wrappings, stacked very high. There must have been hundreds and hundreds, maybe thousands, and we all had to stand in line for maybe half an hour to get one—handed to us by a Santa Claus of course. . . . I found the whole experience rather frightening, as I recall, but, naturally, I wanted the gift."

McCollum's art has always been one of dispassion. His paintings from the late sixties and early seventies are in the mainstream of dour, disaffected minimalism. Even if they fall short of Agnes Martin's works, they do manage to squeak out some originality from an overworked formal motif.

Nevertheless, these were traditional paintings, which by their very nature contained something conservative, and that was bad. It was this fact that induced McCollum to make the first of his surrogate paintings, which are essentially frames with nothing in them other than blank red, brown, yellow, and blue spaces. They are variously displayed, either lined up along the wall in single file, or densely stacked one on top of the other as in a nineteenth-century gallery. By the mid eighties, these surrogate paintings have become black against white and various sizes. Exhibited by the hundreds along a bare wall, they create a disconcertingly jazzy effect on the eye. There is an implicit promise of high purposeness to them, but the promise is made only to be broken, leaving us staring at a sequence of voided artifacts.

Several fashionable doctrines dovetail in these surrogates: Derrida's discourse on the frame, Benjamin's questioning of originality, Baudrillard's precession of the simulacra. Perhaps McCollum believed that, with his surrogates, he had gone beyond even conceptualism. After all, conceptualism had won hands down by obliterating the object, but in a way it had cheated, by turning its back on the work of art itself. What McCollum wanted was to preserve the object, but so voided that it could give no more pleasure, have no more meaning. His paintings are emphatically unsatisfying, as though to say that aesthetic pleasure were no longer possible.

The same themes were given still more emphatic expression by McCollum at the 1989 Whitney Biennial, where a huge table, perhaps two hundred square feet, was filled with ten thousand individual turquoise objects, each about the size and shape of a hand grenade, yet no two alike. The artist accomplished this feat with 150 computer-generated parts replicated and combined in thousands of different ways. Each of these is a pure object, slick and generic without function or purpose. And yet, like that toy McCollum received on the assembly line, it is something our consumer society wants without knowing what it is or what we can do with it.

Despite the appeal of obsessive art in exploring, illustrating, and assailing the irreducible artness of art, no strategy has seemed more seductive than appropriation. We encountered this concept already in the paintings of David Salle. But as paintings, they necessarily had to be shaped and formed by the artist. A more radical kind of appropriation had to be found, and its discoverers were Jeff Koons and Richard Prince.

Prince's career consists in the parasitic photographing of other people's photographs and the telling of other people's jokes. Now it would be naive to imagine that Prince appropriates because he is uninventive, though that he may well be, or that he wishes to claim these works as his own, which he clearly does not. Rather, appropriation is ironical in the extreme, and this radical act of possession, approaching forgery, is in a way the most emphatic form of rejection.

Beginning in the seventies, many of Prince's "rephotographs," as he calls them, were lifted bodily out of magazines. One set, taken from the *New York Times Magazine*, comprises four Ektachrome prints of sumptuous designer living rooms. They are oak-lined and plush, and adorned with Victorian armchairs and oval portraits from the Federalist era. And yet they are not elegant. Because they embody the ambitions of middle-class, middle-American white people, they are, we understand, fatally tainted and compromised.

These images were followed by rephotographed Marlboro cigarette ads of cowboys roping cattle and doing other things that cowboys do. Prince's manipulations of images, according to Lisa Phillips, take a variety of forms: "The following eight variable elements [define] the range of possible manipulations: 1. the original copy, 2. the rephotographed copy, 3. the angled copy, 4. the cropped copy, 5. the focused copy, 6. the out-of-focus copy, 7. the black-and-white copy, 8. the color copy."

But Prince's appropriations are not limited to images. They extend to words as well. As early as 1976, he published a piece in the alternative journal *Tracks*, "Eleven Conversations," consisting of quotes lifted from the back of Elvis Presley bubble-gum cards. These were followed by Prince's *Jokes*, which consist of words stenciled onto canvas. Their sources are either the borscht belt or *New Yorker* cartoons. Some of these jokes are classics of their kind: "I went to see a psychiatrist. He said, 'Tell me everything.' I did and now he's doing my act." Naturally, you are not to find them funny under any circumstances, except in the parasitical way of mocking the idea that anyone could find them funny at all.

By now everyone must have his favorite pseudo-statement about Richard Prince, who is, to be perfectly frank, one of the more swollen mediocrities in contempoary art—no mean distinction. My own personal favorite comes from David Ross: "[Prince's works] are not so much radical statements as they are quests for a new paradigm. In what may be called a postideological moment, Prince is clearly not an ideologue, but rather an artist who insists on questioning the implicit values embedded in any work of art produced well after the age of mechanical reproduction."

It is hard to imagine what Ross was thinking of or looking at when he called these works nonideological. Rather, they fit hand in glove with the prevailing orthodoxies of the art world, whose cloistered members delight one another with "radical" questionings of the establishment. The only possible explanation for Ross's lapse is that the attitude is so pervasive, and he has been around it for so long, that it has become invisible to him.

Last and, for once, least, is Jeff Koons. In a perfect world we would not be discussing him at all. We would view his art as a roguish prank which, though it inspires laughter, is ultimately bound for oblivion. But because Koons persists in being taken very seriously by people who take themselves more seriously still, no discussion of contemporary art can avoid him.

To my knowledge he has never made a work of art that was formally or even spiritually ambitious. Indeed, he has never really made a work of art at all. Sometimes he appropriates objects unchanged; sometimes, as in his infamous porcelain statue of Michael Jackson in white-face embracing Bubbles the chimpanzee, he commissions the work from professional craftsmen thousands of miles away.

It is one of his strategies of provocation to be always coming into and going out of focus. He is oddly familiar and unlike anything ever seen before. Superficially he is a what you might call a "nice looking young man," with light hair, blue eyes, and a clear complexion. Rather than being the hairy anarchist we expect subversives to be, he is the clean-cut boy next door whom mothers would want their daughters to marry.

And yet, listen to him for only a second and you begin to hear something distinctly incongruous. Sometimes this former bond-trader adopts the tone of nauseous beneficence that you find in self-help books: "Don't divorce yourself from your true being, embrace it. That's the only way that you can truly move on to become a new upper class and not move backwards." At other times, he sounds like the sort of deceptively well-scrubbed young man who hands out roses and leaflets in New York's Port Authority: "I am interested in love, I am interested in the reunion, I am interested in the spiritual, to be able to show people that they can have an impact and achieve their desires."

Irony is the means and banality the end of Koons's art. While the rest of the art world strained to see how far it could descend into abjection, Koons was the first to see that the real danger zone could be reached by moving laterally into the land of midcult. This was the Ultima Thule of abjection, that which was categorically alien to art as usual. Since Postimpressionism, popular culture has figured so prominently in art that it has almost become one of the terms of high art. Since pop art, camp as well has been a fixture of high culture and so presents no real threat. But schlock, which deflects from itself all the sympathy for the underdog that accrues to popular art, schlock which caters to the most banal elements of middle-American complacency, seemed permanently off limits until Jeff Koons paraded it into the mainstream. Other artists surely had alluded to it in a pussy-footing way, but Koons was the first to ride this particular tiger.

In earlier works like *New Hoover Convertible*, the gleaming appliance is displayed in a plexiglas container illuminated with fluorescent lights. As with all of Koons's work, the gimmick here is the complex ambiguity of intent with which the artist separates the object for art. Representing consumer culture in all its surprisingly affordable glory, this vacuum cleaner comes attached to an imaginary owner. She is a Donna Reed for the nineties, white, middle class, in her late thirties or early forties. The art world loves this woman. Her existence assures them that they, being either too wealthy or too bohemian for housework, are different from her, and the thought fills them with joy.

By approaching the appliance, we are flirting with one of the few taboos the art establishment still understands: The allure of mid-cult. It is only by recognizing this as a taboo that the art world can approach it at all. For taboos, as the whole art world knows, were made to be transgressed. And the thought that one is entering a zone so perilously unfashionable that art world outsiders might not know that one is doing so in the spirit of irony, is not unlike what entering a bull ring was to Ernest Hemingway.

Koons's interest in basketball is another stage in his exploration of mid-cult. *Three Ball Equilibrium* is an aquarium tank filled with purified water and three perfectly good Spalding basketballs. Another of his acts of appropriation consisted in framing a poster of basketball star Julius Irving (Doctor J.) in a physician's robe in a laboratory, with basketballs lying all about, and at the base the words *Dr. Dunkenstein*.

What is it about basketballs that intrigues Koons? Basketball is seen, at least at the professional level, to be a sport played by astoundingly tall black people. But unlike graffiti or other forms of protest art, which emphasize the apartness of the black experience, basketball is free of anger. It is what inner-city youths play for the sheer exhilarating sport of it. Like most other professional sports, it is seen as a black entrée into the mid-cult American experience. Therefore it is attainted with kitsch. Therefore it has been untouched by the art world, and therefore it has none of the redemption of what black artists like Carrie Mae Weems and Glenn Ligon make and discuss. In short, basketball seems to be the farthest one can get from the abstruse, acidulated ironies of the art world, and that, for Koons, is its exclusive appeal.

Sometime around 1986, however, Koons turned away from the mid-cult of basketballs and Hoovers and decided to devote himself to kitsch and its suppurating vulgarity. Sometimes this interest expresses itself by way of camp, as in a silver-plated bust of Louis XIV resplendent in armor and flowing locks. It is the sort of thing you might expect to find in the lobby of Caesars Palace. At other times Koons goes the way of kitsch, selecting objects whose cloying, sugar-coated cuteness is intentionally intolerable. *Two Kids*, representing a big-eyed boy and girl, is the sort of sentimental statuette advertised in the *Saturday Evening Post*. In *John the Baptist*, a porcelain bust, the saint holds in his arms a pig and a penguin, and, as he gazes heavenward, his face is suffused with an expression of stomach-churning piousness.

Koons's wife, Cicciolina, the Hungarian-Italian porn star whose real name is Ilona Staler, is a kind of living, breathing example of the kitsch Koons likes to appropriate. She is your basic platinum-blond-bimbette flower child, the sort who has said on more than one occasion, "Make love not war," and who tried to resolve the conflict in the Persian Gulf by offering to sleep with Saddam Hussein. Koons's marriage to Cicciolina, which recently ended in divorce, can be seen as an extended performance piece, especially since she speaks no English and Koons speaks only English. "To me, Cicciolina is the Eternal Virgin," Koons says in his typically hyperbolic prose. "She's been able to remove guilt and shame from her life, and because of this she is a great liberator." Their courtship and nuptials were duly solemnized with massive Ectachrome images of the couple having anal sex. These were later converted into life-size polychrome porcelain simulacra. Koons also had smaller statuettes made, like *Jeff Eating Ilona*, that illustrate the Kama Sutra in pleasant pink glass.

In his obsession with kitsch and appropriation, in his preoccupation with the empty gestures of artistic production, Jeff Koons is both the reduction to absurdity and the logical consequence of art's obsession with art. He and the other artists discussed in this chapter merely externalize and incarnate the sickly obsessiveness, which has little to do with love, that art seems to inspire in an ever-growing subset of the population. We have reached the point at which our misplaced devotion to art has drained the art object of all its joy. We prefer the niche to the statue and the frame to the painting. Good, bad, or indifferent, as long as it is art, we will very gladly bow down before it.

It is precisely this misdirected, uncritical adulation which, more than anything else, accounts for the general paltriness of most art in our time. Never has art been more adulated than now; never has it been less deserving of that adulation. The regeneration of visual culture will come about when we awaken to the fact, which we should always have known and which earlier ages never doubted, that art is ultimately far less important than we now believe.

E P I L O G U E

The Art of the Future

Has any critic ever been able to predict the future? I don't mean the ability to see into the next season, or the season after that, but into the next epoch of human culture. Who in the 1450s could have predicted Michelangelo and mannerism? Who in the ancien régime could even have conceived of impressionism? And what impressionist of 1870 would ever have imagined the art of Jackson Pollock and Ad Reinhardt?

By comparison with art, political or economic projections are child's play. Population and gross national product can be extrapolated in a general way from what we know now. Because of a circumscribed number of themes and variables into which the chaotic welter of human social behavior can be set, the general terms of the future are often knowable, even when the specifics are not. But the next phase of culture is always inconceivable until it happens. Only then does it promptly acquire the logic of destiny.

Few self-respecting artists believe they are making contemporary art. Contemporary art is what others produce. What they, in their heart of hearts, suspect and hope is that they are creating the art of the coming age. Their vanity assures them that they are the point where the present bends into the future. Theirs is always the art that is just coming into being, just on the verge of its fullest acceptance, no matter how acclaimed it may already be. It is like fruit that arrives in the stores not yet ripe, so that it will be ready to eat at the time of purchase or soon thereafter.

But is the art of today, postmodernism, in fact the art of the future, the next phase of human artifice after the demise of the modern tradition? Indeed, is it, as some have suggested, the terminal point in the unfolding drama of visual culture in the West, the destination toward which our art has been hastening since its very inception?

Our collective vanity answers yes to both questions. It is the vanity of every age, at least in modern times, to imagine that it occupies the summit of history, that it is the predestined point upon which converge all the earlier and disparate filaments of human culture. At the same time, it is pleasant to assume that we have left nothing for the future to do but to carry on in our footsteps.

Yet when we look at the art examined in this book, the art that, for the past fifteen years, has been taught in academies, admired in museums, and bought at auction, it is difficult to escape the impression that we remain entrenched in the terminal phase of one epoch rather than in the initial phase of the next. We have expanded the range of what art depicts and discusses, but aside from a few technological tricks we have discovered no new formal territory. As for those older formal terms that we preserve, only rarely have we lived up to the brilliance of their originators. Even our rebellious antagonism toward modernism, which we imagine to be at the very core of contemporary art, is really little more than the modernist rebelliousness, the spirit of Courbet and Pollock, through other means.

In the words of Matthew Arnold we are "Wandering between two worlds, one dead,/ The other powerless to be born." There is movement for movement's sake, but no sense of direction. We find ourselves, surprisingly, in the same condition we were in during the seventies, a decade characterized by a pluralistic proliferation of trends and mini-fads. Except that artists in the seventies seemed to be standing still, whereas today we seem, for all our exertions, to be running in place.

But the real parallel is not with the 1970s but with the 1850s, that last great period of stagnation in Western Art that followed the death of the old masters and preceded the emergence of modernism. Just as important older artists like Ingres continued to do memorable work in the earlier style, so Serra and Agnes Martin still create very respectable modernist art. As the academicians imitated Titian, younger painters like Schnabel and Terry Winters, being alienated from the true sources of modernism's strength, spawn weak retreads of the New York School. And just as the orientalists and the realists of the Second Empire increased the scope of what a painting could refer to or depict, so we have found it far easier to expand art's content than to broaden by a single degree its formal terms.

Many reasons could be adduced for the state of contemporary art, but surely the most potent is the fact that ours is the first age in which the mass of mainstream artists have rejected form in favor of content and thus have repudiated even the quest for formal excellence. Perhaps someone will ask: "Because they have found what they were looking for and not found what they were not looking for, are they not to be counted a success?"

By way of answer, I begin with an axiom that the reader either will accept or not: The excellence of art must be artistic excellence. Art may have other excellences than this, but the two must not be confused. To use a somewhat homely analogy: Food often looks good in addition to tasting good, but if it doesn't taste good, then, no matter how lovely it looks, it is necessarily bad cooking. Eloquence is surely a part of what it takes to be a good lawyer, but if a pleader, for all his eloquence, doesn't know the law and can't win a case, then he is necessarily a bad lawyer. Art that does not excel for artistic reasons is necessarily unsuccessful as art.

Obviously there is more to art than mere form, and it may be that art that is only formally excellent cannot truly be called great art. But no art can be great that is not also formally great, or its greatness is other than artistic greatness. By formal excellence, a necessarily vague term, I emphatically do not mean the mere ability to paint a likeness or to make pleasant patterns on canvas. I refer rather to that mysterious process by which, for example, Rembrandt could paint the sleeve of his Jewish bride, a simple sleeve!, and turn it into one of the noblest moral statements in Western art. I refer to the handling of paint in a Fantin-Latour peach and the lilting lines of an Arshile Gorky abstraction. This is what, with fewest exceptions, has been lost from art in our time. These are the ambitions that contemporary art has been unable to live up to or has cynically disowned.

There is a logical problem at the heart of contemporary art. Though most artists overwhelmingly reject the idea of formal excellence, the context of that excellence is preserved intact. In other words, the fact that artists and critics reject notions of excellence doesn't stop them from seeking and awarding praise. Schnabel, Salle, and Koons are all thought of in much the same way that earlier ages thought of Titian or David or Picasso. They occupy the same pedestals. They impress in the same way and receive the same degree of praise for their labors.

For this reason, it may be that today's art is less likely to promote future art than to impede it, in exactly the same way that the bemedaled, belaureled, official salon art of the last century impeded the emergence of modernism. Despite its much-advertised radicalism, the art of the most recent Whitney Biennial and Venice Biennale looks down on the disorganized, impoverished, and unglamorous opposition with a smugness that finds its closest parallel in the very academicians who scoffed at Impressionists as misdirected simpletons. And just as Manet and Picasso succeeded in moving forward only by tearing down the impregnable fortress of the Ecole des Beaux Arts, so it may be that the next stage of art will be accomplished only over the lacerated body of today's art establishment.

But from what quarter is that change likely to come, and is there as yet any evidence of it? Perhaps there is. Far to the east of

SoHo and Cork Street, far to the east of Venice and Cologne, events are occurring that may hold some clue to the future of art. The failed August coup in the former Soviet Union, though obviously unrelated to art, has a symbolic resonance whose implications for all of human culture are almost incalculable.

For the failed coup, together with the collapse of the Soviet bloc and the teetering condition of communist China, have to do with more than the internal politics of a few large and small states to the east. They mark nothing less than an epochal change in human events. During the two centuries following the storming of the Bastille, revolutionary upheaval has been the paradigm for historical change. There were few countries in Europe that were not threatened by it at one time or another. In this century it has dominated the political realities of the East. But on those few days in August two years ago, the epoch of revolutions came to an end.

Art, which reflects political realities, and which has been the mirror in which the revolutionary age expressed itself, has also been fully saturated with the revolutionary temperament. In order to understand the art of the past two centuries, and thus contemporary art as well, one must view it from a higher level of generality than is usually done. It will not do to see it in terms of seasons or movements or even the lifespan of a single artist. Art is rarely thought of in terms of what the historian Fernand Braudel calls *la longue durée*. But only when we conceive it from such a perspective, only when we think of it in almost geological terms, will its true patterns begin to emerge.

Beginning with David, Delacroix, and the other romantics, revolution and rebelliousness altered the mood and subject matter of art. Before that, there was a generally aristocratic or sacerdotal temperament to most art, which favored stability and hated change. Artists like Caravaggio and Salvator Rosa might make angry images, but they did this at the behest of princes of the church and with the intention of delivering a conservative rebuke to the moral decay of their society. There was no talk, as there would be later, of the complete overthrow of society. Only in David and Delacroix do we begin to see art advocating change or at least ratifying the bourgeois state that the revolution had brought about.

But modernism, which emerged three generations after the revolution in the person of Courbet, turned its anger against the bourgeois state itself. Since then, it is difficult to think of a single important movement that has not implicitly criticized or advocated aggression against the bourgeois state or against earlier culture. The Impressionists called into question the academicians and the Symbolists assailed Impressionism. Whereas Cubism attacked Symbolism and Dada attacked everything, the artists of the New York School attacked the European mainstream, and Pop attacked them.

There is no need to elaborate further, or to point out how often social radicalism has accompanied these movements, even when their stated aim was aesthetic. So pervasive has this rebelliousness become in the visual arts, that it is now taken for granted and no longer seems at all remarkable. We have come to feel as though this rebelliousness were the natural condition of the artist, that he is meant to challenge and provoke. Rarely do we see that before the last quarter of the eighteenth century this quality, which can found in almost every work of art in our time, simply did not exist.

Postmodernism is in a sense the reduction to absurdity of this artistic rebelliousness. Divorced from any application to reality, rebelliousness starts to be pursued for its own sake. You see this in the banalities of Koons and the tirades of Wojnarowicz, in Sue Williams's plastic vomit and in the corpses of Andres Serrano. But at the same time, if you listen closely and know what you are listening to, you begin to hear in all of this the despair of an older order increasingly reduced to self-parody.

It seems reasonable, or at least not implausible, that with the decline of the revolutionary paradigm in politics, the revolutionary ethos in art, which was its reflection, will also come to an end. Despite many conflicts that remain in the political sphere, cooperation increasingly seems to be the way of the world and conflict the exception—an exact inversion of most earlier history. We should not expect, because of this change, a return to conservatism in art, nor a continuation of the present rebelliousness for its own sake, but something in between, together with a seriousness of artistic ambition such as has been lacking for some years now.

I suspect that the proliferation of computer options will not really disturb the primacy of the traditional media. Most art remains essentially simple: It can be, for example, figures in space or in two dimensions; it can be representational or it can be abstract. No amount of postmodernity can change that, anymore than it is able to add to our five senses.

To believe that technology must inevitably superannuate the traditional media is naive and unobservant. It has been in the nature of post-industrial society not to destroy the past, as the industrial age had largely done, but rather to preserve it where it was found, and to recreate it where it was necessary. The recent extension of the Jewish Museum in New York, which created from nothing a flawless beaux arts annex to a venerable Fifth Avenue mansion, is just the most recent example of an increasingly common sight.

No one can say how much time must pass before the inauguration of the new epoch in culture. Yet we have little reason to doubt that it will come. Western art has been through longer dry spells than this. If our culture can not regenerate itself, that would be the first time in its long history that it failed to do so. Any anxiety one might have on this score is probably the result of the necessary inability, in the realms of culture, to forsee the future. The regeneration could be happening now in obscure academies or in the unvisited studios of neglected genius. Or it may come about through the inspired efforts of a generation of artists each of whose parents have not yet even met. All we can hope for is that it will come sooner rather than later, and that we shall live to see it.

INDEX

Abject Art, 195
Abstract Expressionism, A Critical Record, 49
Accessions, 142
Acconci, Vito, 173
Adam, 145
Adams, John, 15
An Afternoon of Acteon, 112
Age of Anxiety, The, 98
AIDS Timeline, 53, 149, 160
Alberti, 59
Alden, Todd, 22-24
Altman, Robert, 23
American Art of the 1960s, 55
American Psycho, 15
Andre, Carl, 27
Andrejevic, Milet, 112
Anthro/Socio, 53
Antoni, Janine, 150, 153
Applebroog, Ida, 91, 152
Architecture of the Sky, 136-137
Argento, 109
Arnold, Matthew, 214
Art Biz, The, 25
Art Gallery of New South Wales, 164
Art in America, 50, 68
Art in Transit series, 93
Artcards, 22-24
Artforum, 50, 60-61
Ass, 183
Astor, Patti, 86
At the Hub of Things, 145
Auster, Paul, 83, 105

Bachardy, Don, 115
Bad Boy, 125
Baechler, Ron, 44
Bagosian, Eric, 86
Baldy Paints a Masterpiece, 98
Barnes, Ken, 46
Barney, Matthew, 150
Barthes, Roland, 185
Baselitz, Georg, 117
Basquiat, Jean Michel, 16, 74, 86, 99-101
Baudelaire, 20, 63-64
Baxandall, Michael, 37
Baziotes, William, 134
Beardsley, 93
Beham, Sebald, 156
Ben's Museum, 197

Ben's Window, 197
Benjamin, Walter, 33-34
Benning, Sadie, 150
Beuys, Joseph, 11-12, 17, 46, 201
Bidlo, Mike, 74, 97, 199
Birthday, 28
Birthday Boy, 125-126
Bits and Pieces, 11
Black Jesus, 190
Black Males exhibit, 186-187
Black Mary, 190
Bleckner, Ross, 74, 130, 136-137
Bloodpool, 177-178
Blue Poles, 77, 158
Bofill, Ricardo, 82
Boltanski, Christian, 201-202
Boone Gallery (Mary), 133
Botticelli, Sandro, 37, 42
Bougereau, 76
Bourgeois, Louise, 185
Boulez, Pierre, 77, 105
Boy in a Blue Suit, 28
Brillo Boxes, 50, 68
Broodthaers, Marcel, 23
Brueghel Series (A Vanitas of Styles), 135
Bruno, Giordano, 57
Bryson, Norman, 61
Buggery Faith, 183
Burden, Chris, 3-8, 9, 11, 12, 17, 35, 46, 151, 167, 204
Burning Bush, The, 122
By Night and By Day, 133

Cage, John, 49
Calle, Sophie, 92, 199
Canaday, John, 48-49
Caravaggio, 42, 76
Casanova, 109
Castelli Gallery (Leo), 25-26, 203
Chagall, Marc, 28
Chambre Claire, 185
Chang, Christine, 150
Chattington, Sir Basil, 97, 98
Chris Burden Promo, 5
Circumnavigating the Sea of Shit, 123
Clemente, Francesco, 120-121
Clinton, Bill, 82
Cloak and Harlequin, 173
Coe, Sue, 80
Cook, David, 61
Cooper Gallery (Paula), 45, 190
Coplands, John, 179
Corigliano, John, 82, 109
Corporal Politics exhibit, 174
Courbet, Gustave, 8, 157, 218
Couture, 76
Crouching Man, 178
Cutrone, Ronnie, 90, 91

da Vinci, Leonardo, 1
Daddy's Girl, 125
Darboven, Hanne, 203
David, Jean-Louis, 156, 217-218
De Chirico, Giorgio, 106-108, 114
de Kooning, Willem, 49, 134, 149
de la Tour, Georges, 35-36
Death, 183
Death of American Spirituality, The, 102
Deitch, Jeffrey, 68, 175
della Francesca, Piero, 42
Delacroix, Ferdinand, 156, 217-218
Demoiselles D'Avignon, 68
Derrida, Jacques, 57
Descartes, 66
Development of Modern Art, The, 24
Dog Boy, 183
Doorway to Heaven, 6
Dreams exhibit, 110, 114
Dubuffet, Jean, 46, 203
Duchamp, Marcel, 4, 52, 153, 173
Durham, Jimmie, 61, 150, 199
Dutch Masters, 115
Dying Marat, 156

Eco, Umberto, 57, 109
Ecole des Beaux-Arts, the, 25, 76
"Eleven Conversations," 207-208
Ellis, Bret Easton, 15
Elroy and Leroy, 95-96
Equicola, Mario, 1, 12, 18
Eunuch, 192
Exile, 124

F Space, the, 6
Father and Sunshine, 98
Fear of Evolution, 102

Feldman Gallery (Ronald), 11, 200
Fertile Region, 134
Fetting, Rainer, 117
Fifth of May, 159
Finlay, Ian Hamilton, 113-114, 123
Finley, Karen, 14, 15, 45, 180
Fischl, Erich, 56, 124-126, 152
Five Day Locker Piece, 6
Flash Art, 50, 61
Flavin, Dan, 27
Flynt, Henry, 196
Fortune Teller, The, 35-36
Foucault's Pendulum, 109
Four Quad Cinema, 138
Fouratt, Jim, 86
Francesco Clemente Pinxit, 120
Frank, Peter, 86
Fraser, Andrea, 199
Fried, Michael, 73
From Manet to Manhattan, 42
Fugue, 28
Fun Gallery, the, 86

Gagosian Gallery, the, 22, 51-52, 121
Gandert, Miguel, 150
Garçon!, 3-5
Garden at Little Sparta, 113-114
Garouste, Gerard, 112-113
Gauguin, Paul, 8
Geldzahler, Henry, 115
Gere, Richard, 185
Gericault, Jean Louis, 68
Ghosts of Versailles, 109
Gide, André 42
Gigantomachy, 158
Gilbert and George, 181-183
Glass, Philip, 13, 83, 105, 185
Glowing Cell with Conduits, 139
Gober, Robert, 23, 90-91, 178-179
Gold Piece, 143
Golub, Leon, 157-159
Good Government, 134
Goodman Gallery (Marian), 30-31, 173-174
Goodman, Sam, 195
Gopnik, Adam, 87
Gorky, Arshile, 134
Goya y Lucientes, 159
Green, Denise, 199
Greenberg, Clement, 64, 71-73, 79-80
Greenblatt, Rodney Allen, 91
Grimes, Ken, 46
Group Material, 53, 146, 149
Grünewald, Matthias, 59
Guernica, 158
Guggenheim Museum, 27-30, 31, 117, 160
Gund, Agnes, 23
Guston, Philip, 106, 107, 114

Haacke, Hans, 160-161, 168
Halley, Peter, 130, 135, 137, 138-139
Hallowell, Mavis Grace, 98
Hanson, Fuller Gallery, 3
Happy Land and Empty Heart, A, 133
Haring, Keith, 85, 86, 91, 92-95, 98
Hawkes, John, 82
Helms, Jesse, 44, 45, 189
Hercules Protecting the Balance Between Pleasure and Virtue, 75
Hesse, Eva, 140-142
High and Low exhibit, 87
Hill, Charles, 6
Hirshcl & Adler Modern, 110
Hockney, David, 84, 114-116, 185
Hodicke, K.H, 117
Hoffman von Fallersleben on Helgoland, 119
Holliday, George, 153
Holzer, Jenny, 15, 53, 165-168
Hopper, Edward, 49
Hughes, Holly, 15
Hughes, Robert, 18, 118
Hunger, 120
Huysman, Joris-Karl, 59

I Got Up, 204-205
I Talk to the Devil, 98
Inventory of Objects That Belonged to a Woman of Bois-Colombes, 201
Ippolito de' Medici, Cardinal, 147
Irving, Julius, 210
Isenheim Altarpiece, 59
Isherwood, Christopher, 115

Jackson, Michael, 209
Jacobs, Mark, 82

Jeff Eating Ilona, 212
Jencks, Charles, 70
Jewish Museum, 219
Joe, 187
Joe and Tom, Sausalito, 187
John the Baptist, 211
John Herring, Person with AIDS, Posed as Flora with Lover and Mother, 193
Johns, Jasper, 18, 42
Johnson, Samuel, 57
Jokes, 208
Jong, Erica, 82
Joyce, James, 13
Judd, Donald, 27, 29, 60

Kabakov, Ilya, 200-201
Kahn, Louis, 77
Kandinsky, Wassily, 9, 28
Kapoor, Anish, 144-146
Kauffman, Angelica, 149
Kawara, On, 204-205
Kerouac, Jack, 77
Kiefer, Anselm, 79, 92, 117, 118-120, 132, 172
Kienholz, Ed, 74
King Kong, 122
Klee, Paul, 46
Klinghoffer, 15
Kochelev, S.Y., 200
Komar, Vitaly, 110-112
Koons, Cicciolina, 62, 211-212
Koons, Jeff, 16, 38, 40, 56, 62, 79, 92, 146, 151-152, 207, 208-212
Kostabi, Mark, 92, 97-99
Kostabi: The Early Years, 97-98
Kosuth, Joseph, 202-203
Krauss, Rosalind, 32, 33, 80
Krens, Thomas, 28, 32-33, 117-118
Kroker, Arthur, 61
Kruger, Barbara, 39, 161-162, 174
Kubota, Shigeko, 196
Kunst Kick, 6

Le Figaro, 25, 50
Le Mercure de France, 25
Leatherman Two, 184
Lenin Lived, Lenin Lives, Lenin Will Live, 111
Les Saltimbanques, 72
Levine, Sherrie, 74, 97, 199
Lewitt, Sol, 142
Leyster, Judith, 149
Liberty Leading the People, 156
Lichtenstein, Roy, 40, 91
Lieberman, Harry, 46
Life, 183
Ligare, David, 75
Ligon, Glenn, 15, 53, 150, 152, 199, 211
Lippard, Lucy, 40
Looking at Pictures on a Screen, 115
Lorrain, Claude, 77
Louvre, the, 24
Ludwig, Peter, 161
Luhring, Augustine Gallery, 11
Lumen, 134
Lurie, Boris, 195

MacLeish, Archibald, 106
Madame X, 193
Madonna, 4
Magic Christian, The, 28-29
Magnason, Ann, 86
Maison, 144
Malevich, Kasimir, 74
Man in Polyester Suit, 186
Man Without Legs 1984, 192
Manet, Édouard, 189
Manzoni, Piero, 195-196
Mapplethorpe, Robert, 14, 15, 73, 182, 183-190
Marden, Brice, 184
Maria Callas series, 124
Mariani, Carlo Maria, 80, 109-110, 112, 123
Mark Stevens (Mr. 10-), 187
Marquis, Alice Goldfarb, 25
Marshall, Richard, 101
Martin, Agnes, 67, 143
Martinez, Daniel, 58
Matisse, Henri, 16
McCollum, Allan, 205-206
McKenzie, Michael, 86

Meier-Graefe, Julius, 24
Melamid, Alexander, 110-112
Mengs, Anton Raphael, 108, 109, 110
Mexican Pin-up, 192
Michelangelo, 36
Miller Gallery (Robert), 135
Modigliani, Amedeu, 28
MoMA Poll Question, 160
Mondrian, 76, 77
Moore, Clementine, 46
Moreau, Gustave, 8
Morris, Robert, 24, 151, 180
Mother and Child, 128
Motherwell, Robert, 49
Mouth of Europa and the Figure of Venus, The, 172
Murray, Elizabeth, 130
Museum of Modern Art, 87, 160, 204

Nauman, Bruce, 53
Neel, Alice, 126-128
Neimans, LeRoy, 126
New American Painting, The, 49
New Hoover Convertible, 210
New Teacher, The, 200
New, Used and Improved, 86
New York School, the, 49, 54, 55, 117
Newman, Barnett, 53, 60, 80, 138
Nichols Canyon, 116
Night Chant series, 135
Nitsch, Hermann, 9-11, 12, 46
Nixon, Nicholas, 184

Obnoxious Liberals, 100
Olitski, Jules, 74
Olympia, 189
On the Composition of Images, Signs, and Ideas, 57
One and Three Chairs, 202
One Million Years, 204
Orgies, Mysteries Theater, 9
Origin of Social Realism, The, 111
Originality of the Avant-Garde and Other Modernist Myths The, 32
Orion the Classi—Orion the Indian, 112-113
Orlan, 170-173
Osmosis Series, the, 32-33
Osorio, Pepon, 154-155, 168
Other Vietnam Memorial, 204
Oulton, Therese, 130
Owens-Corning Fiberglass Center, 141
Oxidation Painting, 196

Paganini, 117-118
Painted Word, The, 52-53
Painting and Experience in Fifteenth Century Italy, 37
Panza, Count Giuseppe di Biumo, 27-30, 31
Parisian Salon, the, 25
Parson's School of Design, 43
Pascal, 55, 149
Pearblossom Hwy, 115-116
Pearlstein, Philip, 124-125
Pellner, Greg, 46
Perot, Ross, 82
Pfaff, Judy, 23
Phillips, Lisa, 23, 155, 208
Picasso, Pablo, 42, 68, 72, 116, 149, 158
Pincus-Witten, Robert, 23
Pink Panther, 62
Piper, Adrian, 61, 152
Piss Christ, 190
Player, The, 23
Polish Rider, 35
Polke, Sigmar, 117-118, 132
Pollock, Jackson, 18, 54, 72, 74, 77, 134, 158
Poons, Larry, 74
Poppy, 186
Posner, Helaine, 174
Post-Human exhibit, 175
Postmodern Scene, The, 61
Pound, Ezra, 13, 14
Poussin, Nicolas, 41
Power, Kevin, 122
Pressed-in Sturges, 121-122
Prince, Richard, 207-208
Prison, 139

Raft of the Medusa, 68
Rahv, Philip, 127
Rain, 120
Raphael, 36, 42, 66, 109
Rauschenberg, Robert, 25, 43
Raynaud, Jean-Pierre, 143-144
Read, Herbert, 42
Reagan, Ronald, 82
Reinhardt, Ad, 77, 80, 105, 129, 138
Rembrandt, 35, 115
Reni, Guido, 41
Repitition Nineteen III, 141
Reserve—Detective, 201
Richter, Gerhard, 117, 131-133
Riley, Bridget, 138
Ringaround Arosie, 142
Rizzoli, 46
Robbe-Grillet, Alain, 105
Roman Clergy's Procession into Hell, The, 156
Rorem, Ned, 13
Rose, Barbara, 73, 170-171, 172
Rosenberg, Harold, 49, 52
Ross, David, 43, 208
Rothenberg, Susan, 130
Rothko, Mark, 18, 155
Rowboat, 126
Royal Academy, 25
Rubens, Peter Paul, 1, 32
Ruskin, John, 20, 57

Saint Orlan as a Baroque White Virgin Armed with a Bouquet, 171
Salle, David, 22-23, 79, 92, 121-123, 207
Sandler, Irving, 55, 78, 157
Sans Two, 142
Savior of the Primates, 192-193
Schapiro, Meyer, 49
Schnabel, Julian, 53, 56, 75, 120, 123-124, 146
Schneeman, Carolee, 180
School of London, the, 116
School of Rome, The, 109
Schwarzenegger, Arnold, 184
Schwarzkogler, Rudolf, 170
Scully, Sean, 133-134
Seedbed, 173
Segal, George, 74, 177
Self-Portrait in a Yellow Hat, 117
Serrano, Andres, 14, 15, 35, 190-191
Sewer, The, 126
Sex, John, 86
Shahn, Ben, 80
Shapiro, Cecile, 49
Shapiro, David, 49
Shapolsky et al Real Estate Holdings, 160
Sharf, Kenny, 74, 86, 91, 92, 95-97, 112
Sherman, Cindy, 23, 179-181
Shit Faith, 183
Shoot, 6
Shulamith, 119
Siegfried, 57-58
Simeon Stylites, Saint 7
Singing Sculpture, The, 181
Smith, Cary, 130
Smith, Kiki, 61, 92, 176-178
Smith, Patti, 184
Sol Goldman and Alex Dilorenzo Manhattan Real Estate Holdings, A Real Time Social System, 160
Something From Sleep II, 102
Sonnabend Gallery, 173
Sontag, Susan, 109
Spero, Nancy, 152
Splash, The, 114
St. Augustine Florida, 152
Stable Gallery, the, 26, 50
Staler, Ilona, 211-212
Stedelijk Museum, 201
Stein Gallery (Gertrude), 195
Steir, Pat, 135-137
Stella, Frank, 18, 73, 97
Stevens, Wallace, 13
Still Life, Marseilles, 193
Storr, Roger, 64, 66
Stroke, 111
Sultan, Donald, 130
Summer, 117

T.B., Harlem, 128
Taafe, Phillip, 130, 137-138

Tate Gallery, 202
Taylor, Simon, 195
Telescopic Life, 137
Tennyson, 122
Text/Context, 202
Third Dream—Fragments, 110
Three Balls Equilibrium, 210
Three Urinals, 178
Thyssen, Francesca, 185
Tillim, Sidney, 73
Times Square Show, the, 68-70
Tisdall, Caroline, 11
Titian, 65
Torvan, Michael, 29
Total Art Match Box, 196-197
Towards Bathesda Fountain, 112
Transfixed, 5-6
Trinity, 138
Truisms series, 165
20 Jahre Einsamkeit, 173-174
Two Black Girls, 128
Two Kids, 211
Two Puerto Rican Boys, 128

Untitled (Rope Piece), 142

Van Gogh, Vincent, 20, 28, 36
Vasarely, Victor, 138
Vatican Parnassus, 109
Vautier, Ben, 196-197
Velvet Water, 6
Venetian Caprice in the Manner of Veronese, 106-107
Venice Bienniale, 53, 216
Virgin and Child, 37
Visit to/ A Visit From/ The Island, A, 125
Viti, Timoteo, 66
Volcano Lover, The, 109

Wagner, Richard, 57
Walker Art Center, 196
Warhol, Andy, 25-26, 50, 68, 91, 97, 196
Waterfall of Ancient Ghosts, 135-136
Waterfall of the Asian Night, 135-136
Waterfall of Reverie, 135-136
Watson, Peter, 42
Ways of Wordly Wisdom: Arminius Battle, The, 119
We Are Not Afraid, 138
Webb, Alex, 152
Weems, Carrie Mae, 152, 211
Weiner, Lawrence, 30-31, 32, 35, 38-39
Weisman, Fred, 115
Weisman, Marcia, 115
Wells, H.G., 20
Weston, Edward, 34
White Squad, 159
White, Edmund, 186
Whitney Museum, 43, 51, 58, 61, 67, 75, 101, 134, 148-156, 181, 195, 196, 199, 206, 216
Wilke, Hannah, 180, 196
Williams, Sue, 67, 75, 79, 153-154, 155
Williams, William Carlos, 13
Wilmarth, Christopher, 84
Wilson, Fred, 199
Wilson, Robert, 185
Winsor, Jackie, 142-143
Winters, Terry, 130, 134-135
Witkin, Joel-Peter, 191-194
Wodiczko, Krzysztof, 162-165
Wojnarowicz, David, 45, 101-103
Wolfe, Tom, 52-53
Wool, Christopher, 53
Woolf, Virginia, 13
"Work of Art in the Age of Mechanical Reproduction, The," 33
Wreath, 136

Zero & Not, 203
Zola, Emile, 13, 82